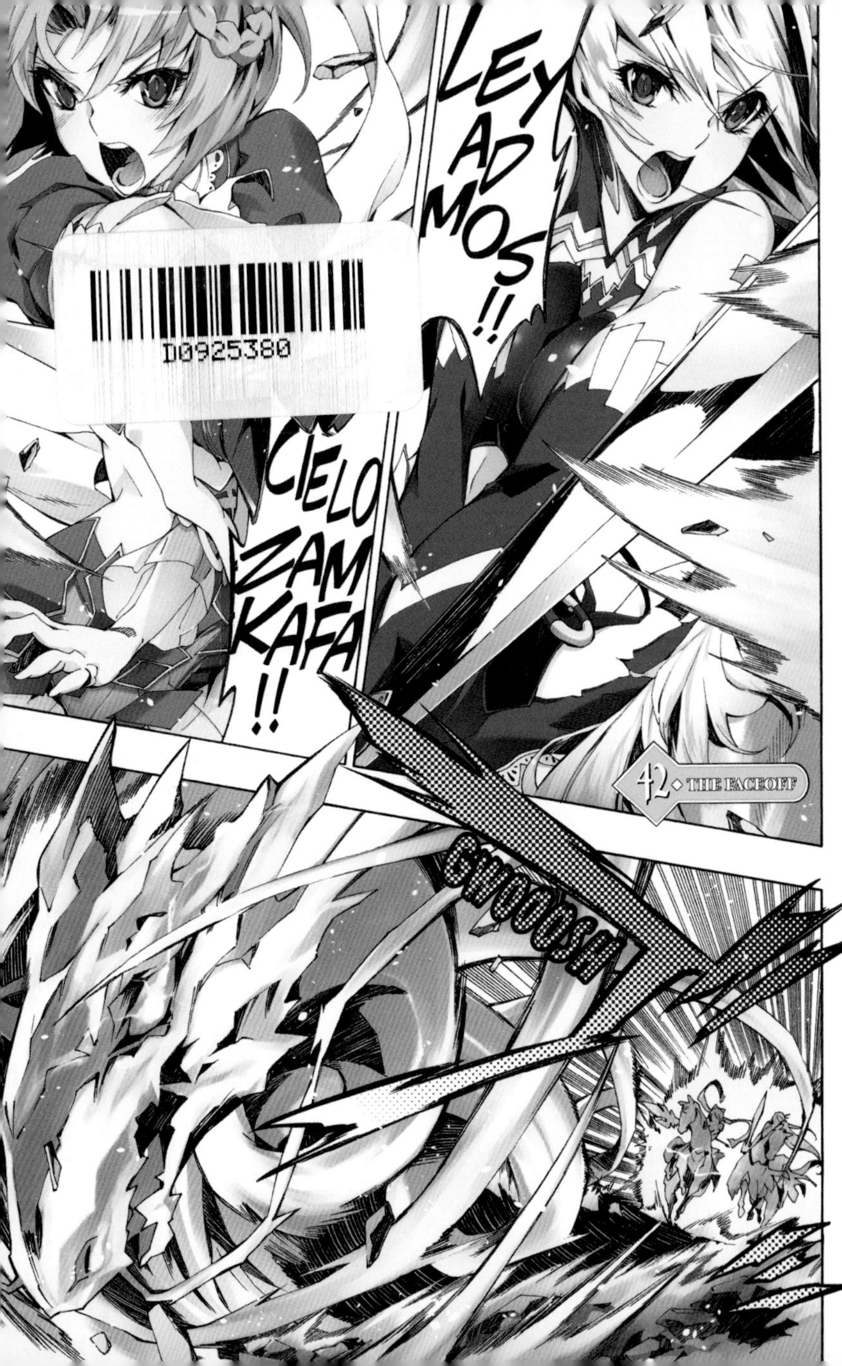
LEY AD MOS!!
CIELO ZAM KAFA!!
42 ◆ THE FACEOFF
GWOOOSH

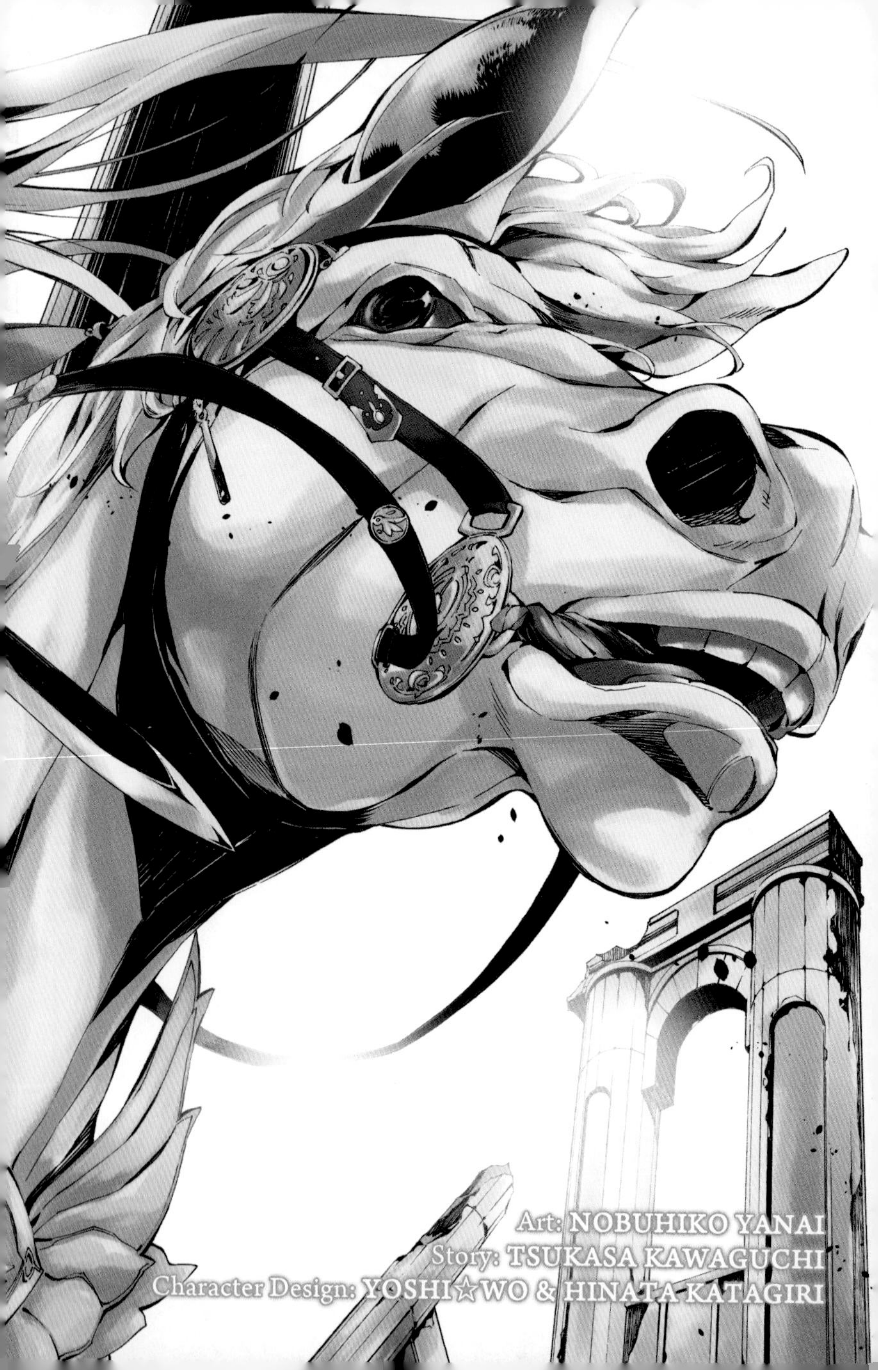
Art: NOBUHIKO YANAI
Story: TSUKASA KAWAGUCHI
Character Design: YOSHI☆WO & HINATA KATAGIRI

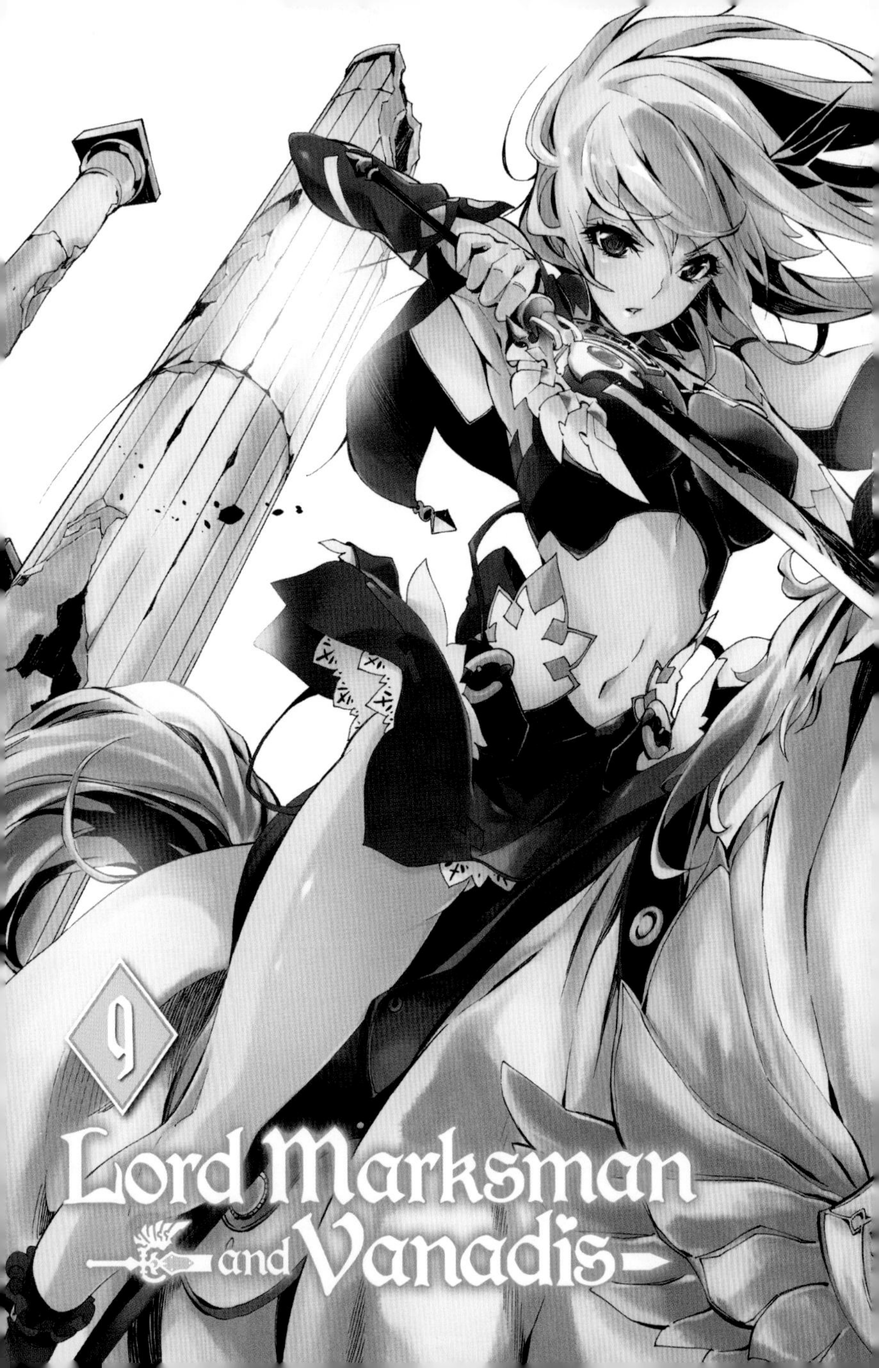
9
Lord Marksman
and Vanadis

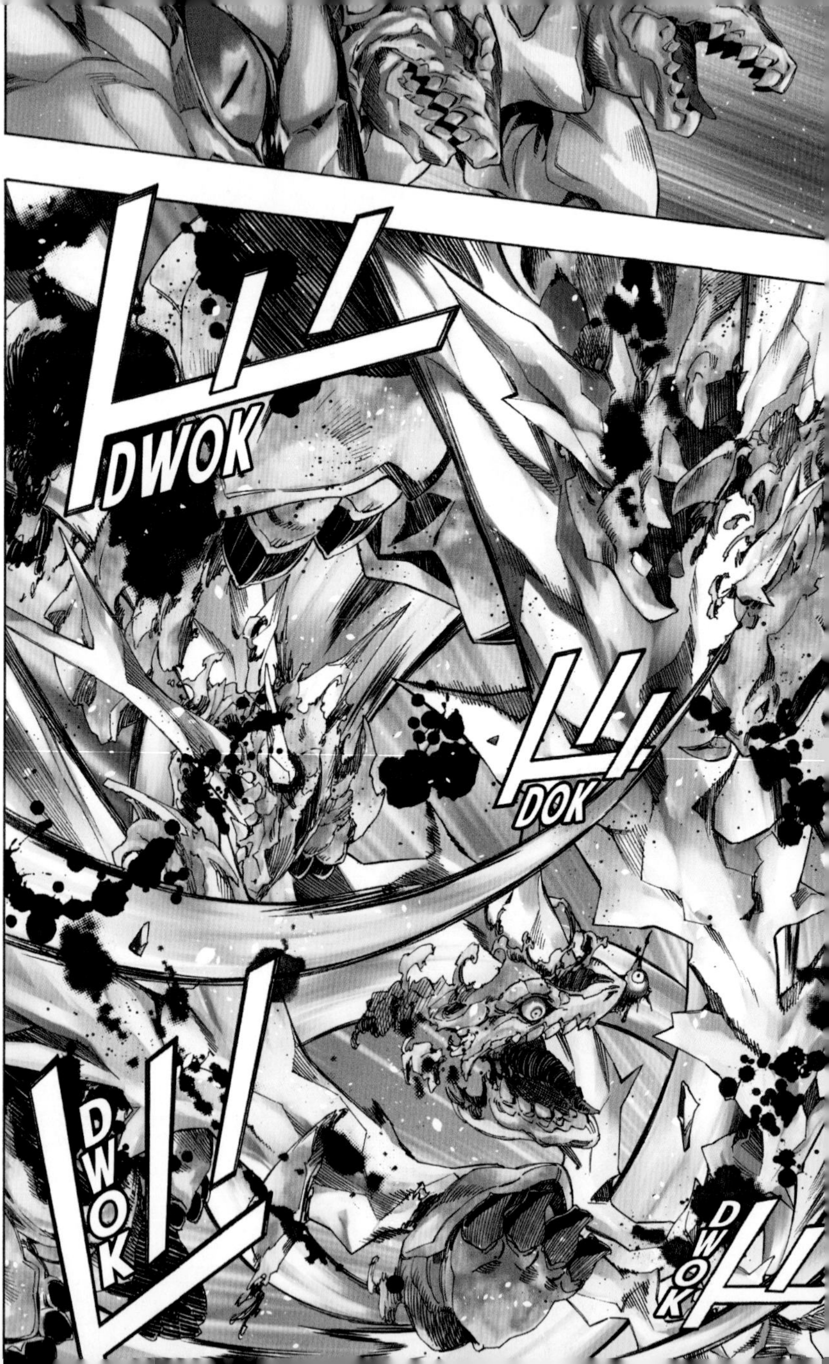
DWOK
DOK
DWOK
DWOK

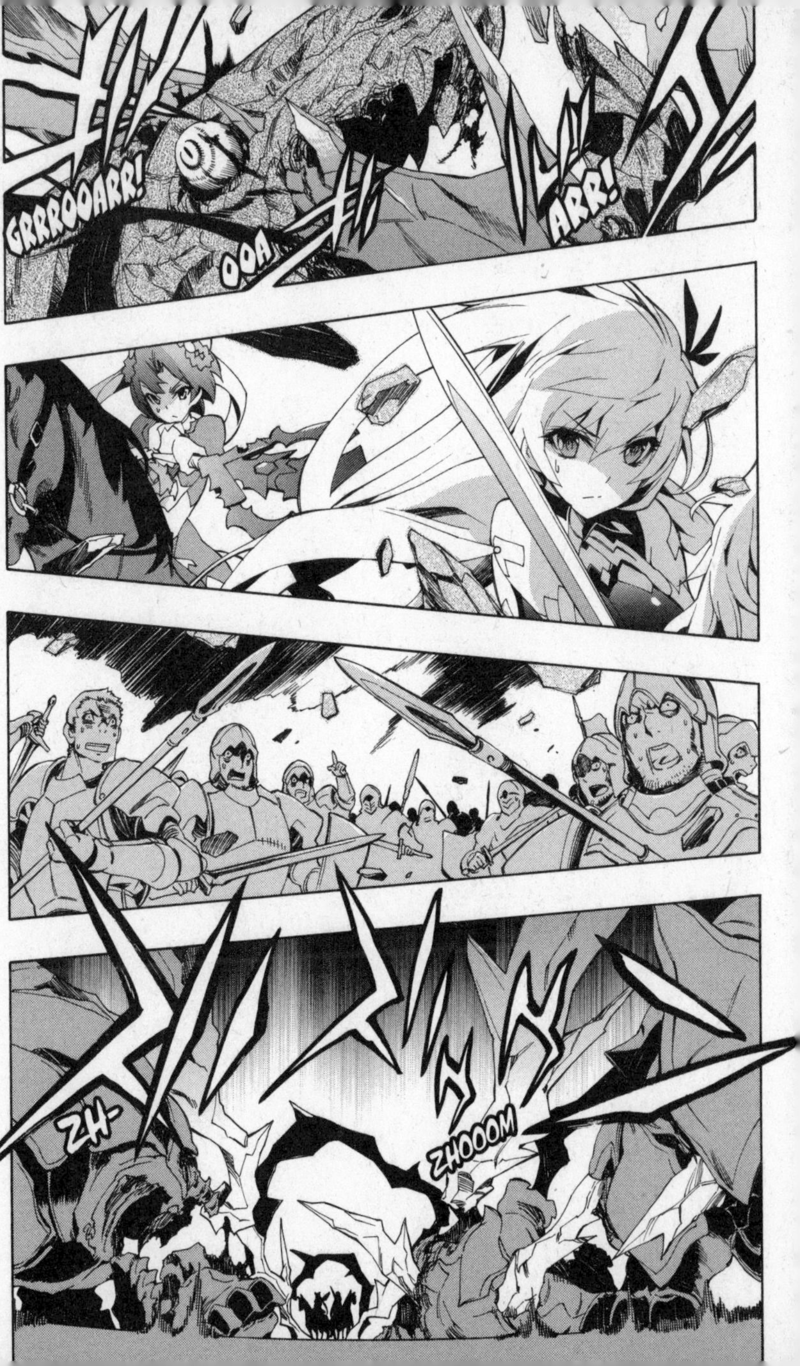
ARR!
OOA
GRRROOARR!
ZHOOOM
ZH-

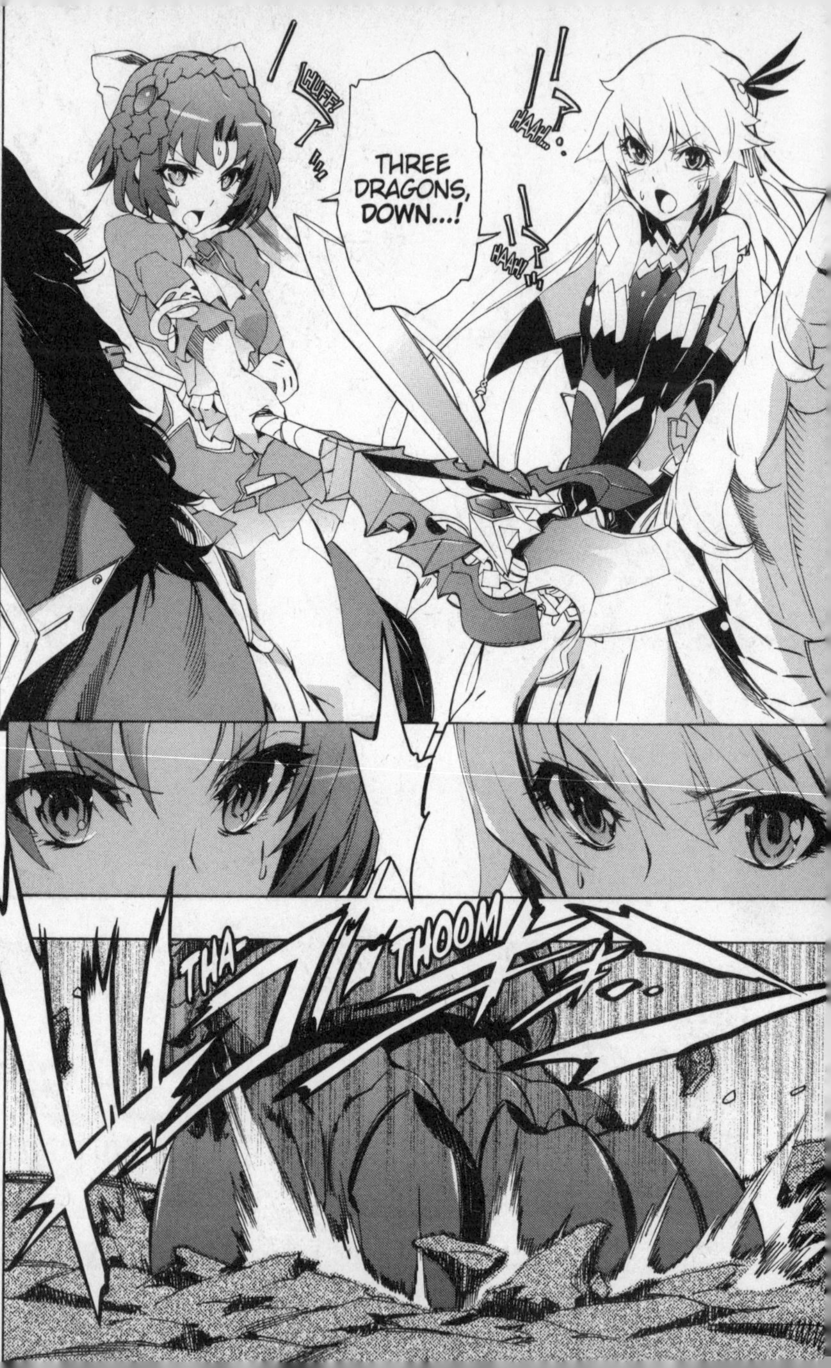
HAAH!...
HAAH!
THREE DRAGONS, DOWN...!
HUFF!
THA-THOOM

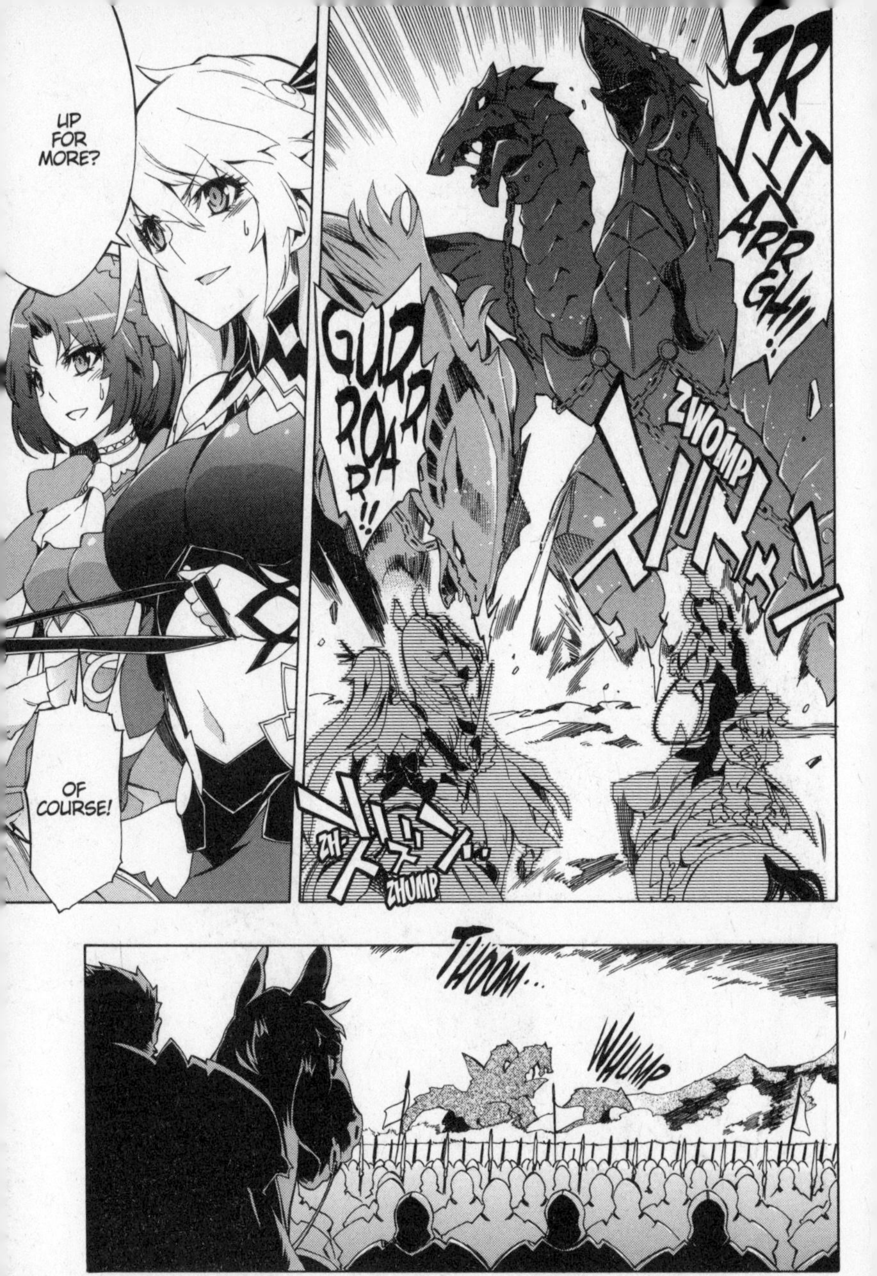
ARRGH!!
ZWOMP
GUDROARR!!
ZHUMP
UP FOR MORE?
OF COURSE!
THOOM...
WHUMP

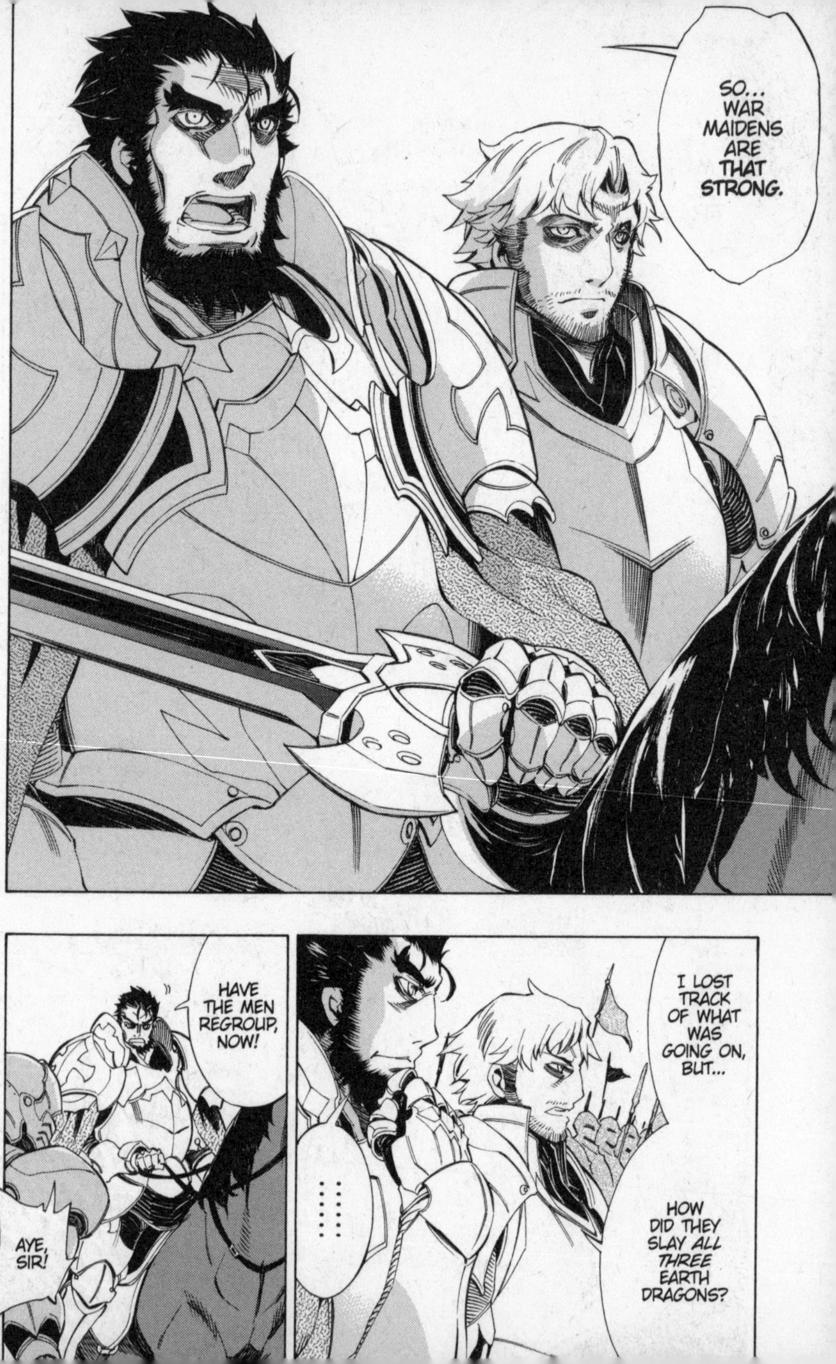
SO... WAR MAIDENS ARE THAT STRONG.
I LOST TRACK OF WHAT WAS GOING ON, BUT...
HOW DID THEY SLAY *ALL THREE* EARTH DRAGONS?
......
HAVE THE MEN REGROUP, NOW!
AYE, SIR!

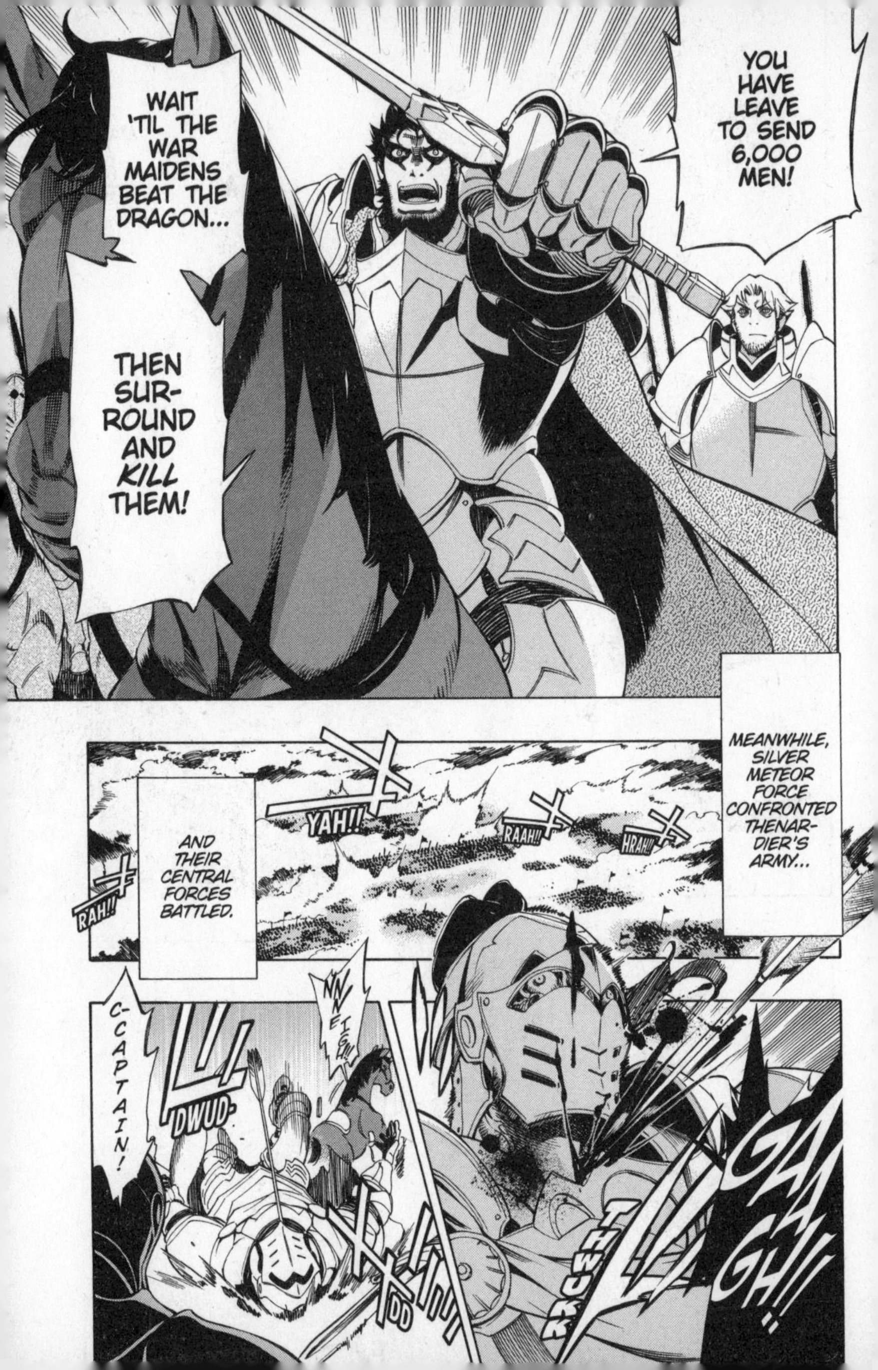
YOU HAVE LEAVE TO SEND 6,000 MEN!
WAIT 'TIL THE WAR MAIDENS BEAT THE DRAGON...
THEN SUR-ROUND AND *KILL* THEM!
MEANWHILE, SILVER METEOR FORCE CONFRONTED THENAR-DIER'S ARMY...
HRAH!!
RAAH!!
YAH!!
AND THEIR CENTRAL FORCES BATTLED.
RAH!!
THWUKK
NNNEIGH!!
DWUD-
C-CAPTAIN!

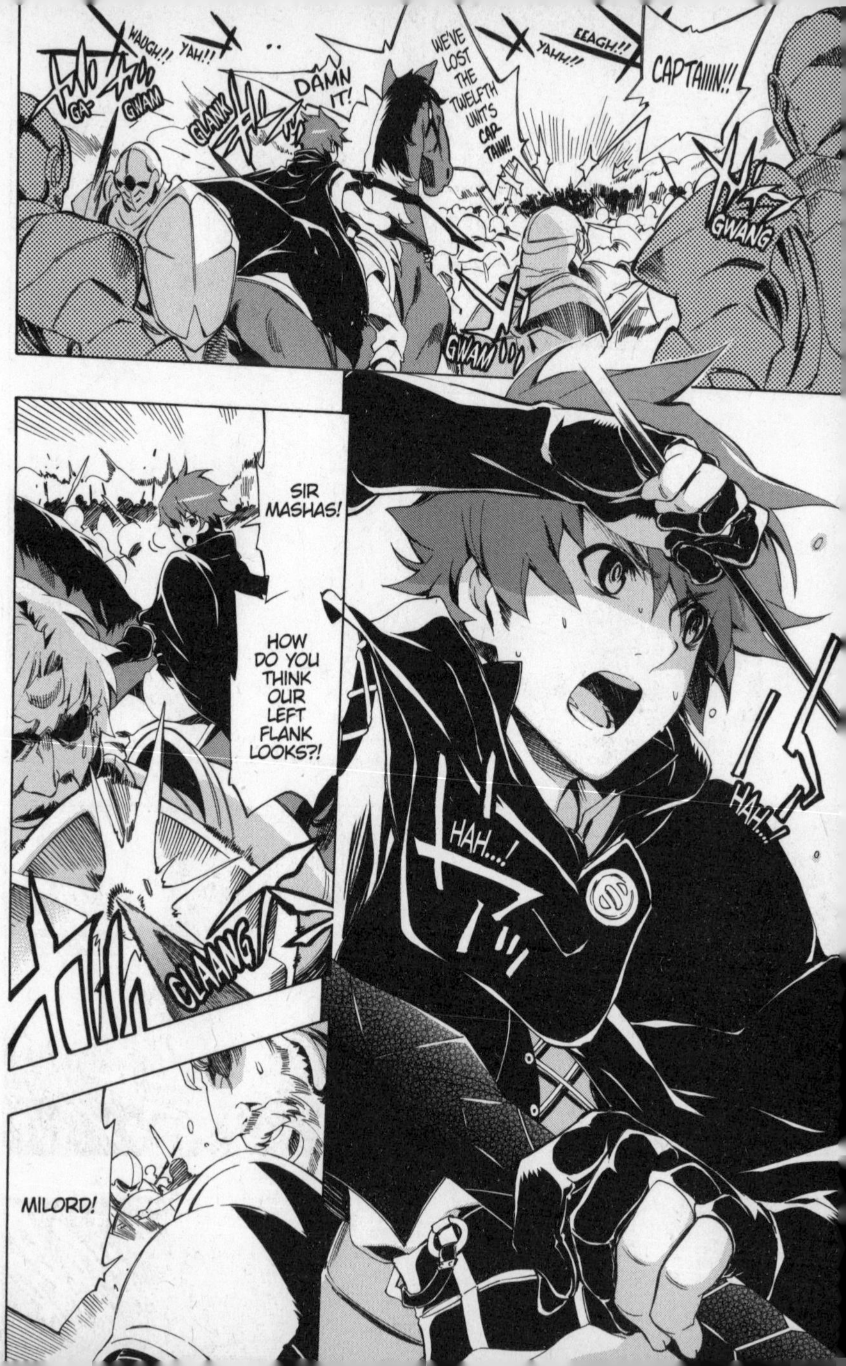
CAPTAIIIN!!
GWANG
EEAGH!!
YAHH!!
WE'VE LOST THE TWELFTH UNIT'S CAPTAIN!!
GWAM
DAMN IT!
GLANK
YAH!!
WAUGH!!
GA-GWAM
HAH...!
HAH...!
SIR MASHAS!
HOW DO YOU THINK OUR LEFT FLANK LOOKS?!
CLAANG
MILORD!

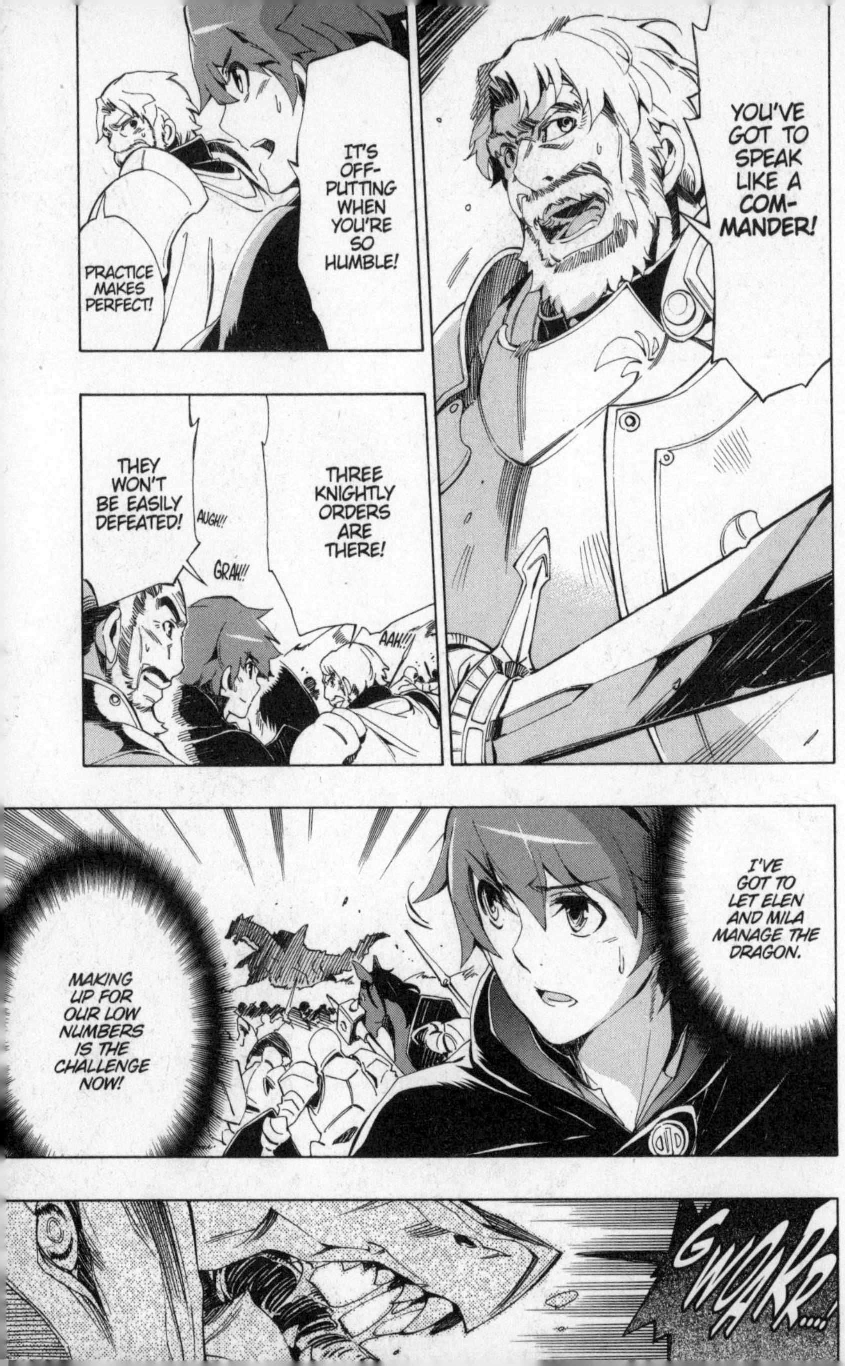
YOU'VE GOT TO SPEAK LIKE A COM-MANDER!
IT'S OFF-PUTTING WHEN YOU'RE SO HUMBLE!
PRACTICE MAKES PERFECT!
THREE KNIGHTLY ORDERS ARE THERE!
THEY WON'T BE EASILY DEFEATED!
AUGH!!
GRAH!!
AAH!!
I'VE GOT TO LET ELEN AND MILA MANAGE THE DRAGON.
MAKING UP FOR OUR LOW NUMBERS IS THE CHALLENGE NOW!
GWAKRR....!

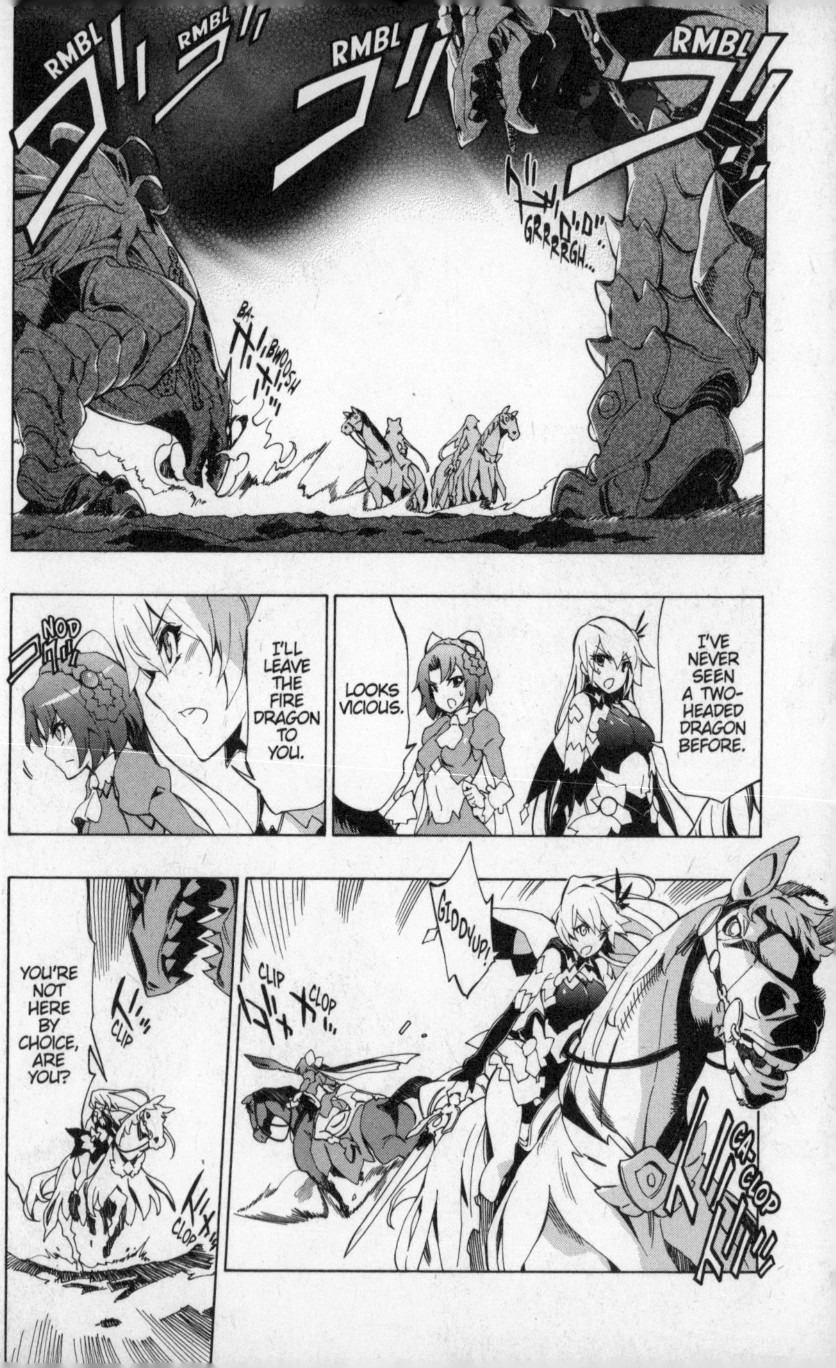
RMBL
RMBL
GRRRRRGH...
RMBL
RMBL
BA-BWOOSH
I'VE NEVER SEEN A TWO-HEADED DRAGON BEFORE.
LOOKS VICIOUS.
I'LL LEAVE THE FIRE DRAGON TO YOU.
NOD
GIDDYUP!
GA-CLOP
CLIP
CLOP
YOU'RE NOT HERE BY CHOICE, ARE YOU?
CLIP
CLOP

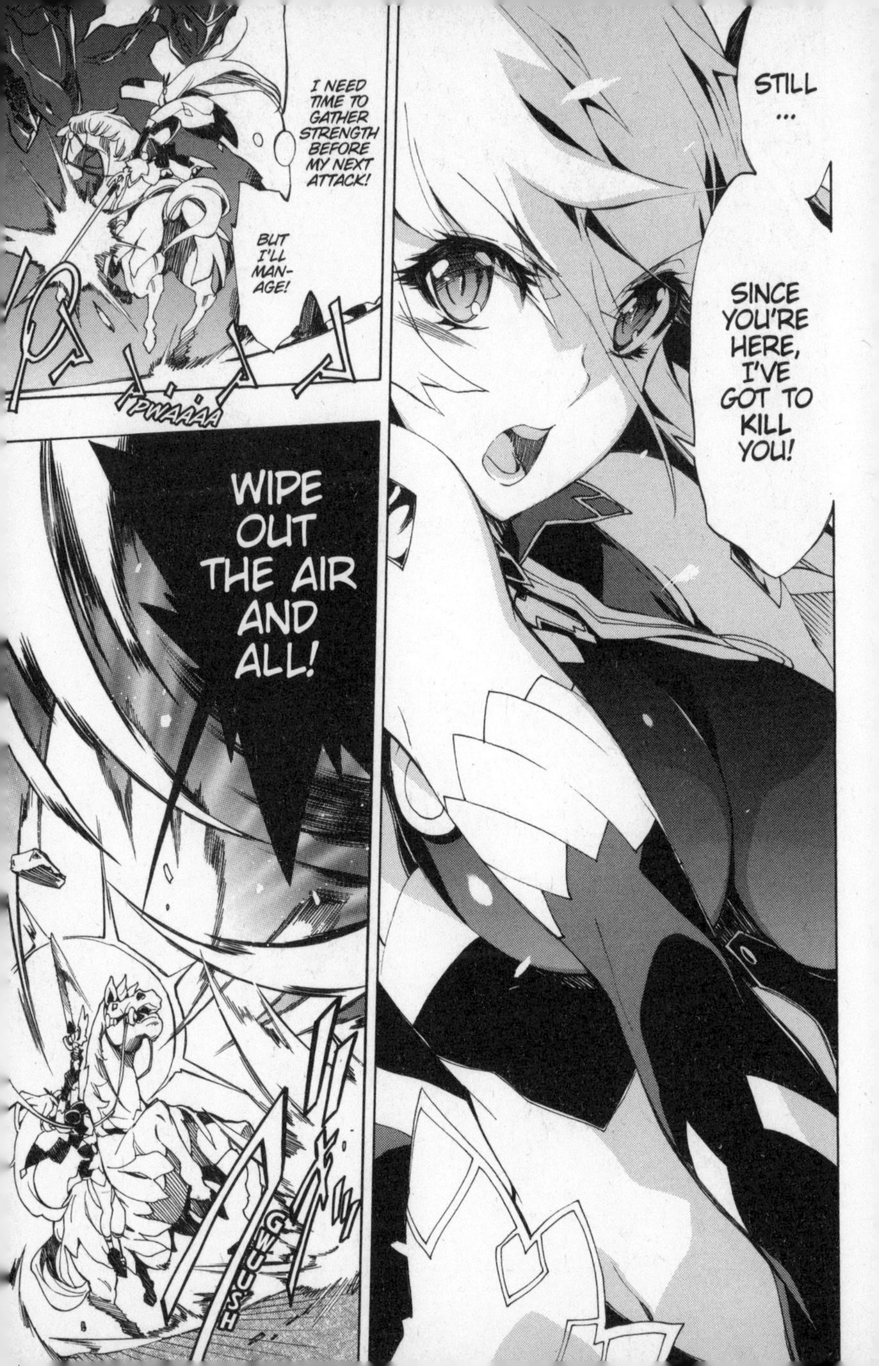
STILL ...
SINCE YOU'RE HERE, I'VE GOT TO KILL YOU!
I NEED TIME TO GATHER STRENGTH BEFORE MY NEXT ATTACK!
BUT I'LL MAN-AGE!
PWAAAA
WIPE OUT THE AIR AND ALL!
GWUUSH

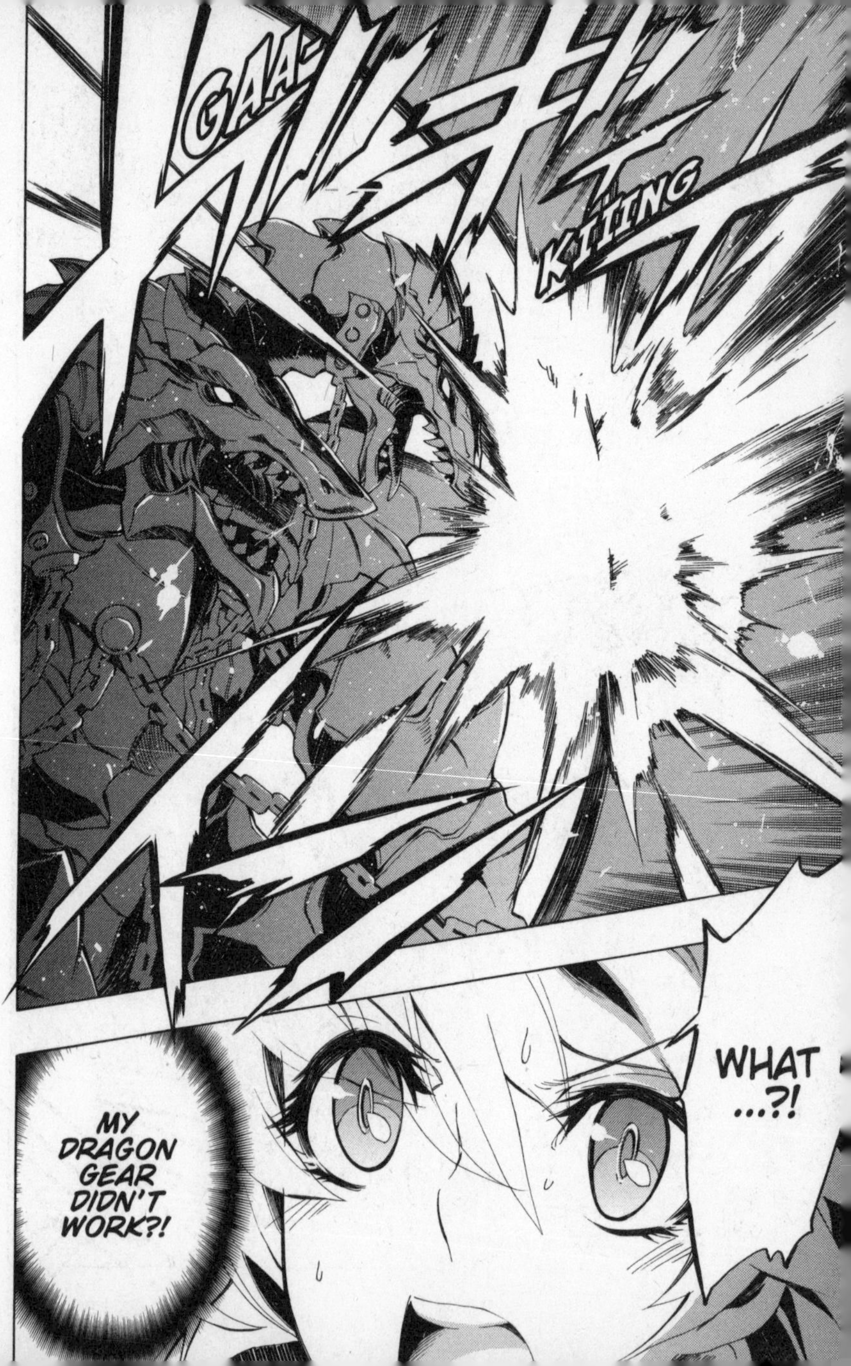
GAA-
KIIING
WHAT ...?!
MY DRAGON GEAR DIDN'T WORK?!

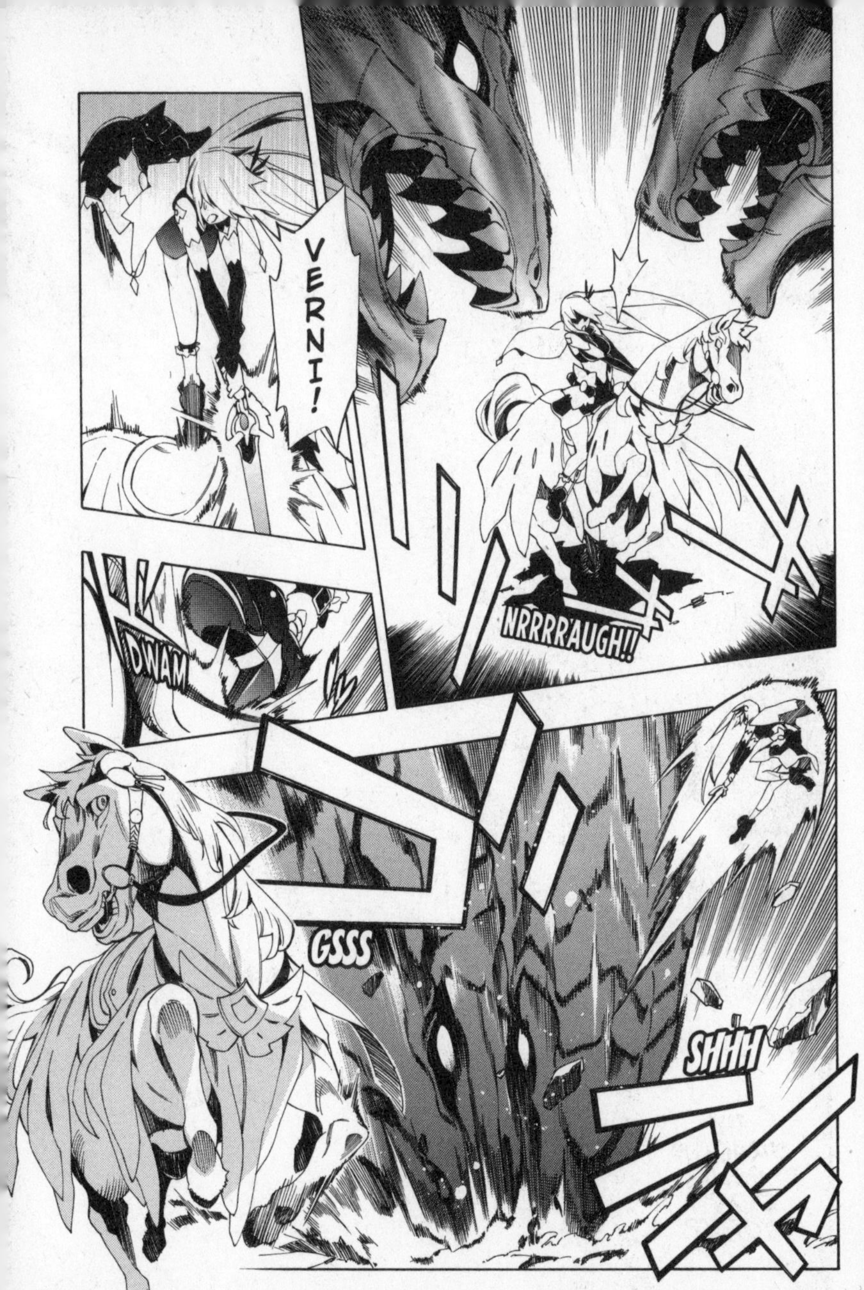
NRRRRAUGH!!
VERNI!
DWAM
SHHH
GSSS

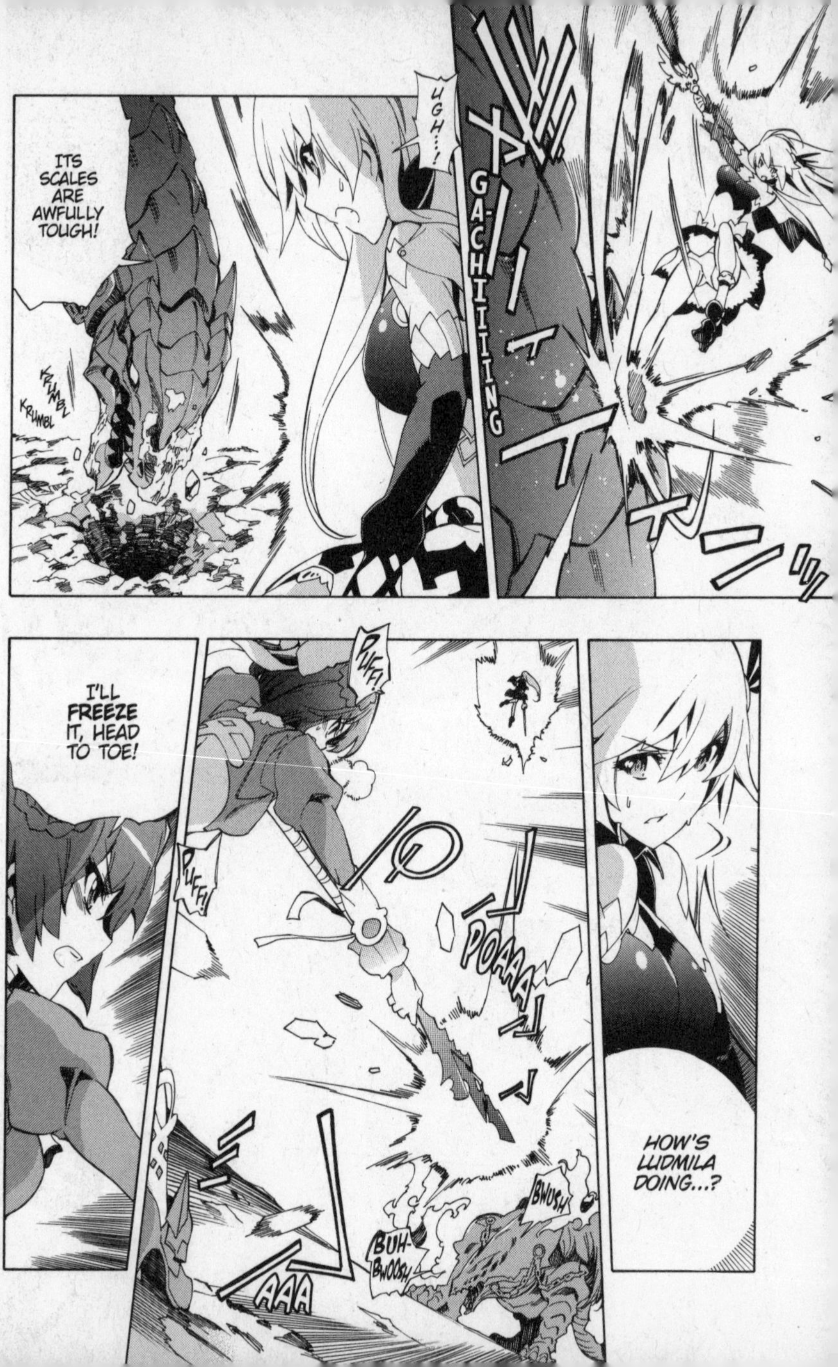
GA-CHIIIING
UGH...!
ITS SCALES ARE AWFULLY TOUGH!
KRUMBL KRUMBL
HOW'S LUDMILA DOING...?
PUFF!
PUFF!
POAAAA
BWUSH
BUH-BWOOSH
AAA
I'LL FREEZE IT, HEAD TO TOE!

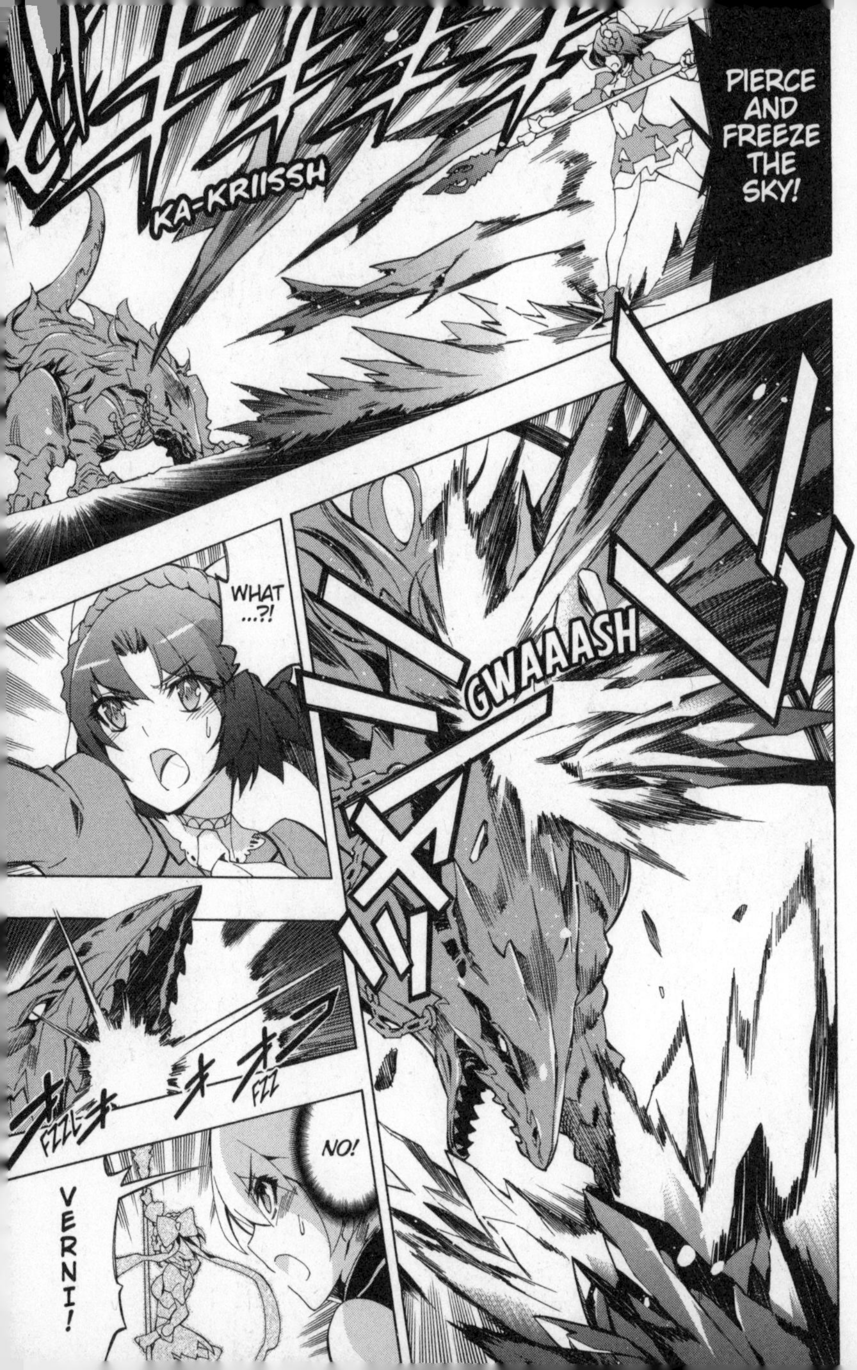
PIERCE AND FREEZE THE SKY!
KA-KRIISSH
GWAAASH
WHAT ...?!
FZZLE
FZZ
NO!
VERNI!

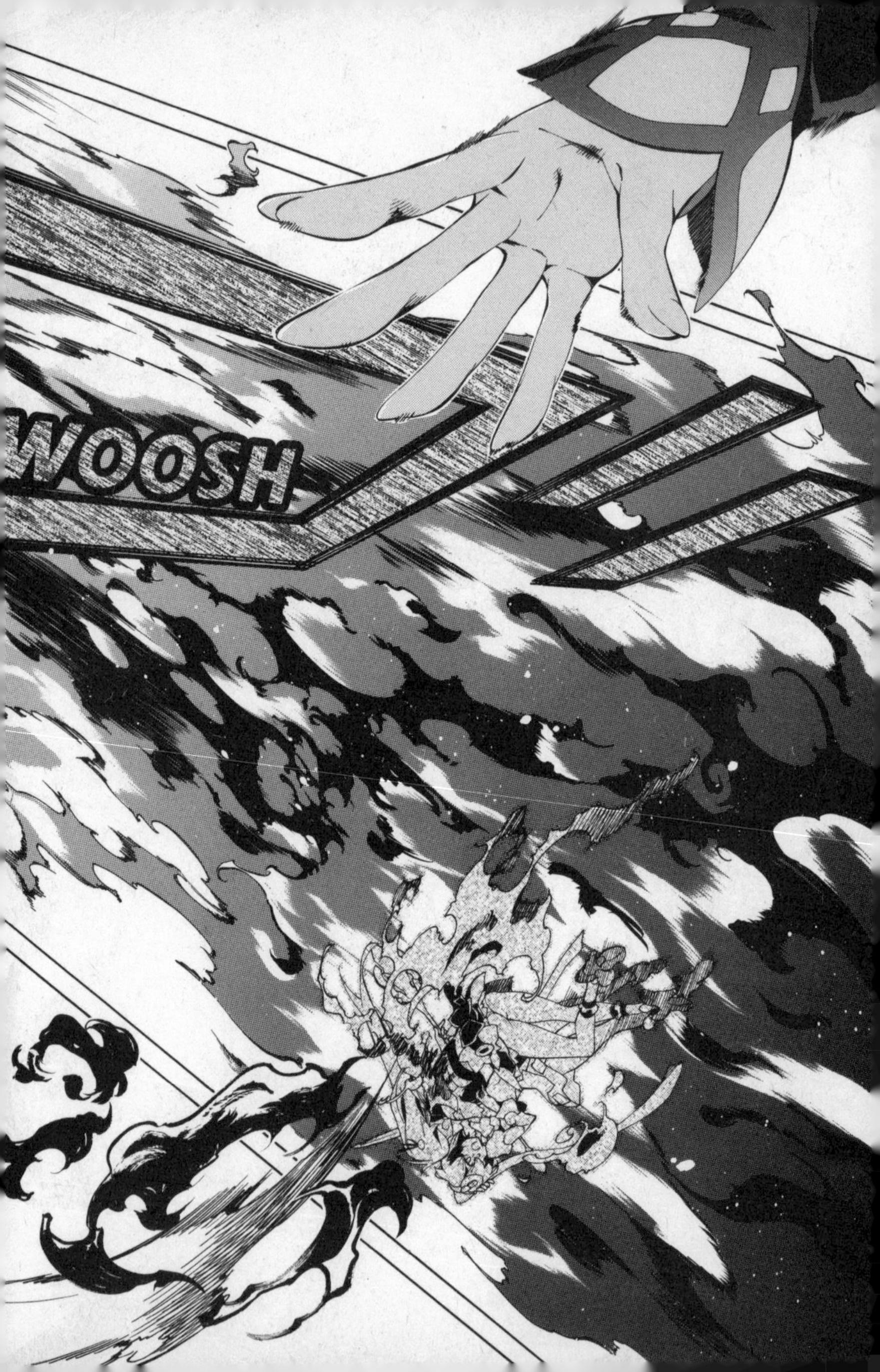
WOOSH

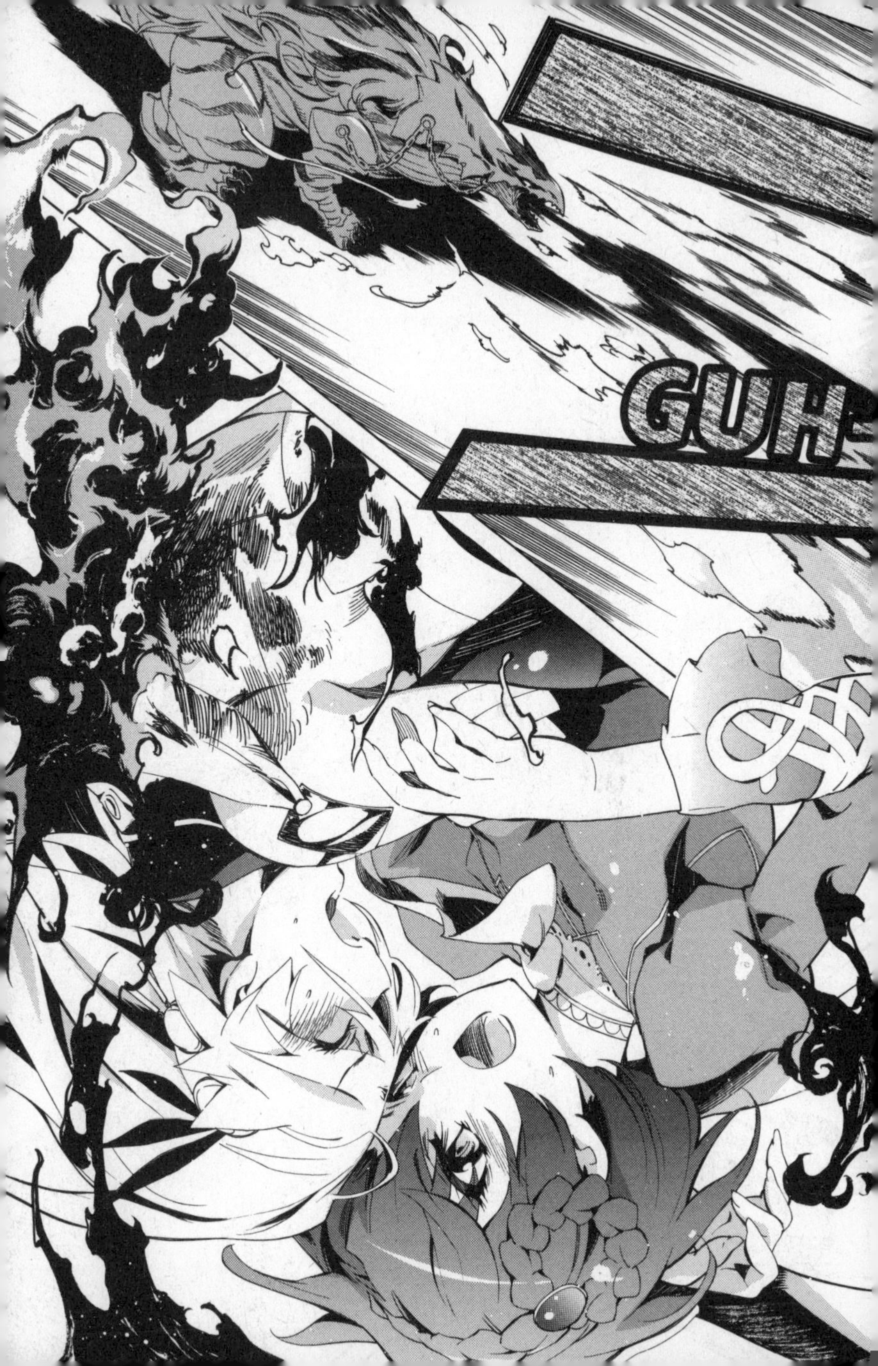
GUH

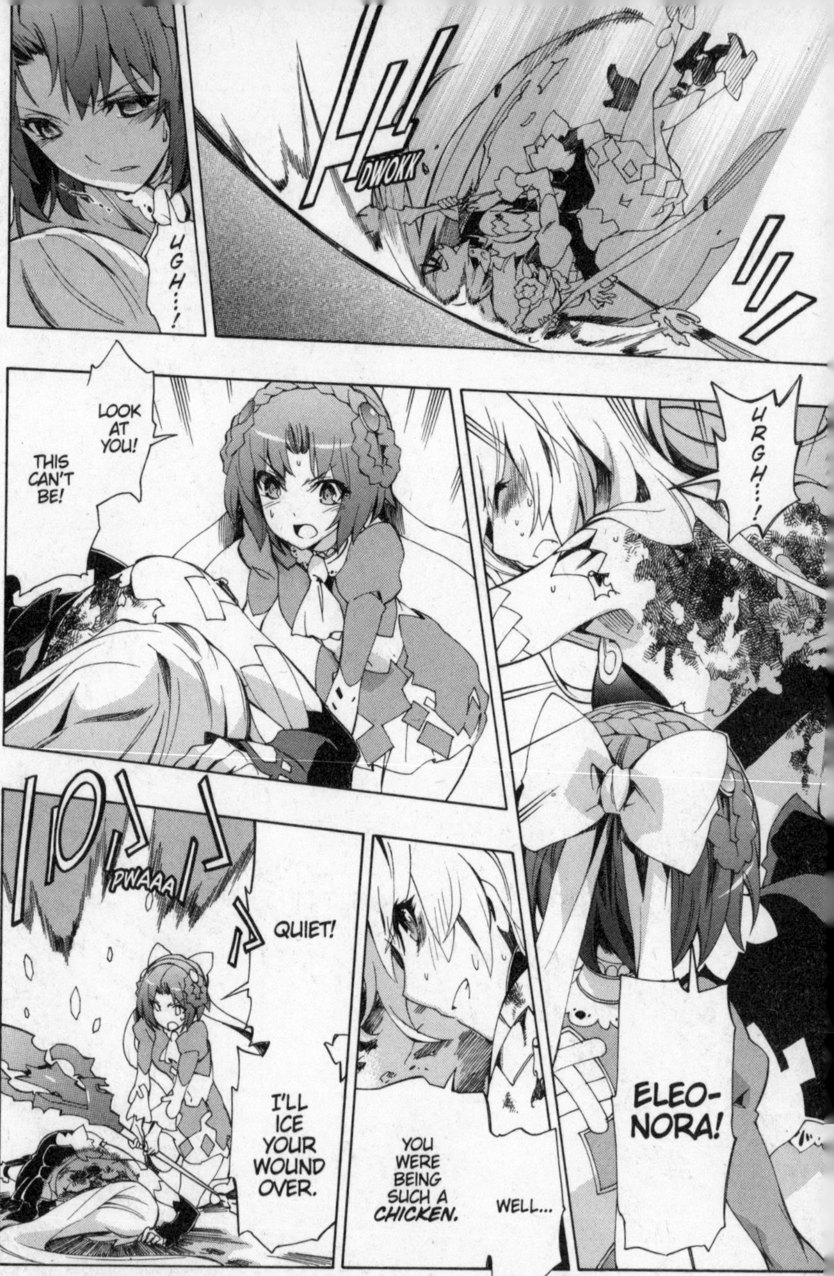
DWOKK
UGH...!
URGH...!
LOOK AT YOU!
THIS CAN'T BE!
ELEO-NORA!
WELL...
YOU WERE BEING SUCH A CHICKEN.
PWAAA
QUIET!
I'LL ICE YOUR WOUND OVER.

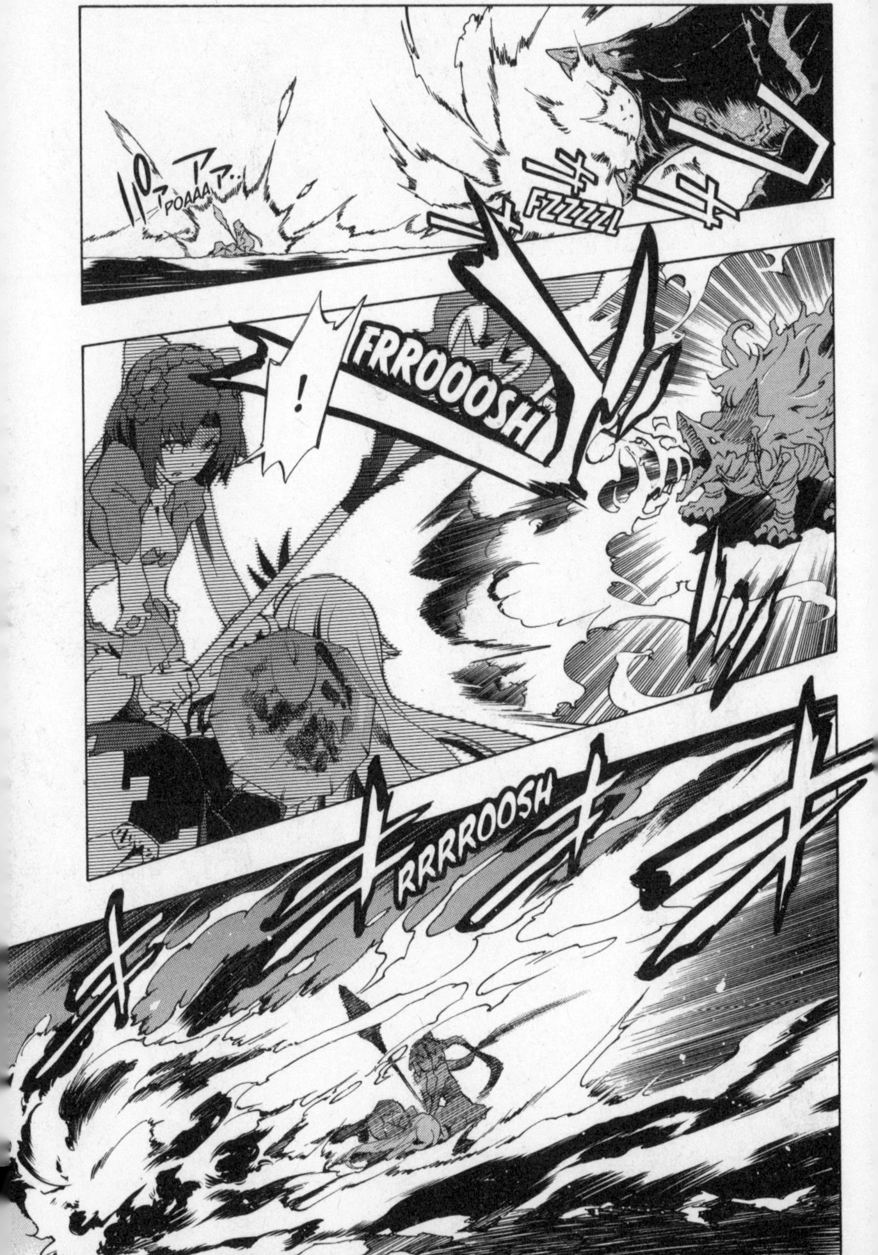
FZZZZL
POAAA
FRROOOSH
!
RRRROOSH

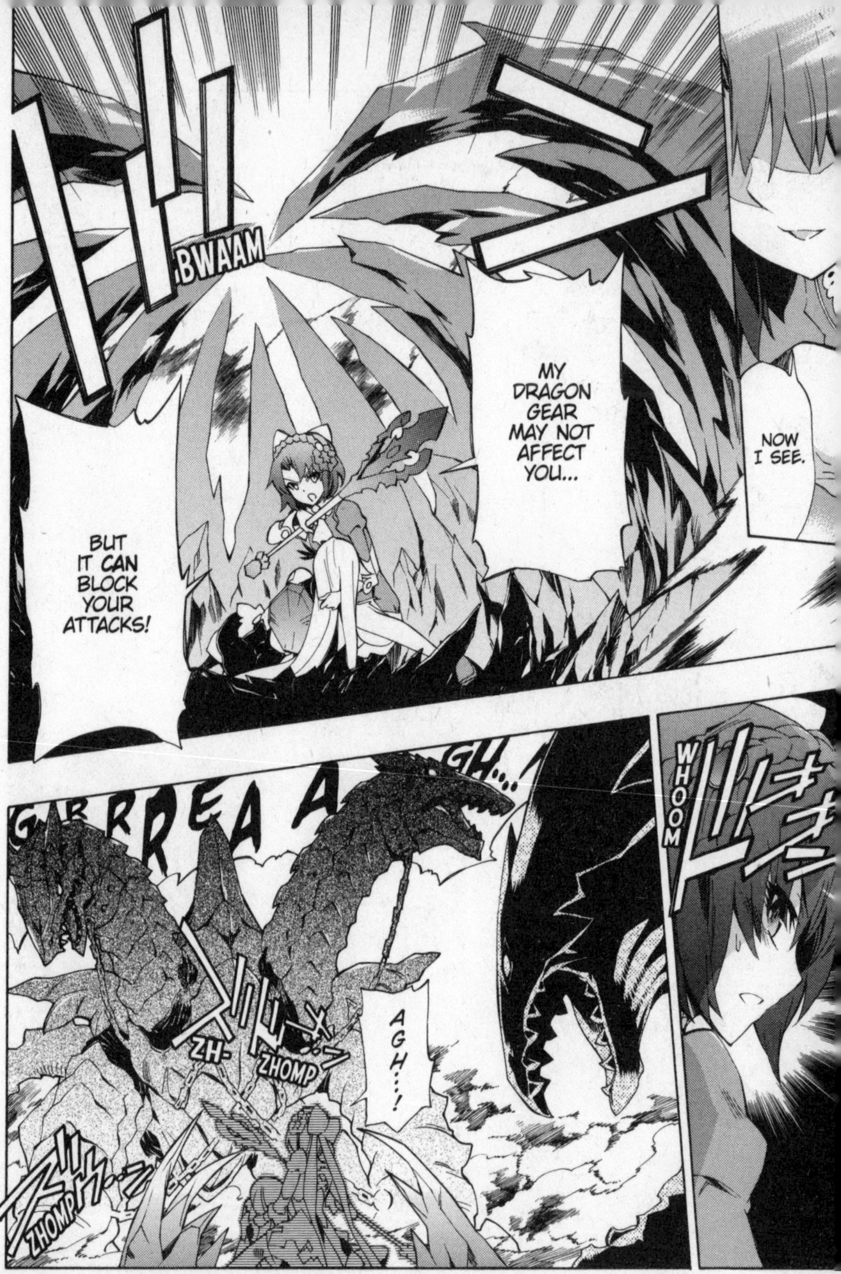
NOW I SEE.
BWAAM
MY DRAGON GEAR MAY NOT AFFECT YOU...
BUT IT CAN BLOCK YOUR ATTACKS!
WHOOM
GRRREAAAGH..!
AGH...!
ZH- ZHOMP
ZHOMP

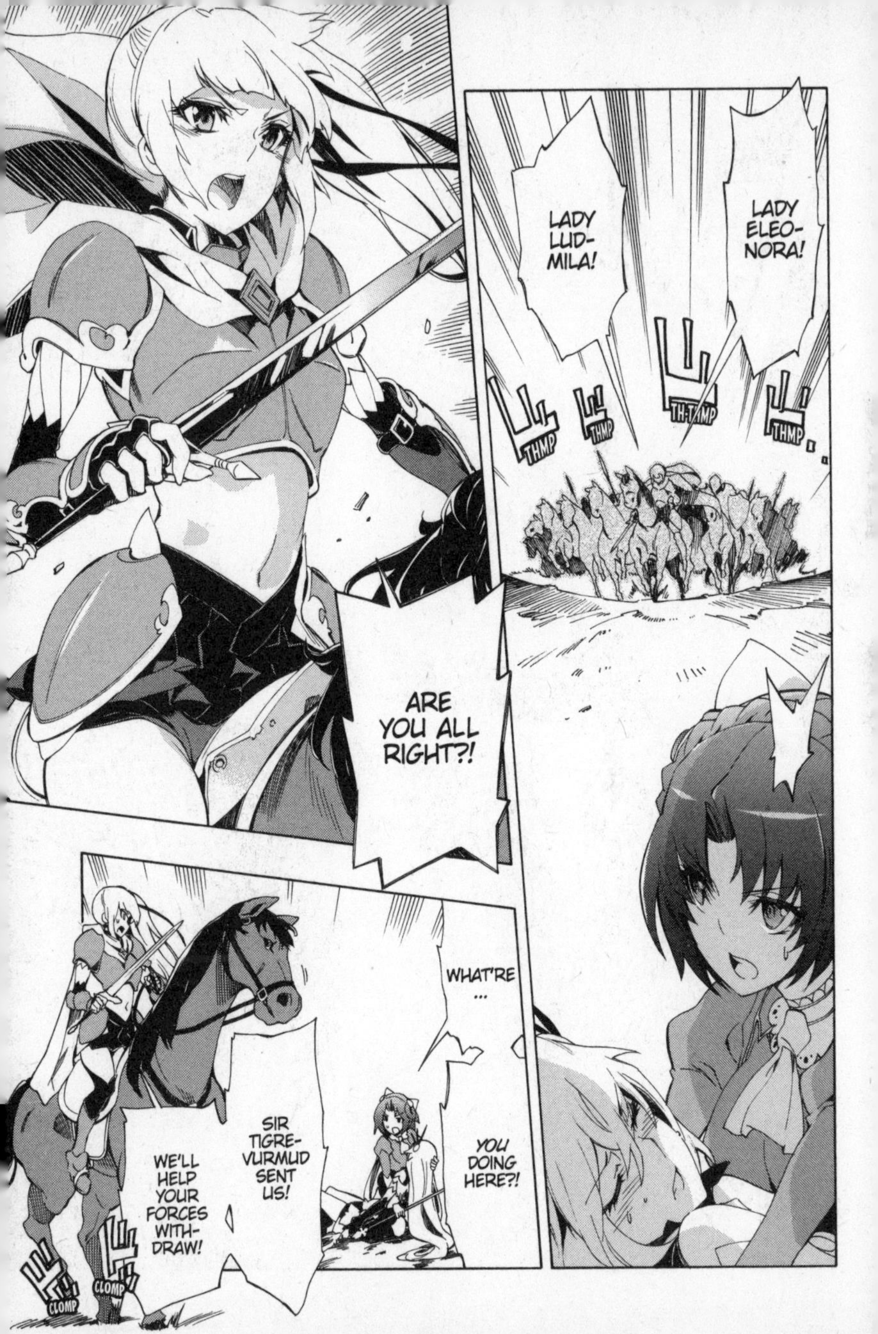
LADY ELEO-NORA!
LADY LUD-MILA!
THMP
TH-THMP
THMP
THMP
ARE YOU ALL RIGHT?!
WHAT'RE ...
YOU DOING HERE?!
SIR TIGRE-VURMUD SENT US!
WE'LL HELP YOUR FORCES WITH-DRAW!
CLOMP
CLOMP

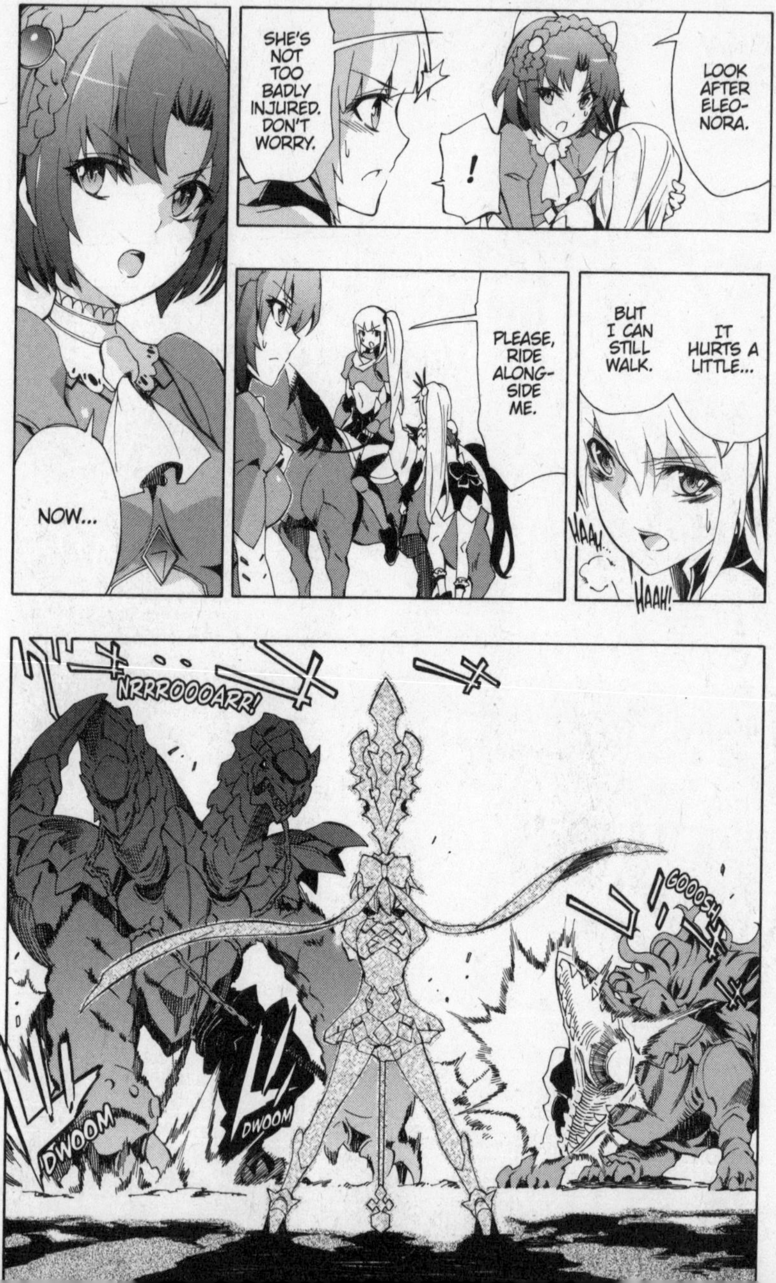
LOOK AFTER ELEO-NORA.
!
SHE'S NOT TOO BADLY INJURED. DON'T WORRY.
IT HURTS A LITTLE...
BUT I CAN STILL WALK.
HAAH...
HAAH!
PLEASE, RIDE ALONG-SIDE ME.
NOW...
GOOOSH
NRRROOOARR!
DWOOM
DWOOM

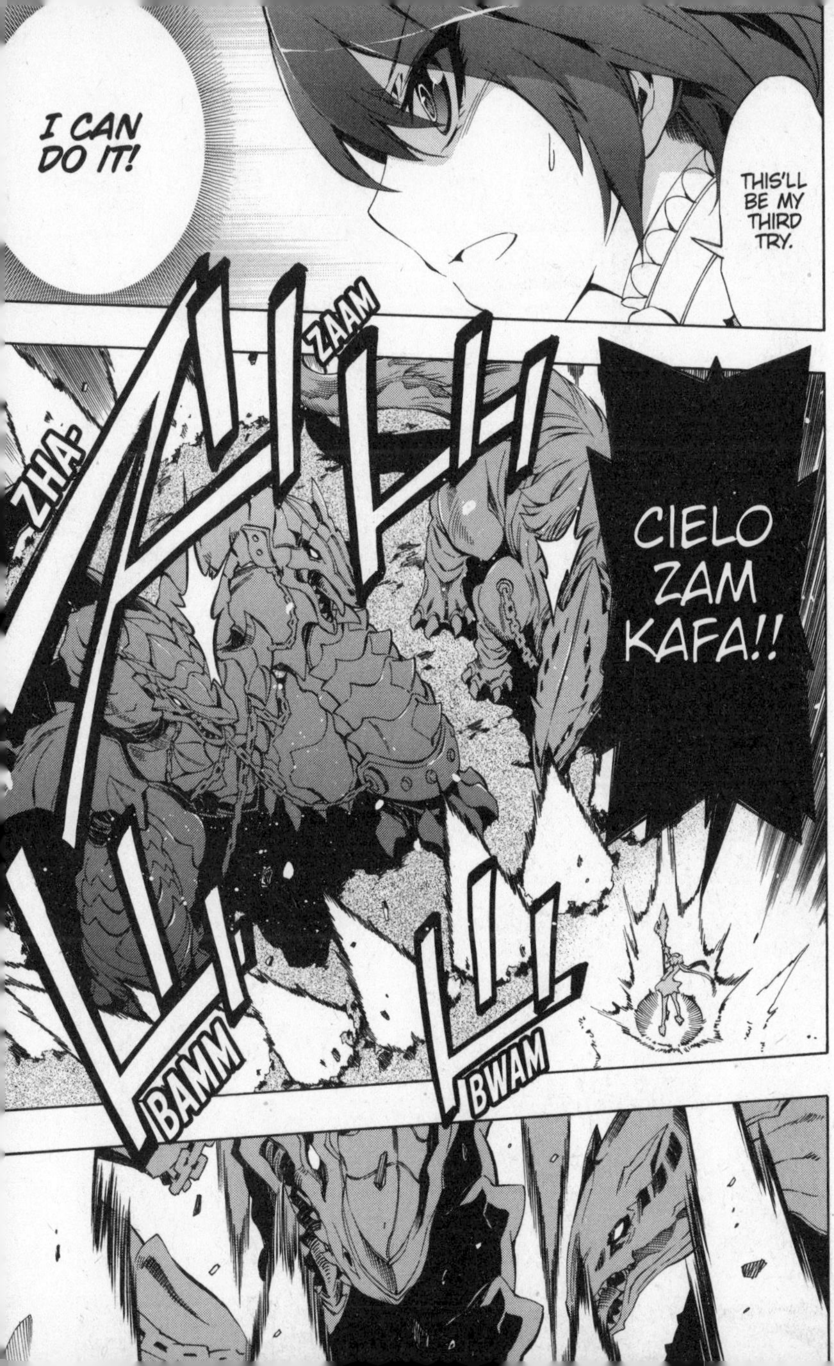
THIS'LL BE MY THIRD TRY.
I CAN DO IT!
CIELO ZAM KAFA!!
ZAAM
ZHA
BWAM
BAMM

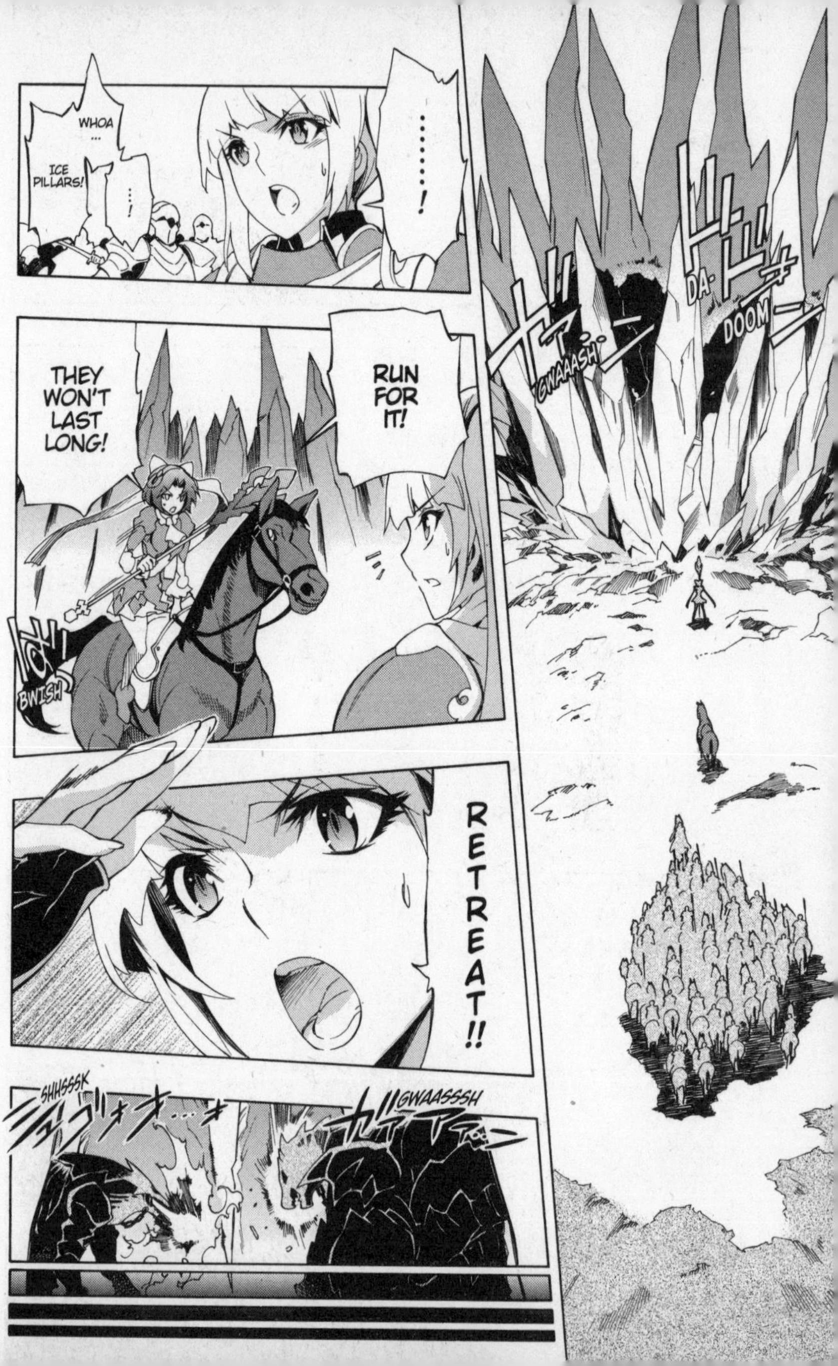
DA-
DOOM
GWAAASH
......!
WHOA ...
ICE PILLARS!
...!
RUN FOR IT!
THEY WON'T LAST LONG!
BWISH
RETREAT!!
GWAASSSH
SHHSSSK

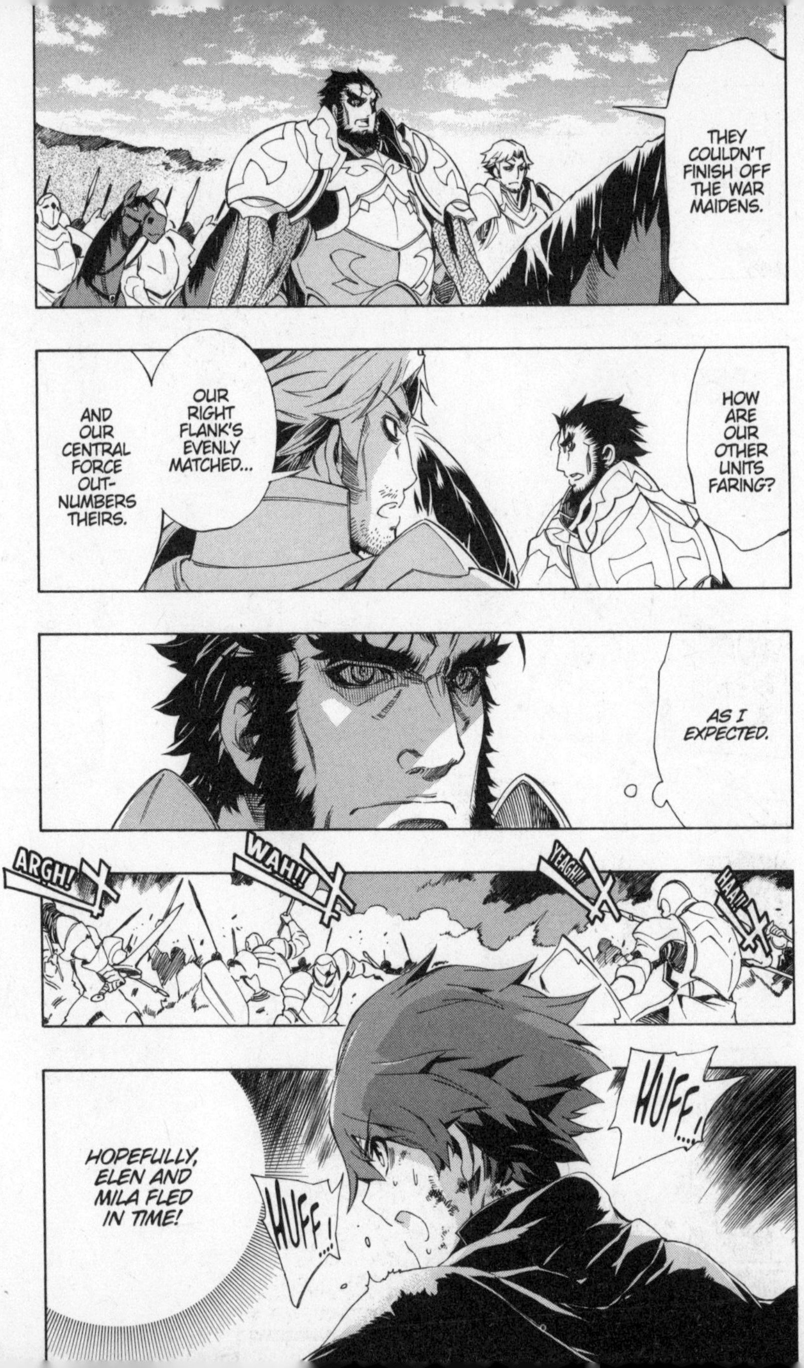
THEY COULDN'T FINISH OFF THE WAR MAIDENS.
HOW ARE OUR OTHER UNITS FARING?
OUR RIGHT FLANK'S EVENLY MATCHED...
AND OUR CENTRAL FORCE OUT-NUMBERS THEIRS.
AS I EXPECTED.
HAA!!
YEAGH!!
WAH!!
ARGH!
HUFF...!
HUFF...!
HOPEFULLY, ELEN AND MILA FLED IN TIME!

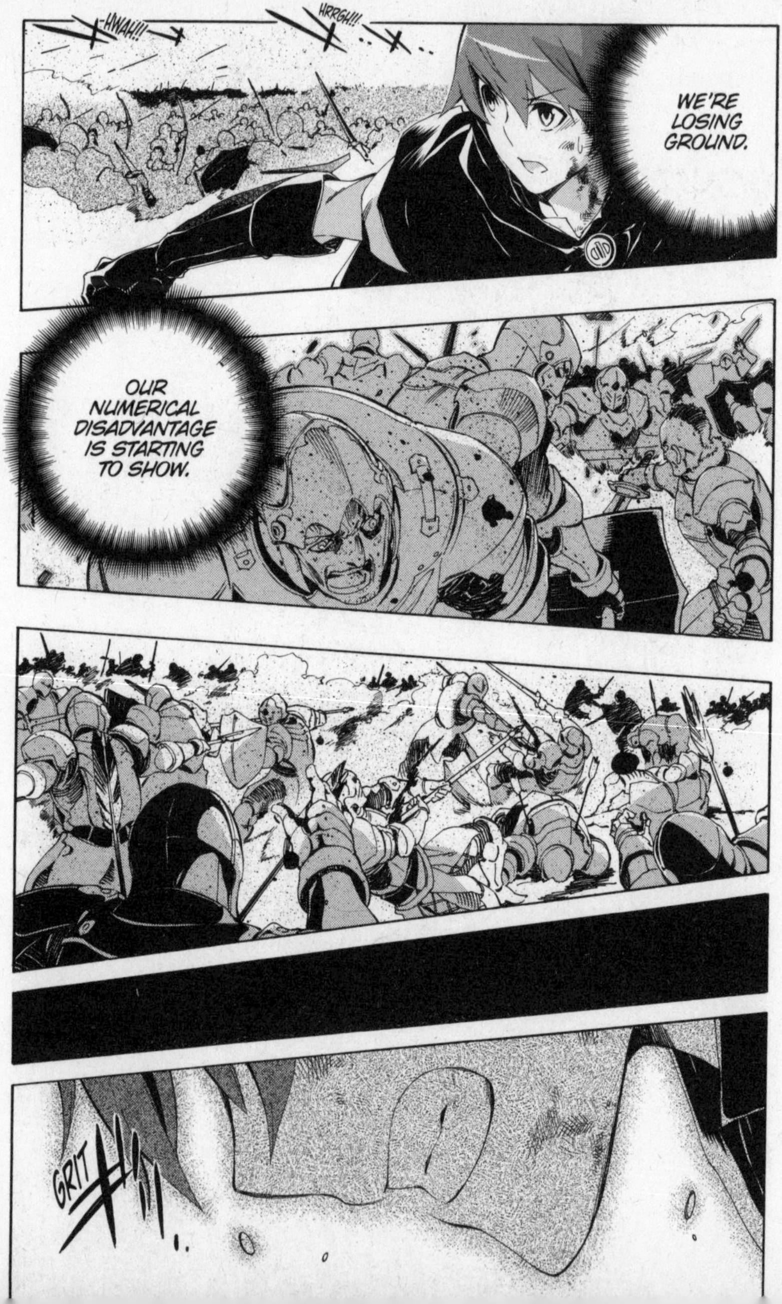
HRRGH!!!
HWAH!!!
WE'RE LOSING GROUND.
OUR NUMERICAL DISADVANTAGE IS STARTING TO SHOW.
GRIT

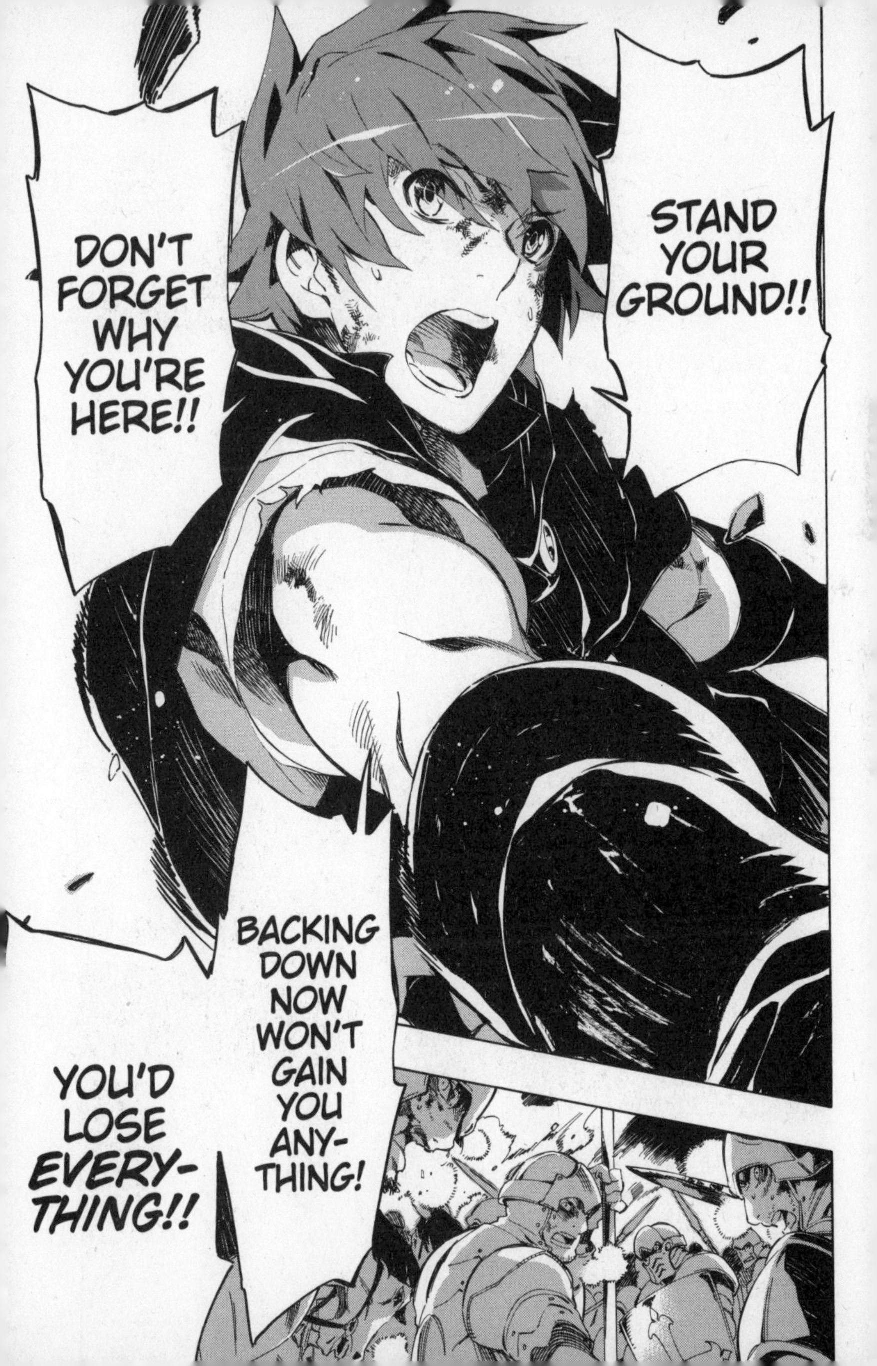
STAND YOUR GROUND!!
DON'T FORGET WHY YOU'RE HERE!!
BACKING DOWN NOW WON'T GAIN YOU ANY-THING!
YOU'D LOSE EVERY-THING!!

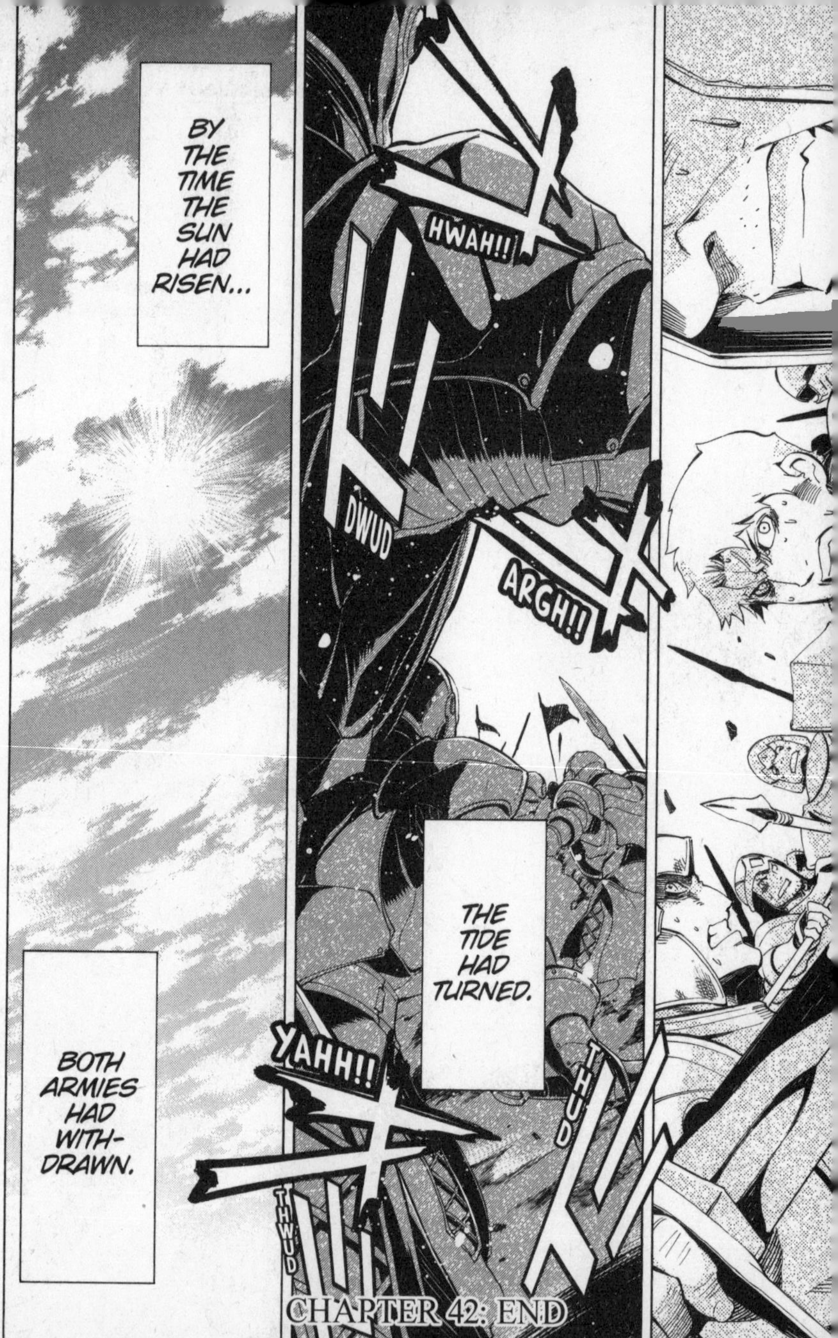
HWAH!!
DWUD
ARGH!!
THE TIDE HAD TURNED.
YAHH!!
THUD
THWUD
BY THE TIME THE SUN HAD RISEN...
BOTH ARMIES HAD WITH-DRAWN.

CHAPTER 42: END

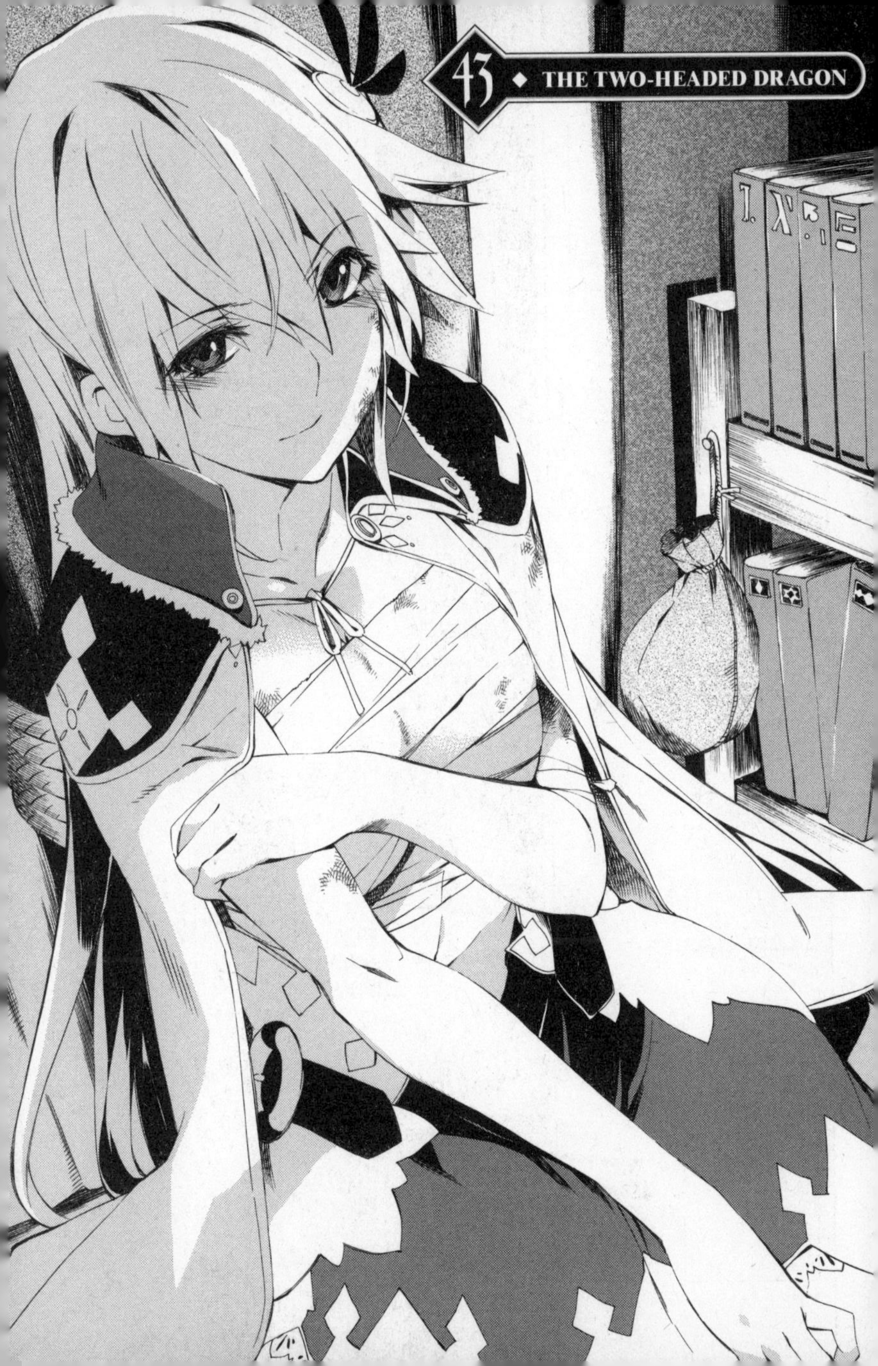
43 ◆ THE TWO-HEADED DRAGON

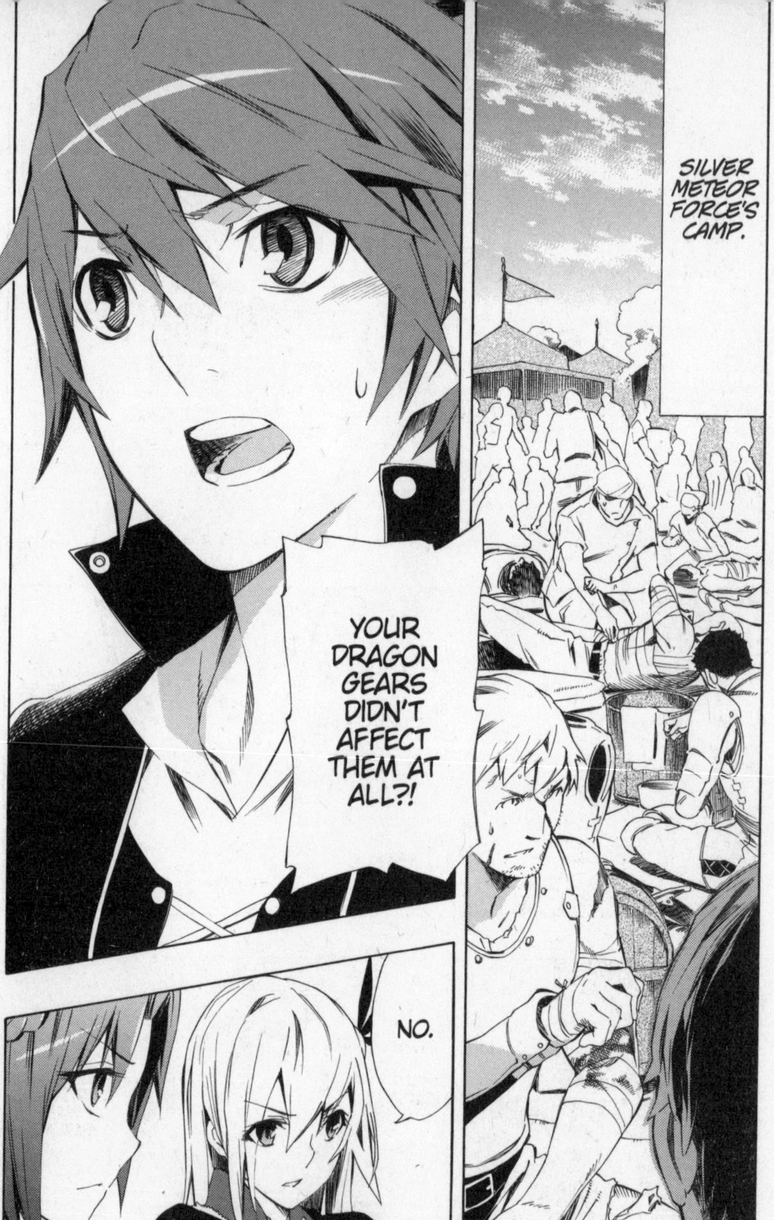
SILVER METEOR FORCE'S CAMP.
YOUR DRAGON GEARS DIDN'T AFFECT THEM AT ALL?!
NO.

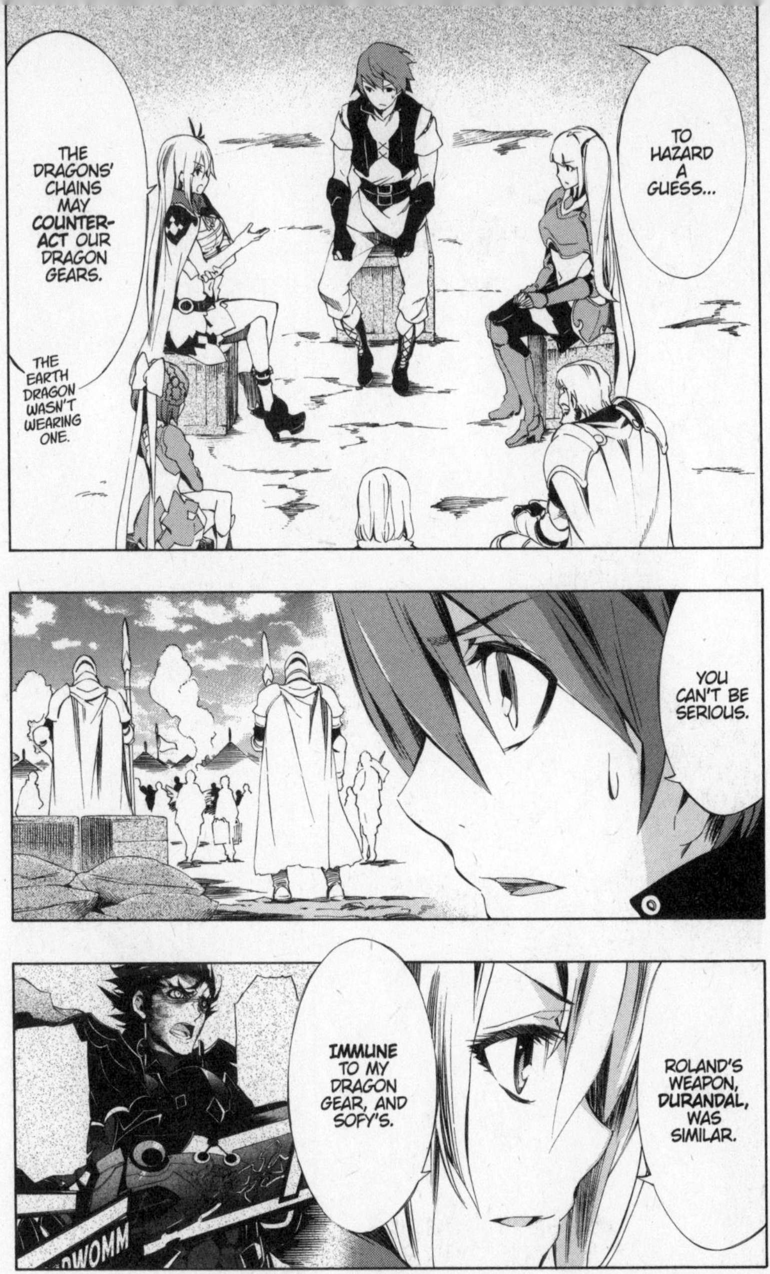
TO HAZARD A GUESS...
THE DRAGONS' CHAINS MAY COUNTER-ACT OUR DRAGON GEARS.
THE EARTH DRAGON WASN'T WEARING ONE.
YOU CAN'T BE SERIOUS.
ROLAND'S WEAPON, DURANDAL, WAS SIMILAR.
IMMUNE TO MY DRAGON GEAR, AND SOFY'S.
DWOMM

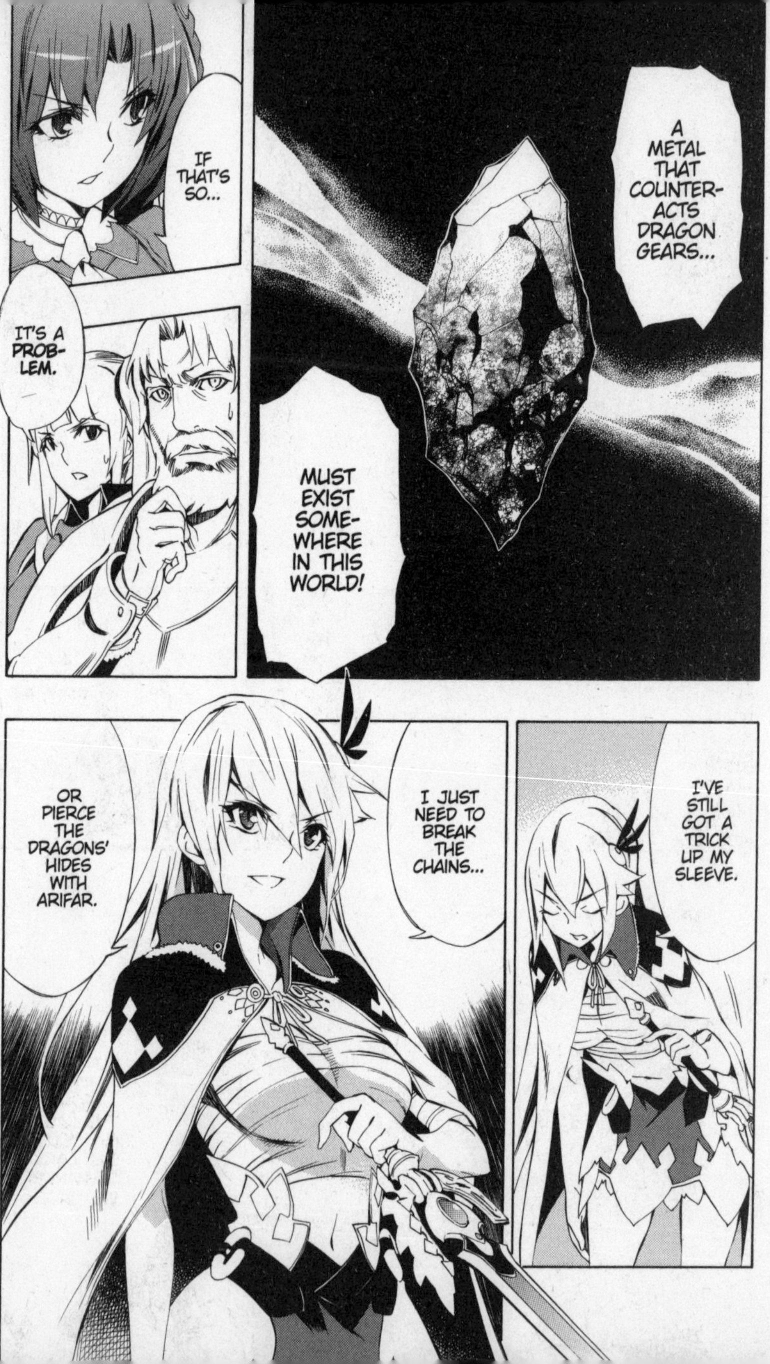
A METAL THAT COUNTER-ACTS DRAGON GEARS...
MUST EXIST SOME-WHERE IN THIS WORLD!
IF THAT'S SO...
IT'S A PROB-LEM.
I'VE STILL GOT A TRICK UP MY SLEEVE.
I JUST NEED TO BREAK THE CHAINS...
OR PIERCE THE DRAGONS' HIDES WITH ARIFAR.

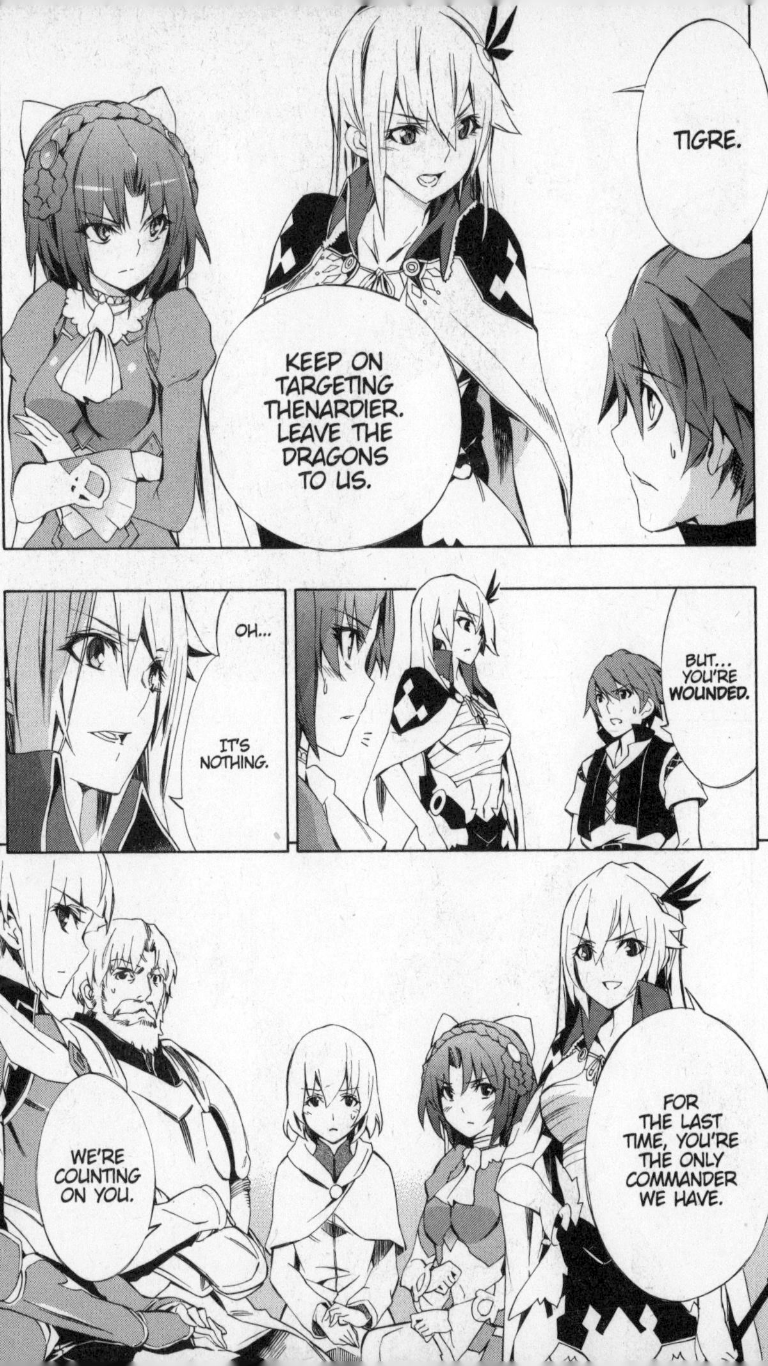
TIGRE.
KEEP ON TARGETING THENARDIER. LEAVE THE DRAGONS TO US.
BUT... YOU'RE WOUNDED.
OH...
IT'S NOTHING.
FOR THE LAST TIME, YOU'RE THE ONLY COMMANDER WE HAVE.
WE'RE COUNTING ON YOU.

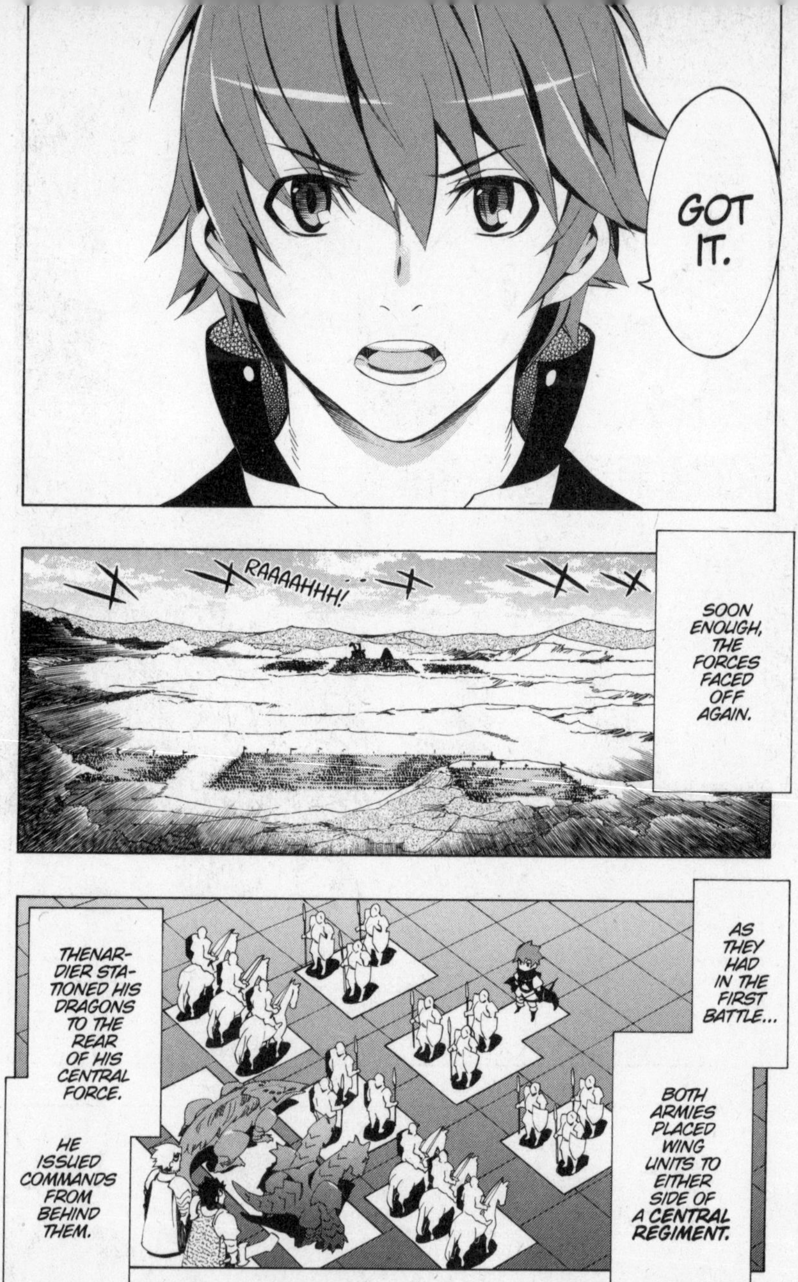
GOT IT.
SOON ENOUGH, THE FORCES FACED OFF AGAIN.
RAAAAHHH!
AS THEY HAD IN THE FIRST BATTLE...
BOTH ARMIES PLACED WING UNITS TO EITHER SIDE OF A CENTRAL REGIMENT.
THENARDIER STATIONED HIS DRAGONS TO THE REAR OF HIS CENTRAL FORCE.
HE ISSUED COMMANDS FROM BEHIND THEM.

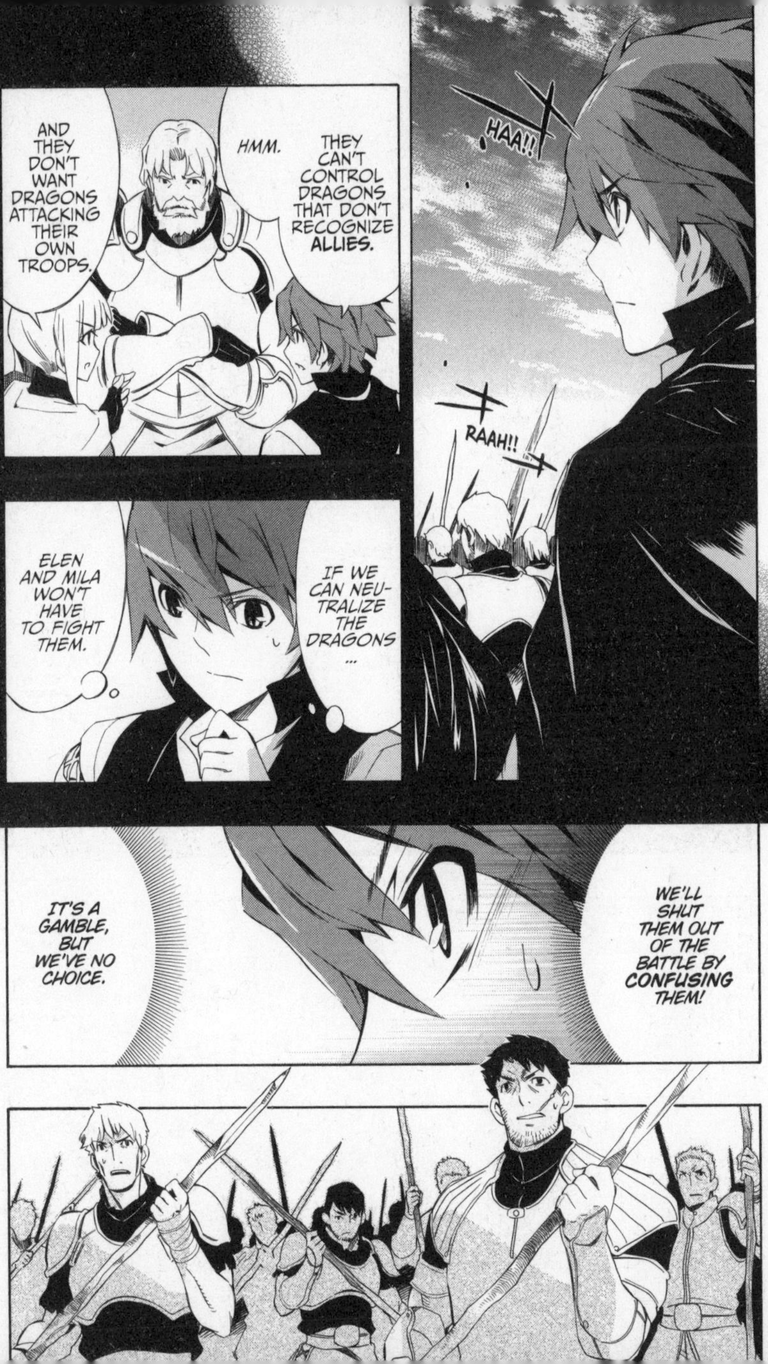
HAA!!
RAAH!!
THEY CAN'T CONTROL DRAGONS THAT DON'T RECOGNIZE ALLIES.
HMM.
AND THEY DON'T WANT DRAGONS ATTACKING THEIR OWN TROOPS.
IF WE CAN NEUTRALIZE THE DRAGONS...
ELEN AND MILA WON'T HAVE TO FIGHT THEM.
WE'LL SHUT THEM OUT OF THE BATTLE BY CONFUSING THEM!
IT'S A GAMBLE, BUT WE'VE NO CHOICE.

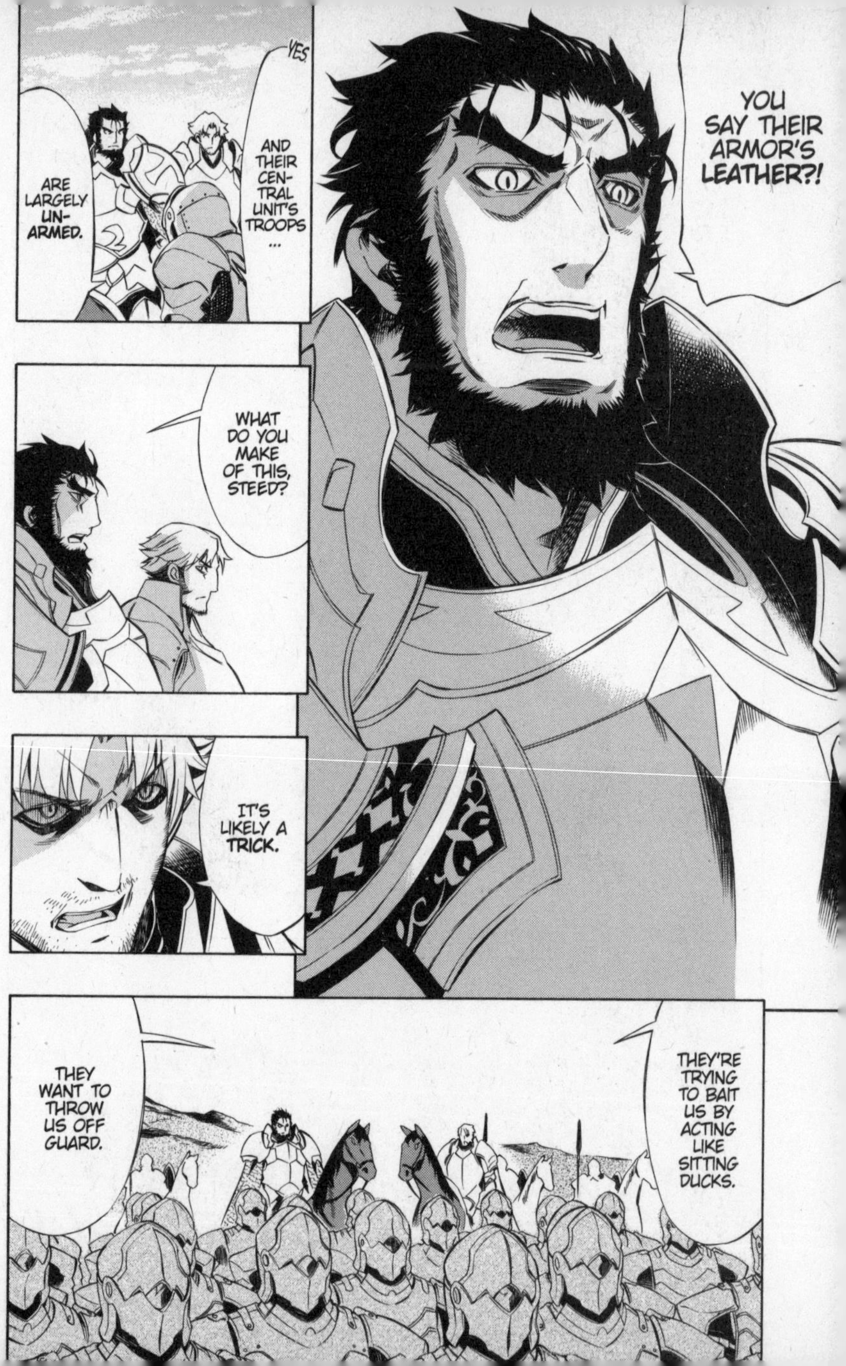
YOU SAY THEIR ARMOR'S LEATHER?!
YES.
AND THEIR CENTRAL UNIT'S TROOPS ...
ARE LARGELY UNARMED.
WHAT DO YOU MAKE OF THIS, STEED?
IT'S LIKELY A TRICK.
THEY'RE TRYING TO BAIT US BY ACTING LIKE SITTING DUCKS.
THEY WANT TO THROW US OFF GUARD.

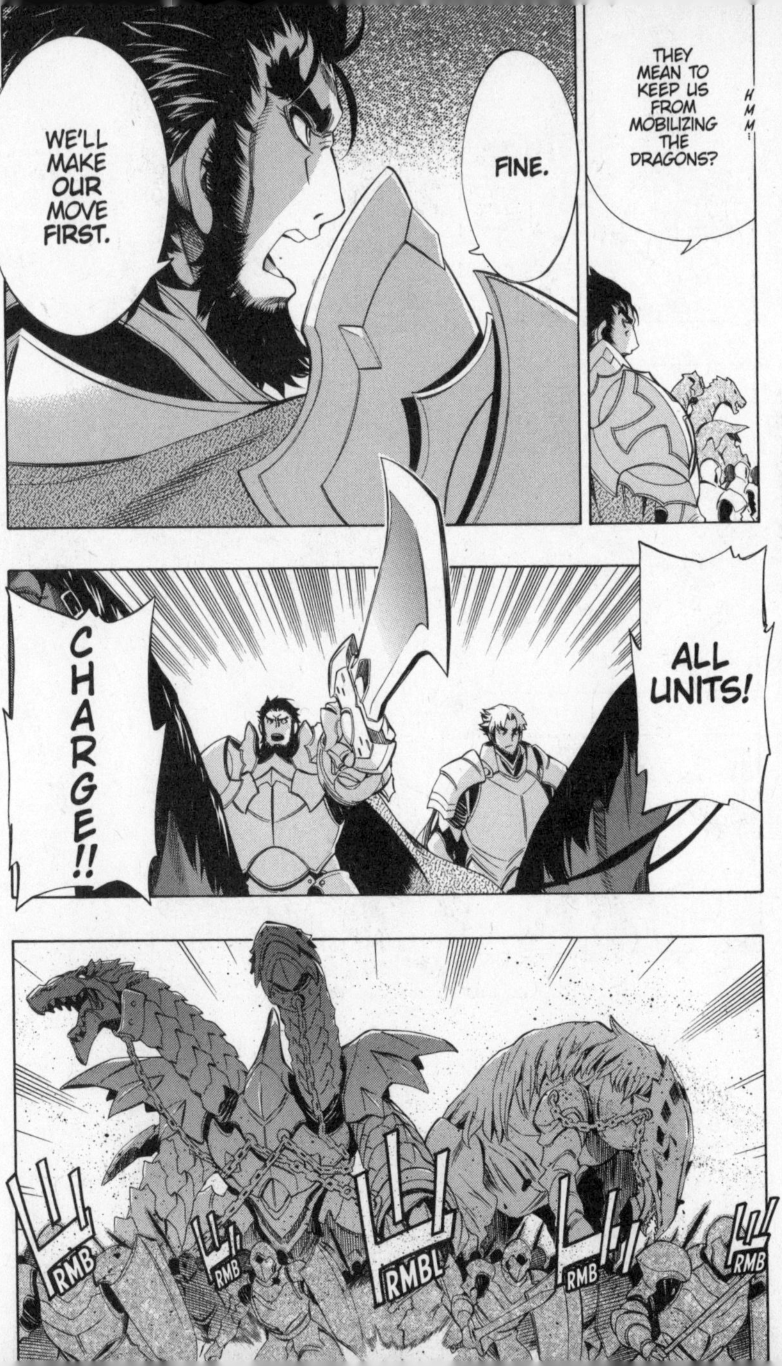
HMM...
THEY MEAN TO KEEP US FROM MOBILIZING THE DRAGONS?
FINE.
WE'LL MAKE OUR MOVE FIRST.
ALL UNITS!
CHARGE!!
RMB
RMB
RMBL
RMB
RMB

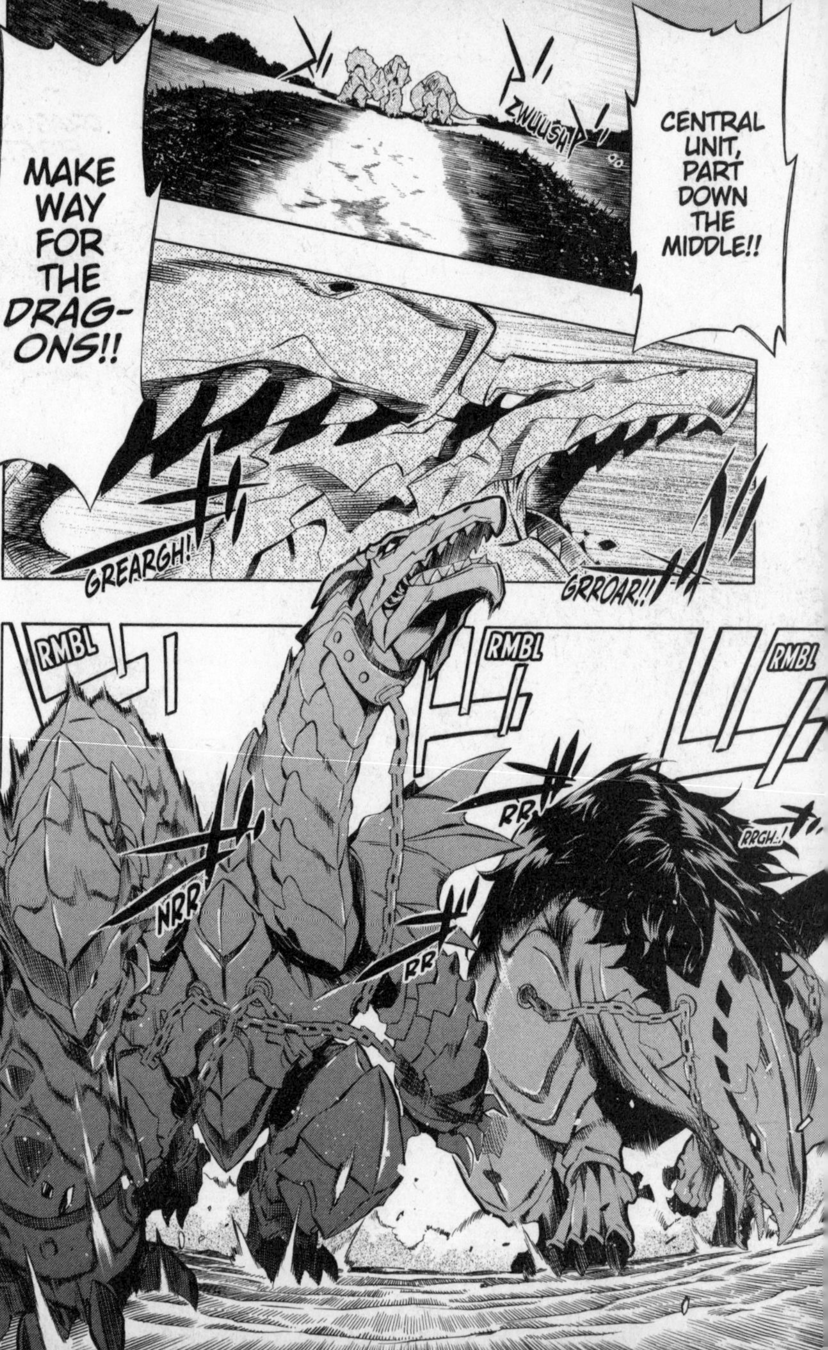
CENTRAL UNIT, PART DOWN THE MIDDLE!!
ZWUUSH
MAKE WAY FOR THE DRAG-ONS!!
GRROAR!!
GREARGH!
RMBL
RMBL
RMBL
RRGH..!
RR
RR
NRR

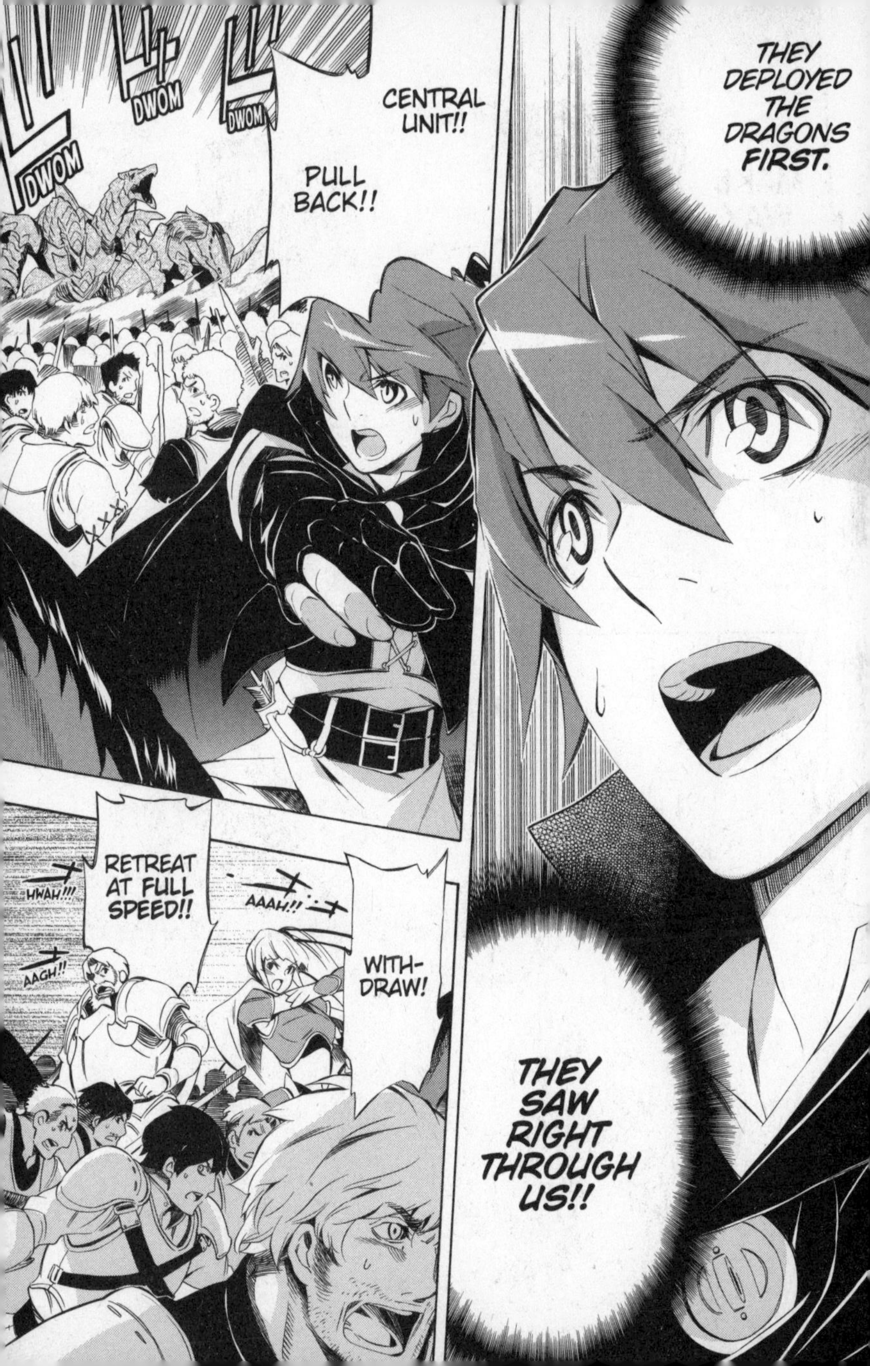
THEY DEPLOYED THE DRAGONS FIRST.
THEY SAW RIGHT THROUGH US!!
CENTRAL UNIT!!
PULL BACK!!
DWOM
DWOM
DWOM
DWOM
WITH-DRAW!
AAAH!!
RETREAT AT FULL SPEED!!
HWAH!!!
AAGH!!

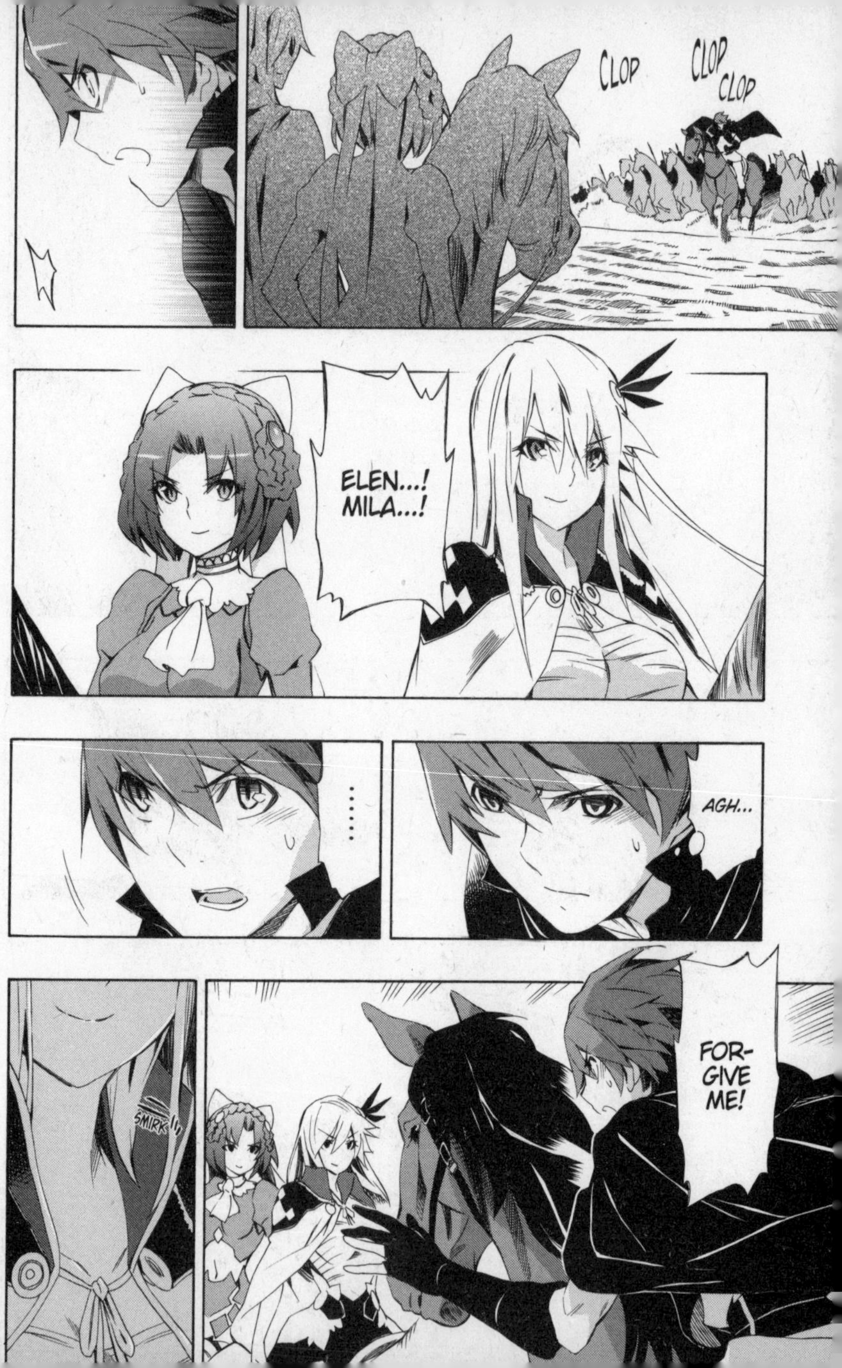
CLOP
CLOP
CLOP
ELEN...! MILA...!
AGH...
......
FOR-GIVE ME!
SMIRK

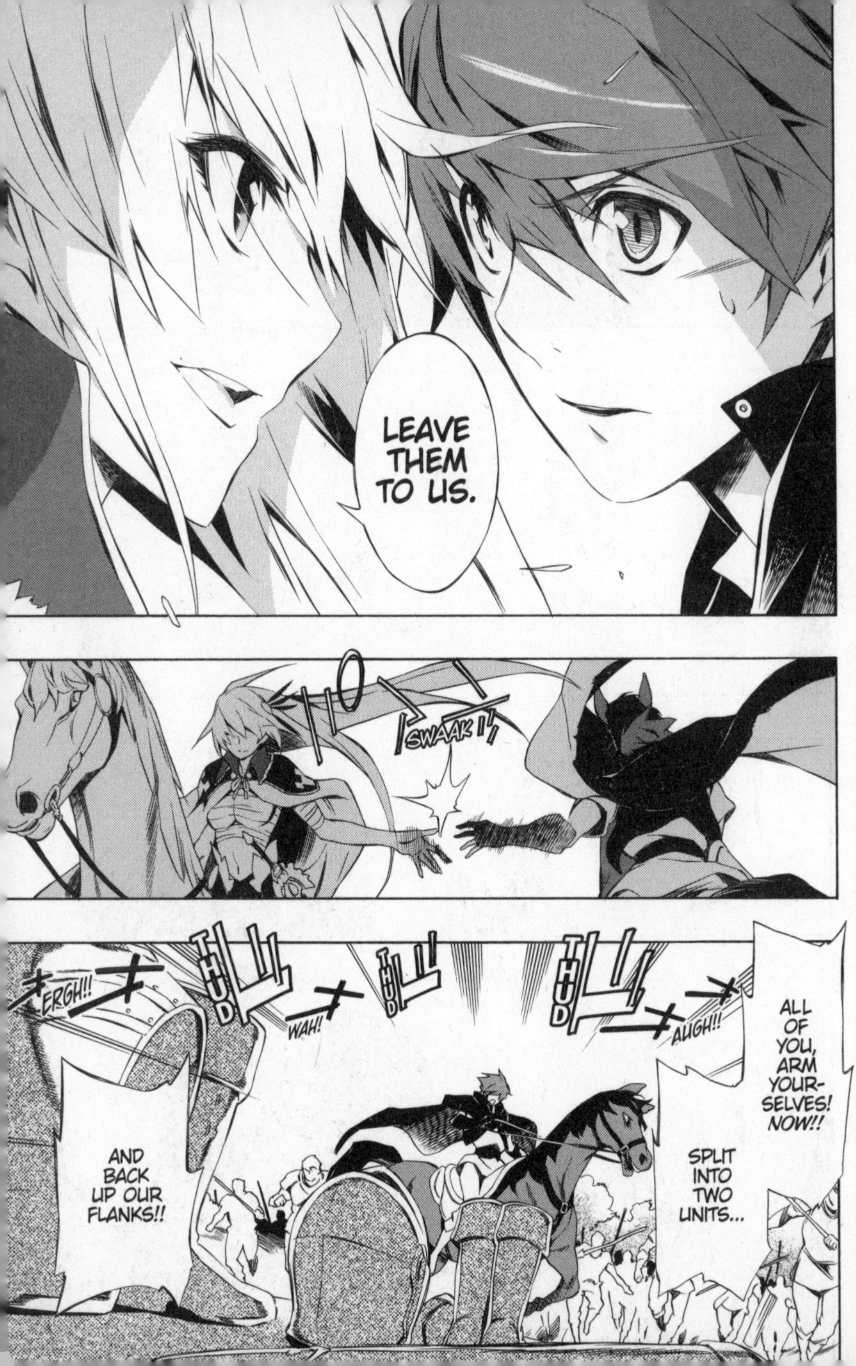
LEAVE THEM TO US.
SWAAK!!
ALL OF YOU, ARM YOURSELVES! NOW!!
AUGH!!
THUD
THUD
WAH!
THUD
ERGH!!
SPLIT INTO TWO UNITS...
AND BACK UP OUR FLANKS!!

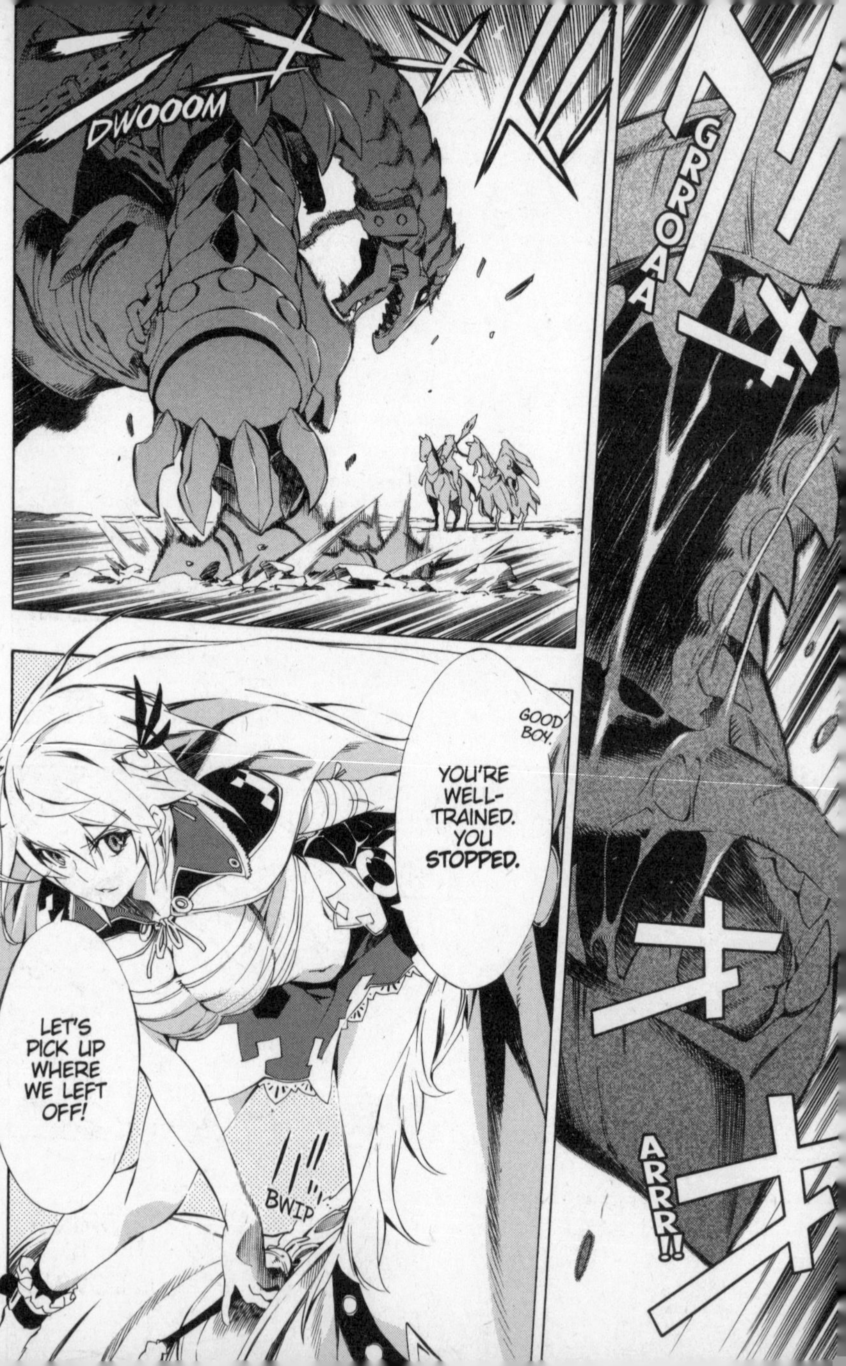
GRRROAA
ARRR!!
DWOOOM
GOOD BOY.
YOU'RE WELL-TRAINED. YOU STOPPED.
LET'S PICK UP WHERE WE LEFT OFF!
BWIP

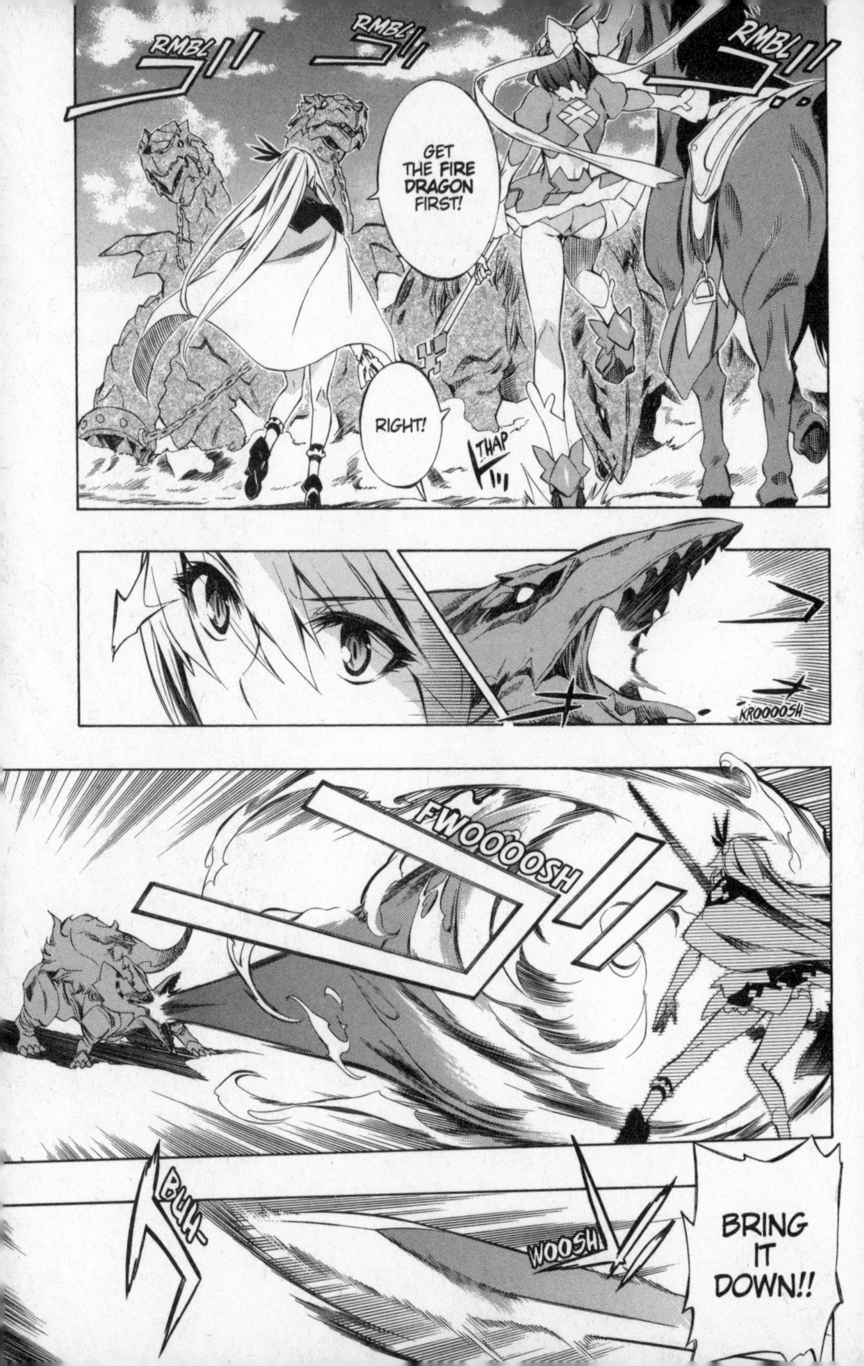
RMBL
GET THE FIRE DRAGON FIRST!
RMBL
RMBL
RIGHT!
THAP
KROOOOSH
FWOOOOSH
BRING IT DOWN!!
WOOSH
BUH-

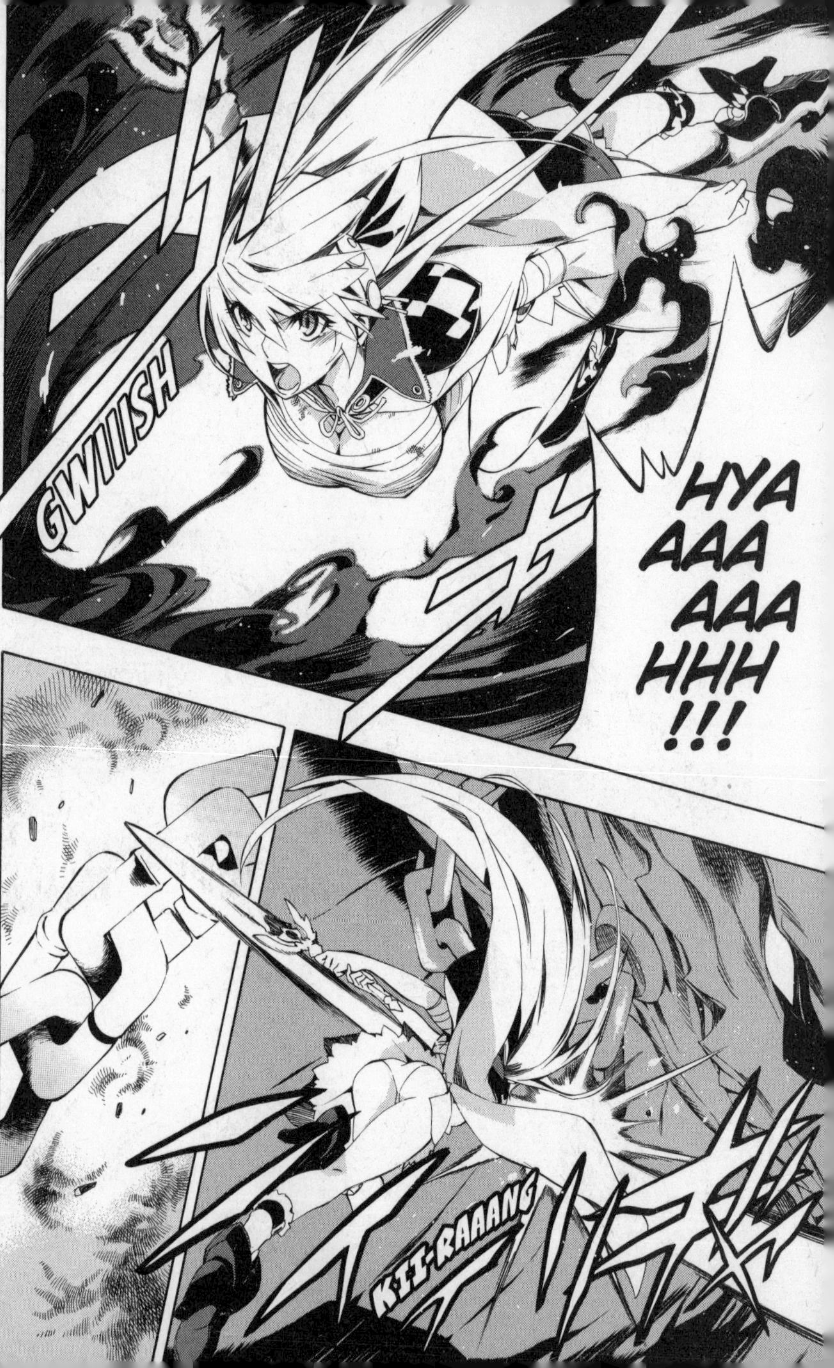
HYA AAA AAA HHH !!!
GWIIISH
KII-RAAANG

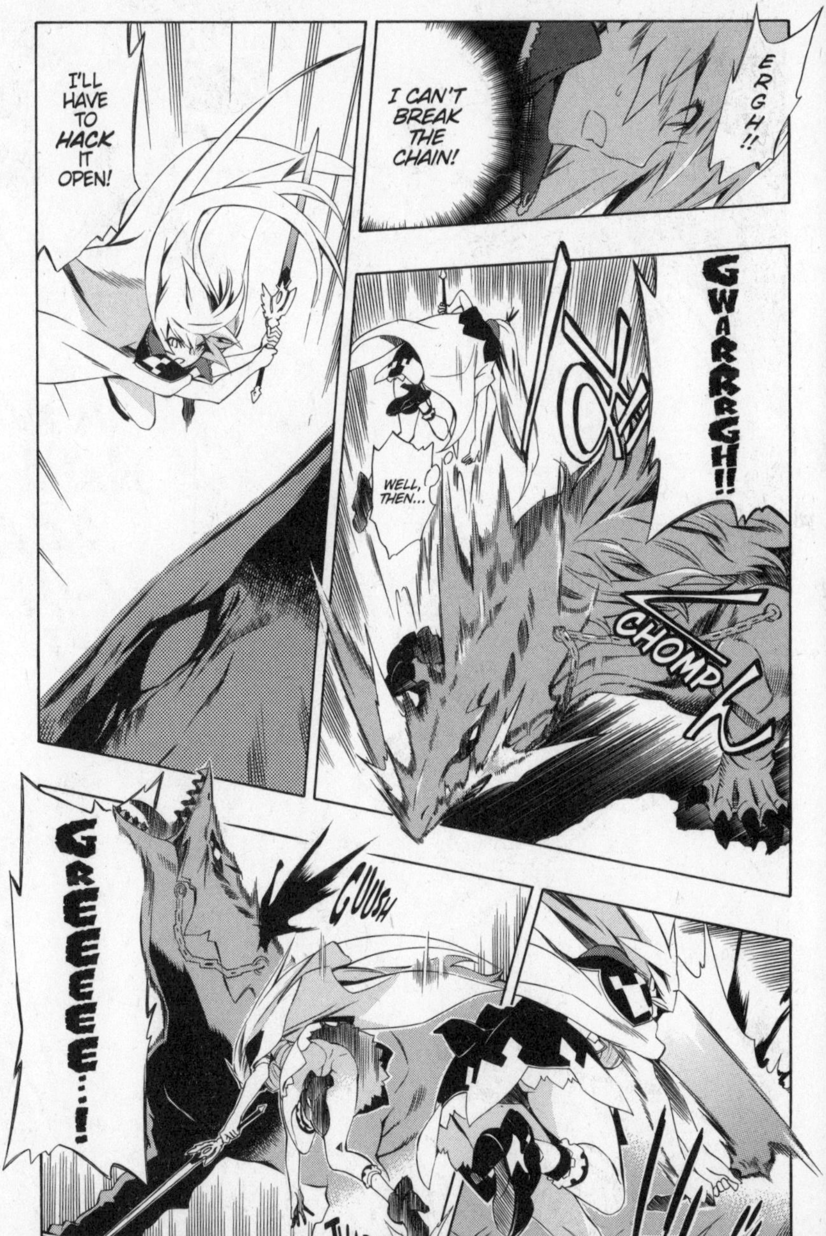
ERGH!!
I CAN'T BREAK THE CHAIN!
GWARRRGH!!
WELL, THEN...
CHOMP
I'LL HAVE TO HACK IT OPEN!
GUUSH
GREEEEE...!!
THWUP
THAP

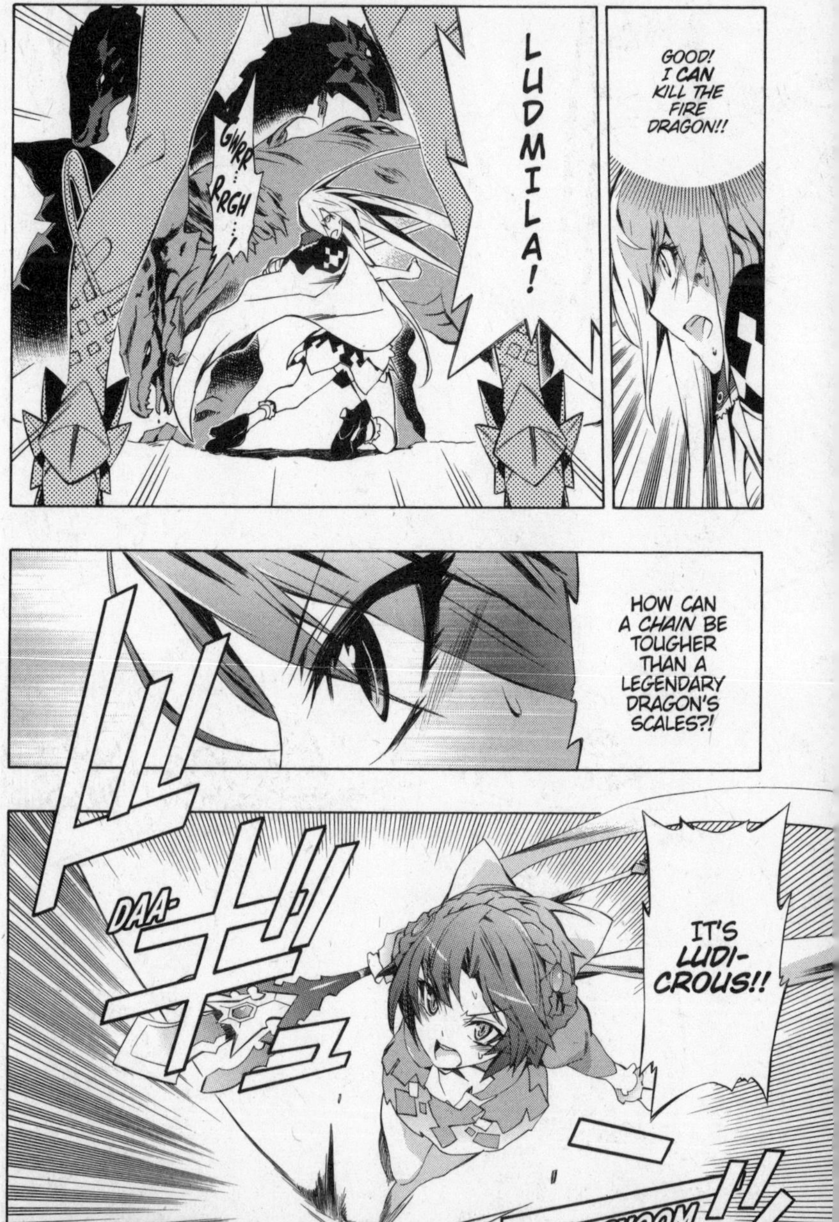
GOOD! I CAN KILL THE FIRE DRAGON!!
LUDMILA!
GWRR... RRGH...!
HOW CAN A CHAIN BE TOUGHER THAN A LEGENDARY DRAGON'S SCALES?!
IT'S LUDI-CROUS!!
DAA-
SHOOM

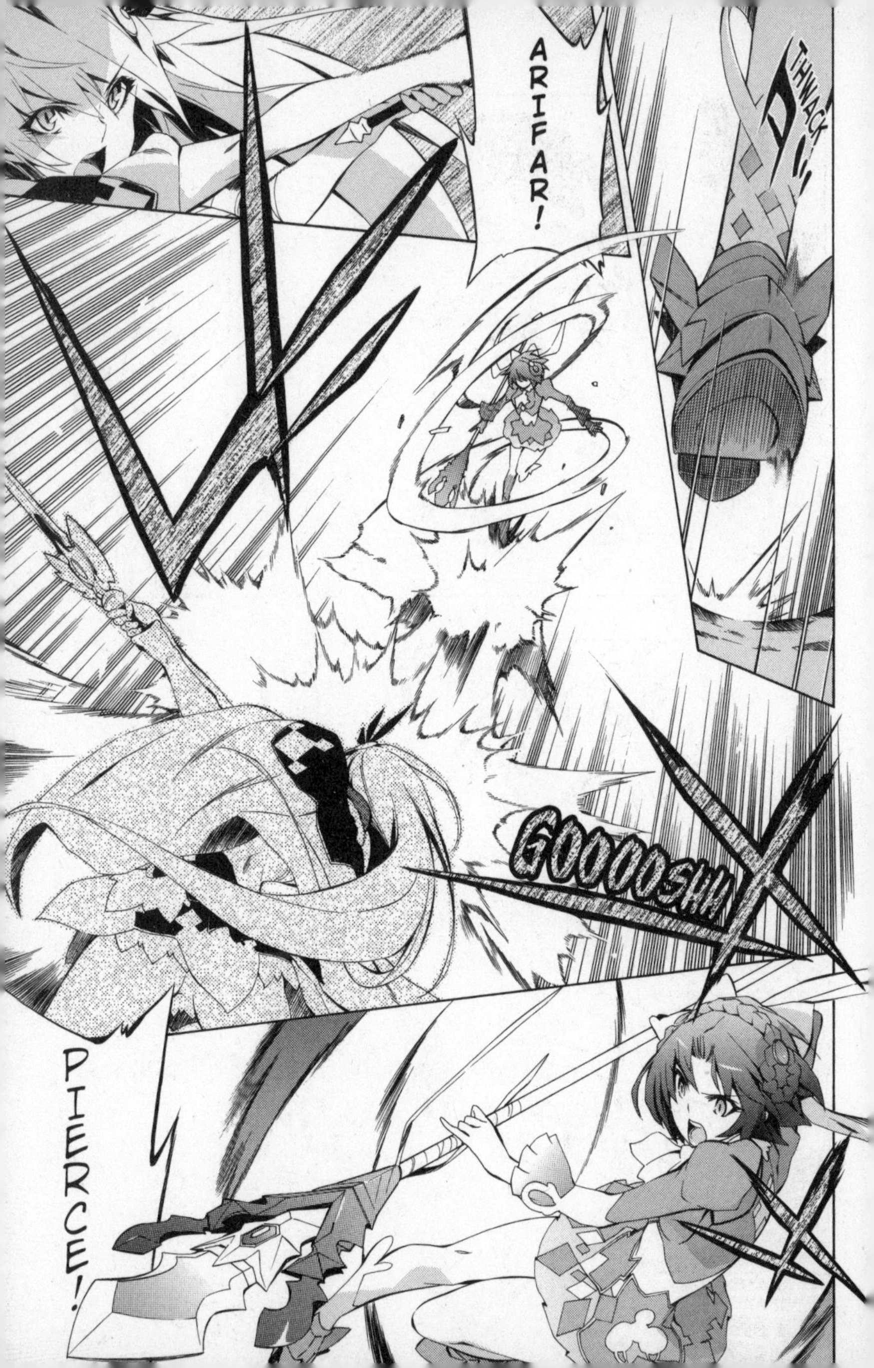
THWACK
ARIFAR!
GOOOOSHH
PIERCE!

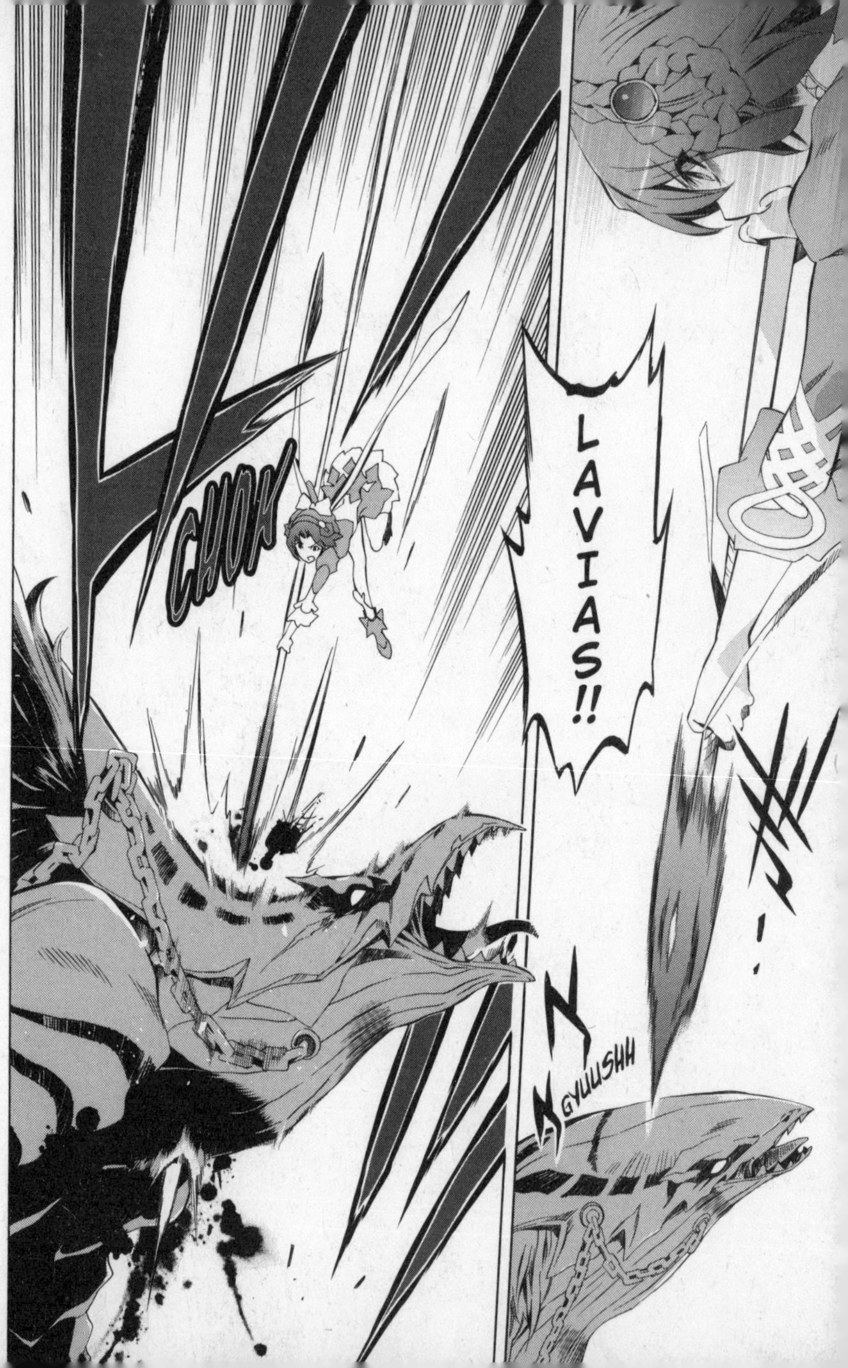
LAVIAS!!
GYUUSHH
CHOK

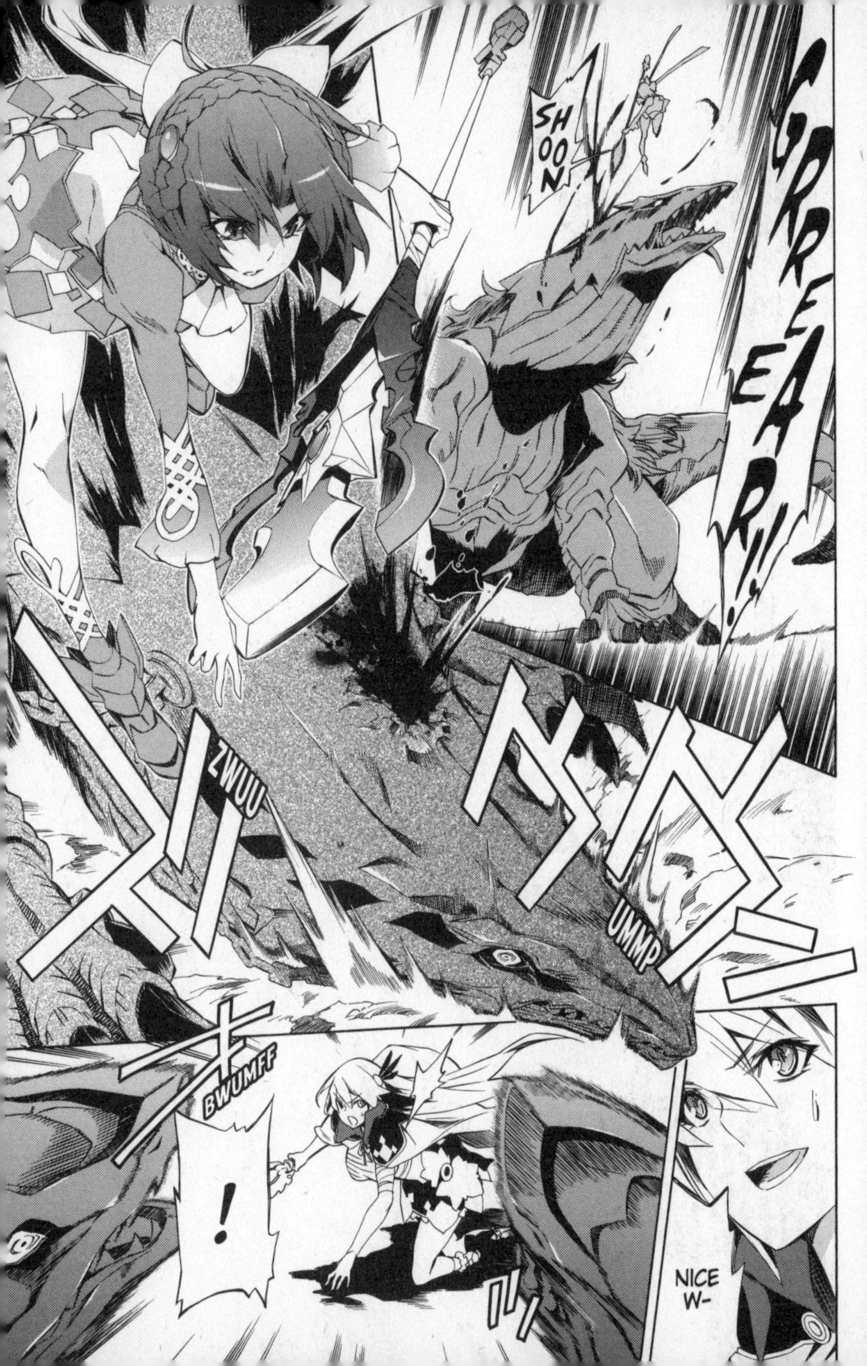
GRREEAR!!
SHOON
UMMP
ZWUU
NICE W-
BWUMFF
!

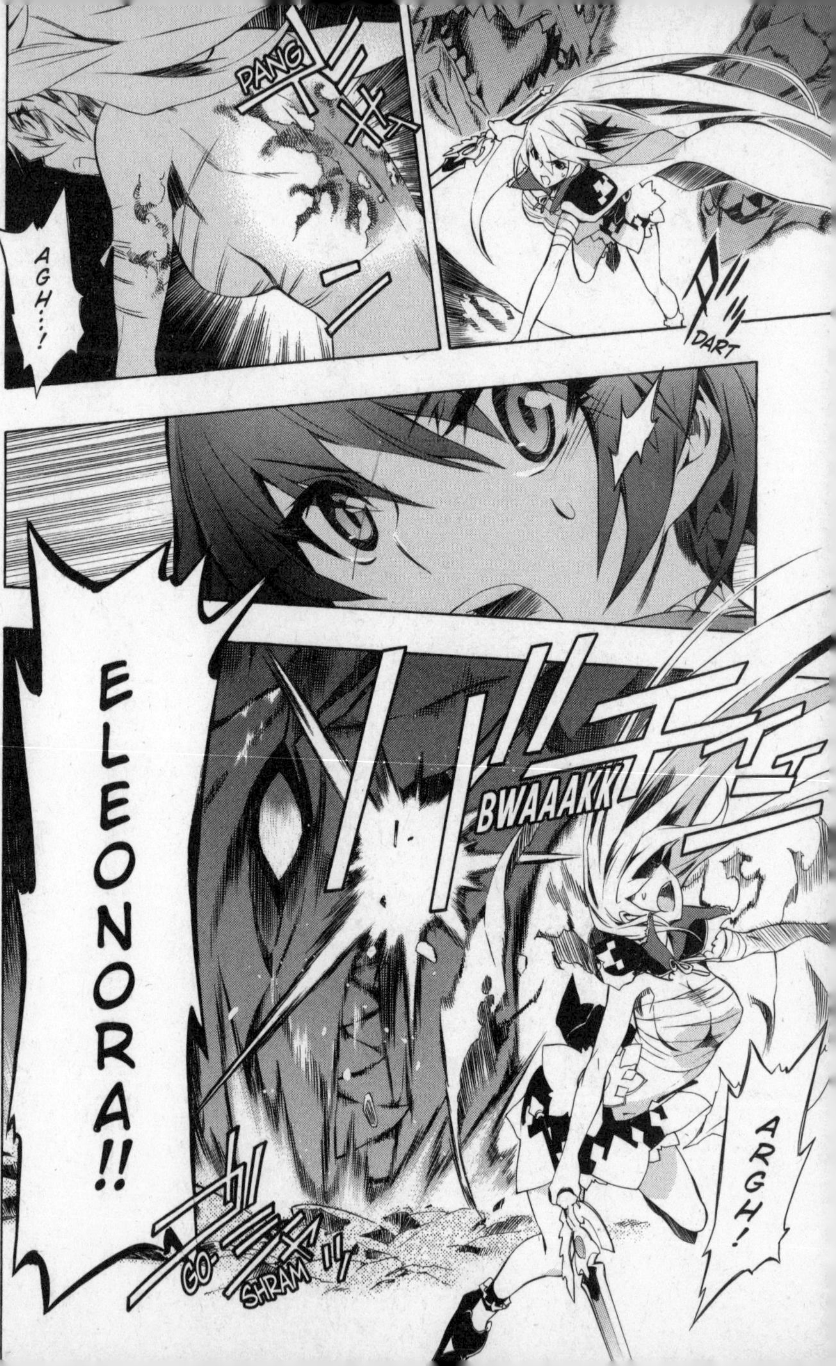
DART
PANG
AGH...!
BWAAAKK
ARGH!
ELEONORA!!
GO-
SHRAM

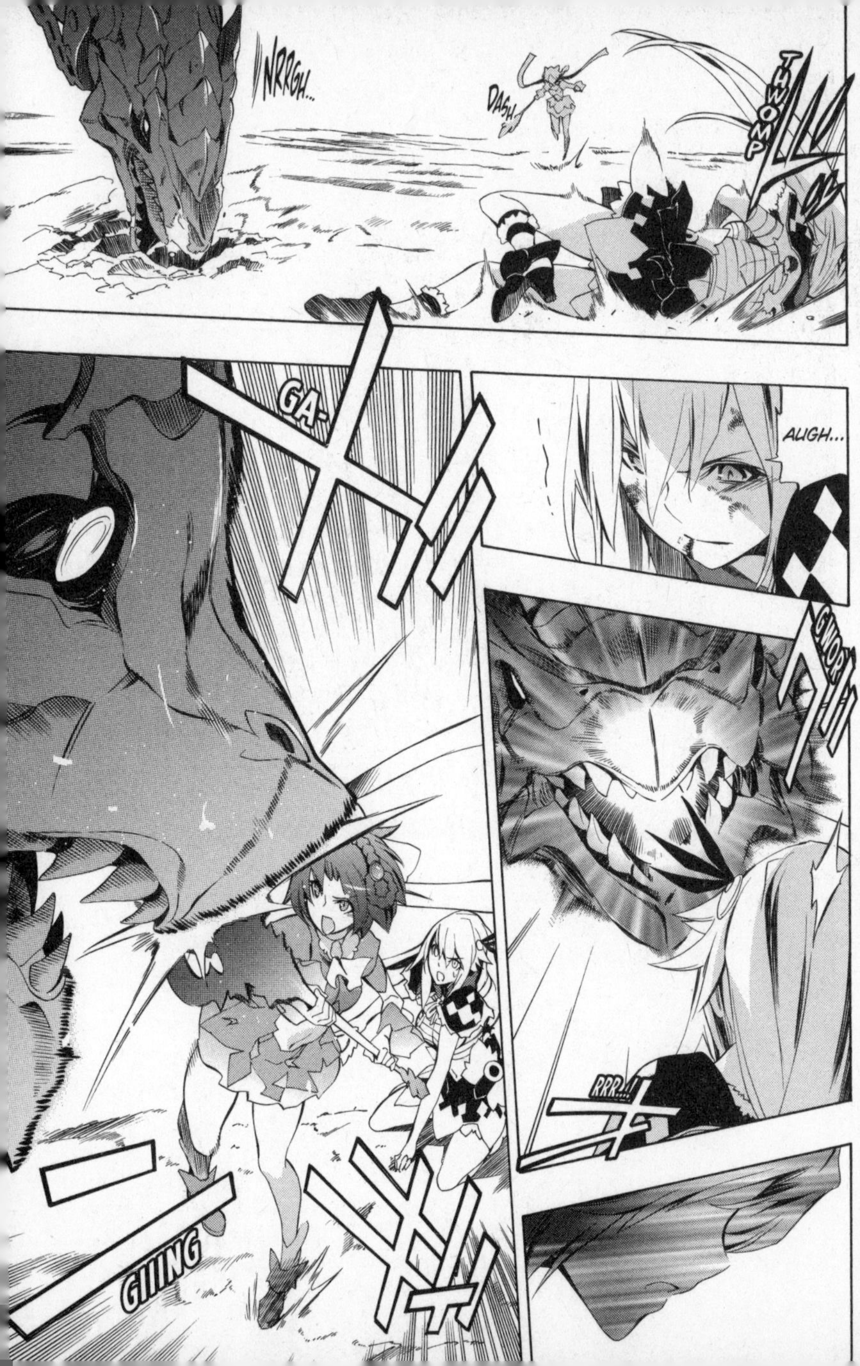
THWOMP
DASH
NRRGH...
AUGH...
GWOR
RRR...!
GA-
GIIING

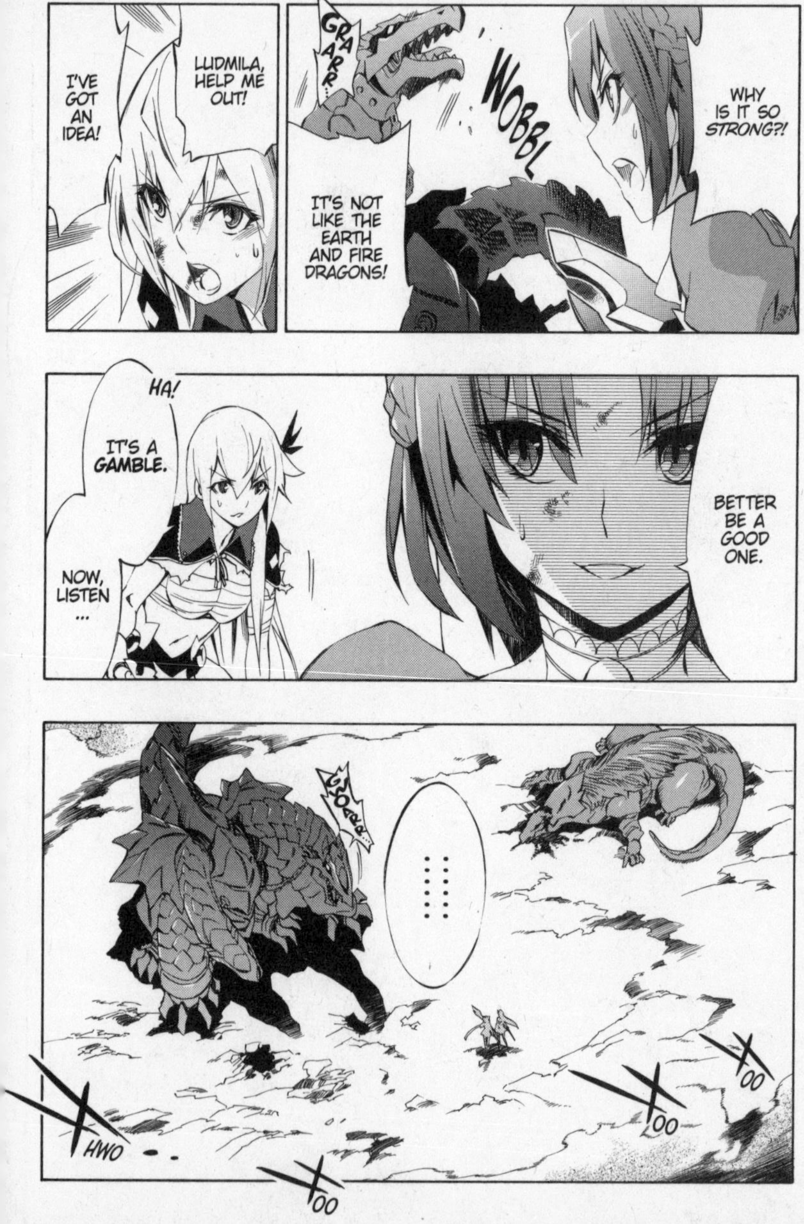
WHY IS IT SO STRONG?!
WOBBL
GRARR...
IT'S NOT LIKE THE EARTH AND FIRE DRAGONS!
LUDMILA, HELP ME OUT!
I'VE GOT AN IDEA!
BETTER BE A GOOD ONE.
HA!
IT'S A GAMBLE.
NOW, LISTEN...
GROARR...
......
HWO

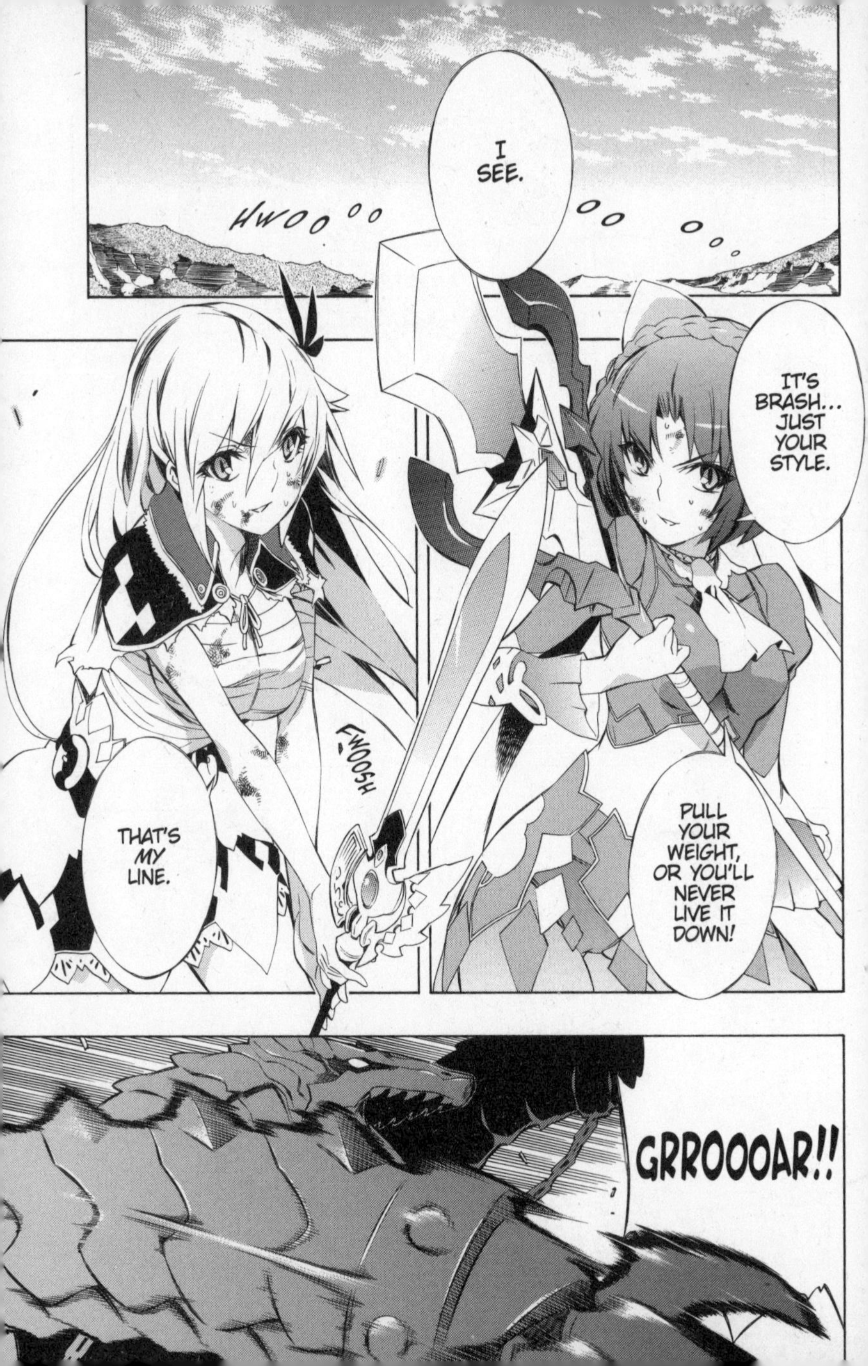
I SEE.
HWOOOOOOOO...
IT'S BRASH... JUST YOUR STYLE.
PULL YOUR WEIGHT, OR YOU'LL NEVER LIVE IT DOWN!
FWOOSH
THAT'S MY LINE.
GRROOOAR!!

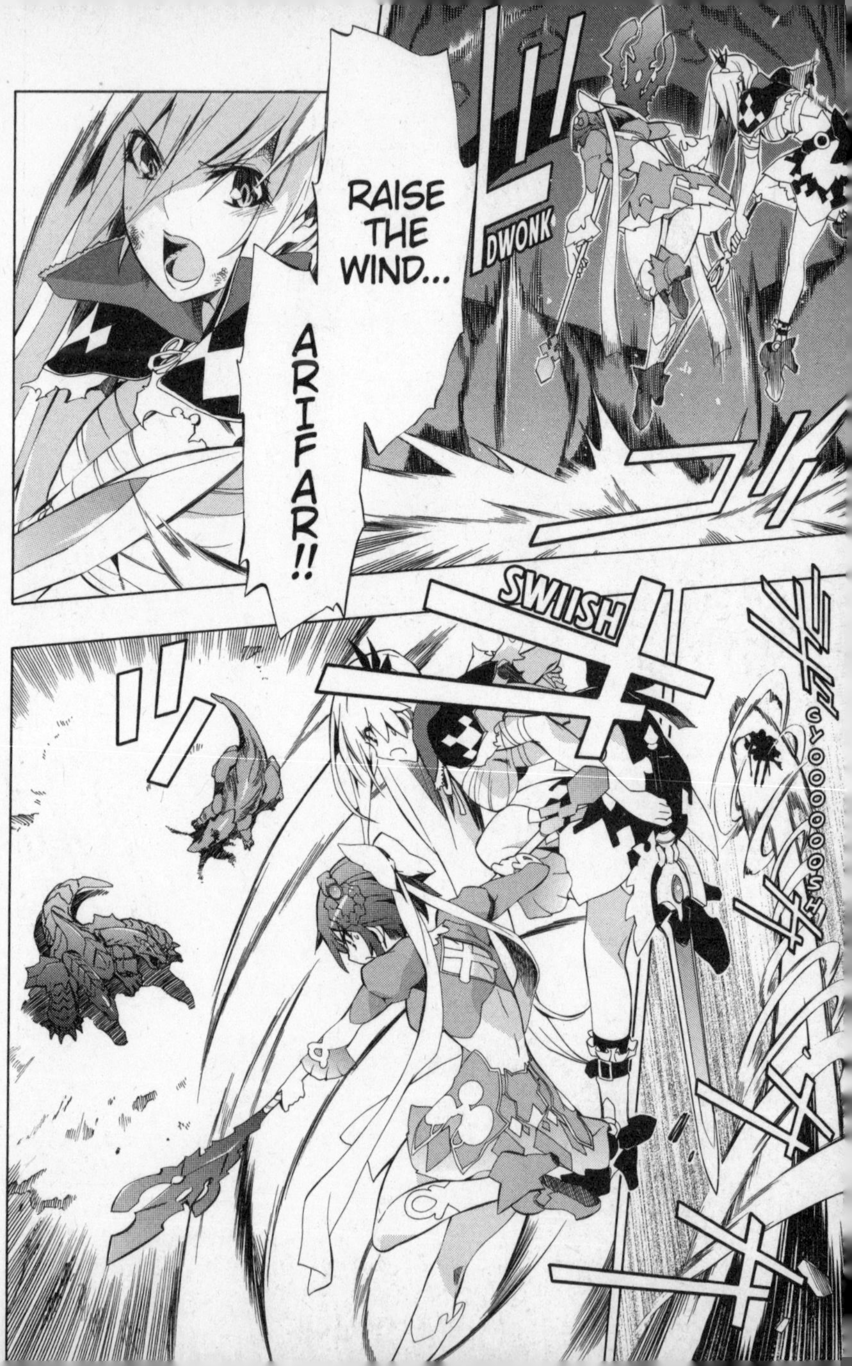
DWONK
RAISE THE WIND...
ARIFAR!!
SWISH
WHOOOOOOSH

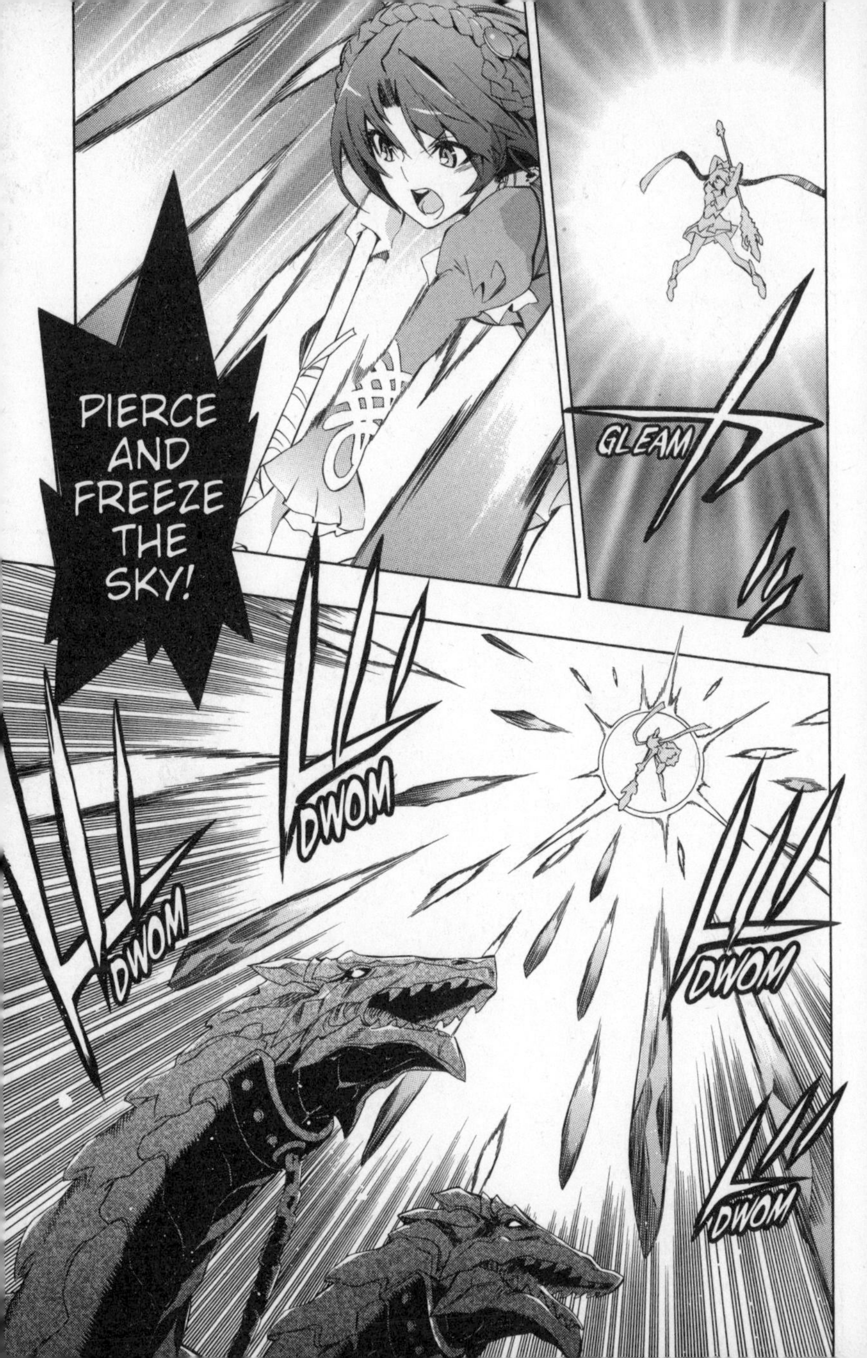
GLEAM
PIERCE AND FREEZE THE SKY!
DWOM
DWOM
DWOM
DWOM

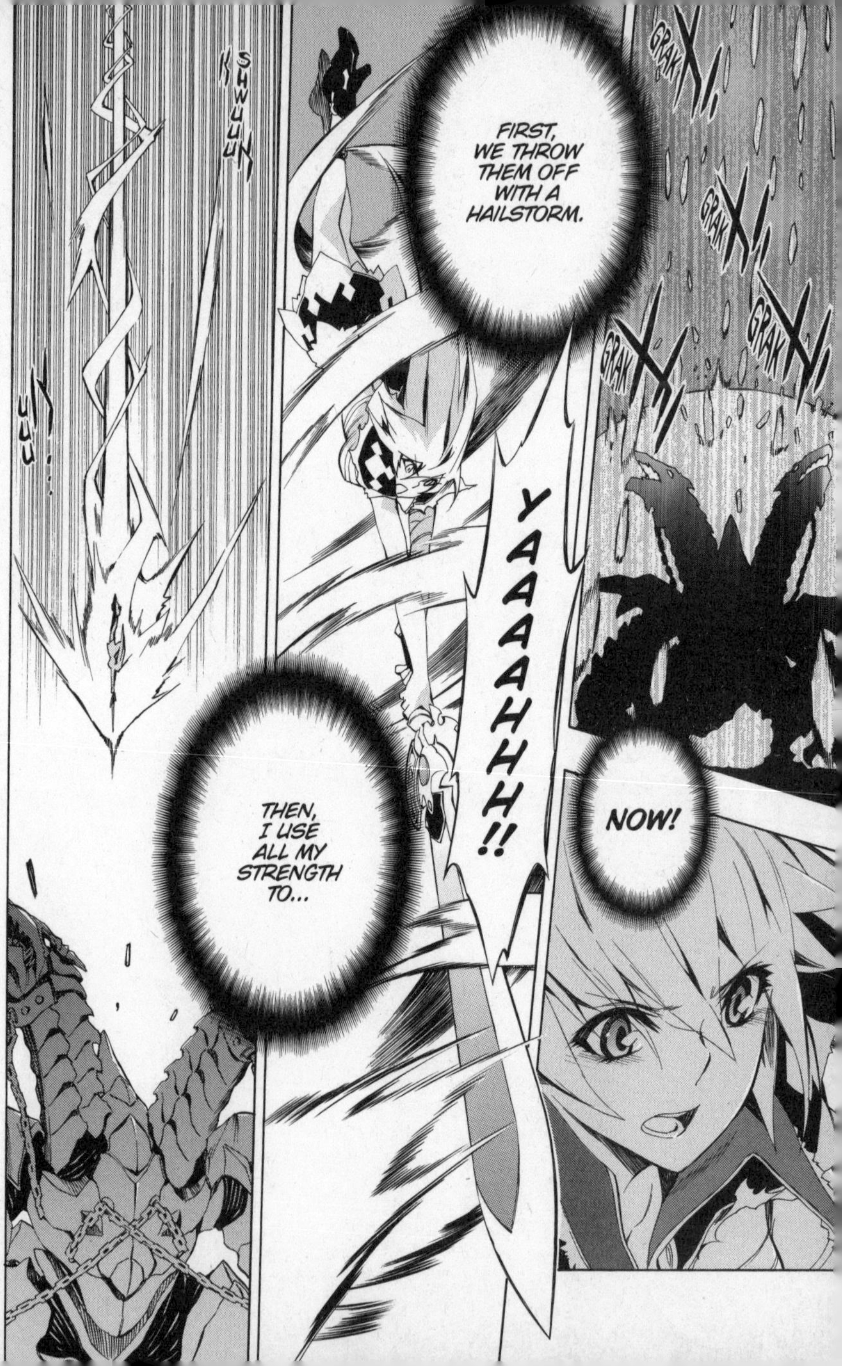
GRAK
GRAK
GRAK
GRAK
FIRST, WE THROW THEM OFF WITH A HAILSTORM.
NOW!
THEN, I USE ALL MY STRENGTH TO...
YAAAAAHHHH!!
KSHWUUUN

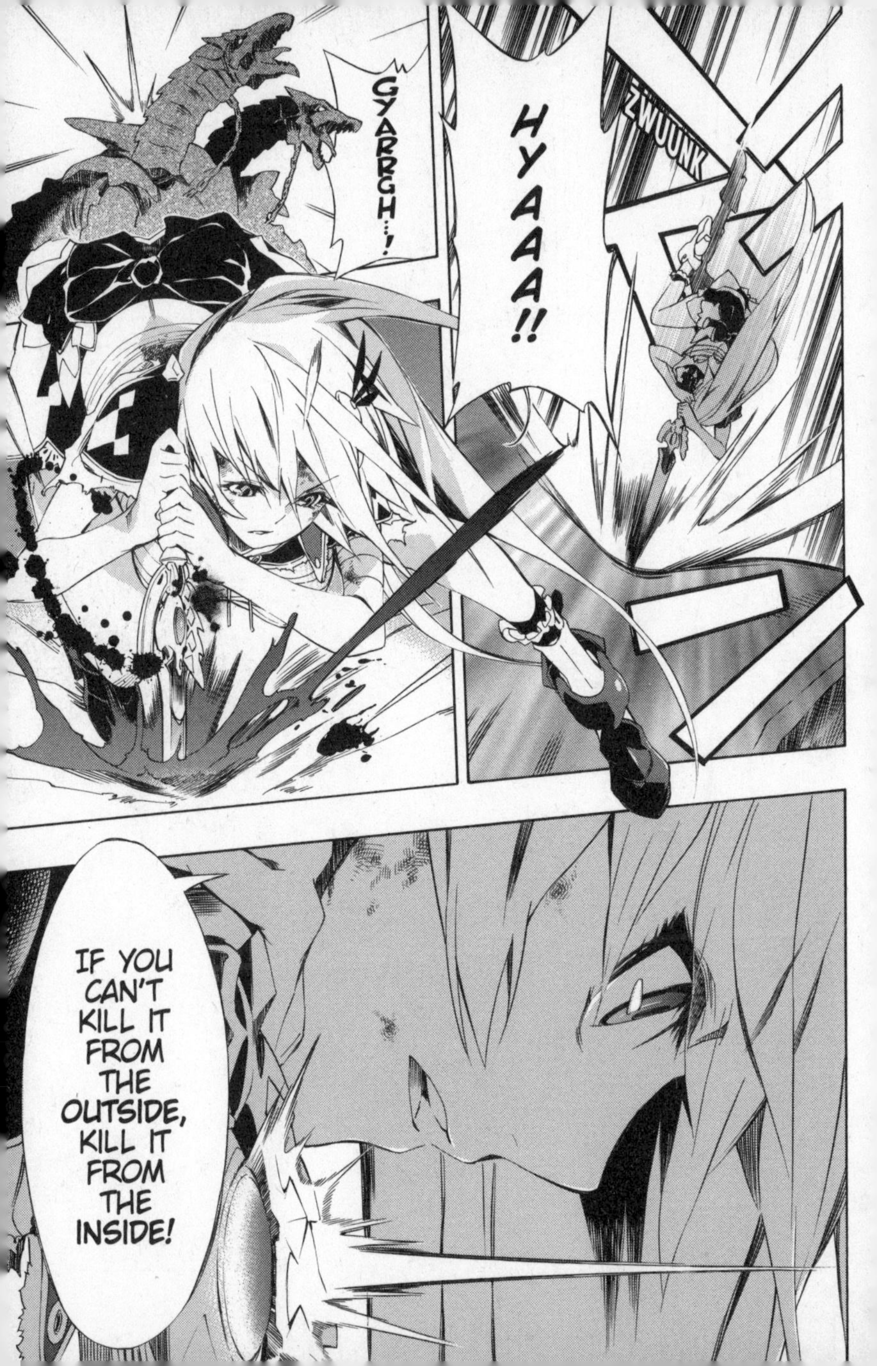
ZWUUNK
HYAAAA!!
GYARRGH...!
IF YOU CAN'T KILL IT FROM THE OUTSIDE, KILL IT FROM THE INSIDE!

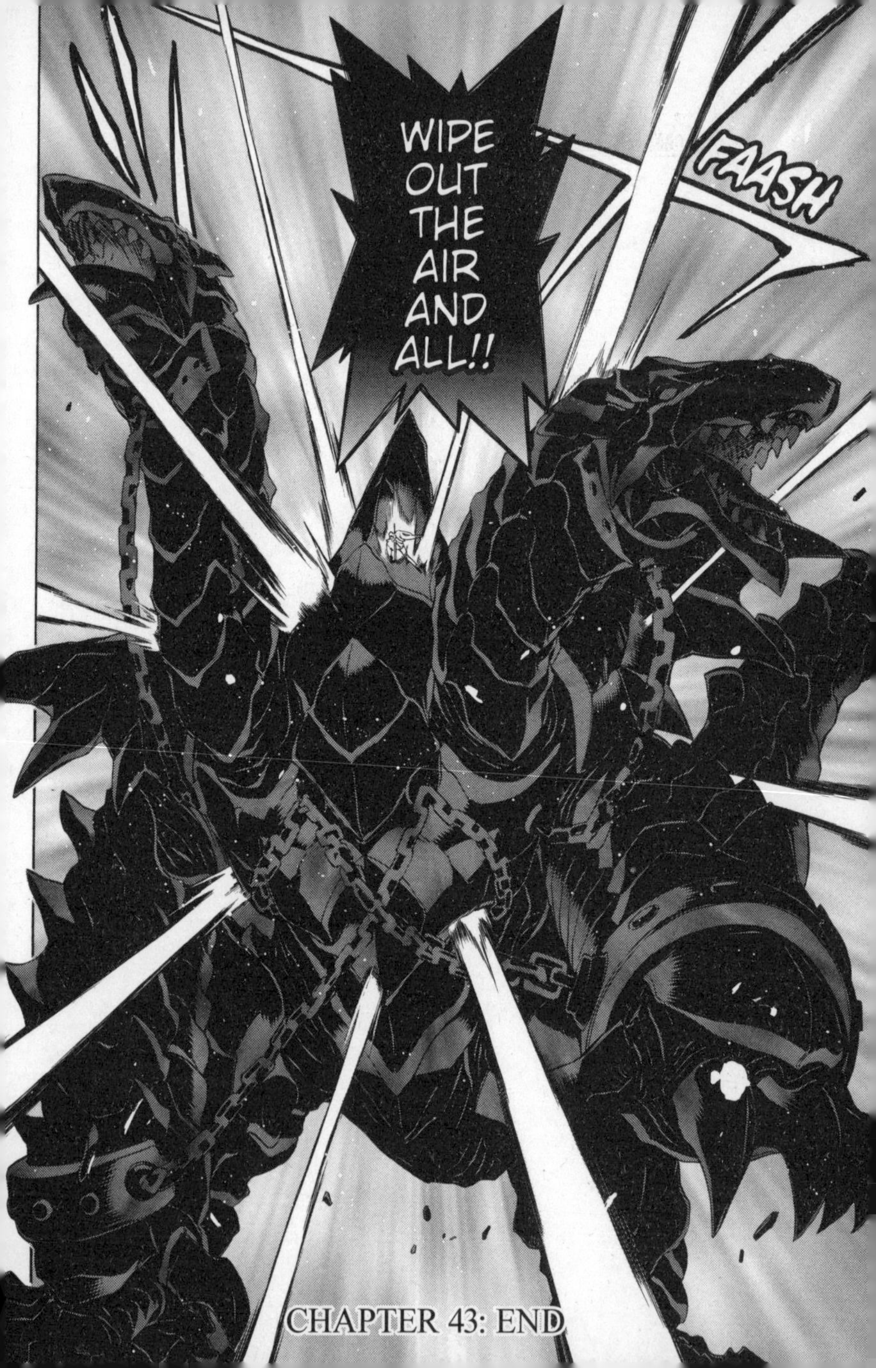
WIPE OUT THE AIR AND ALL!!
FAASH
CHAPTER 43: END

44 ◆ THE HOLY GROTTO

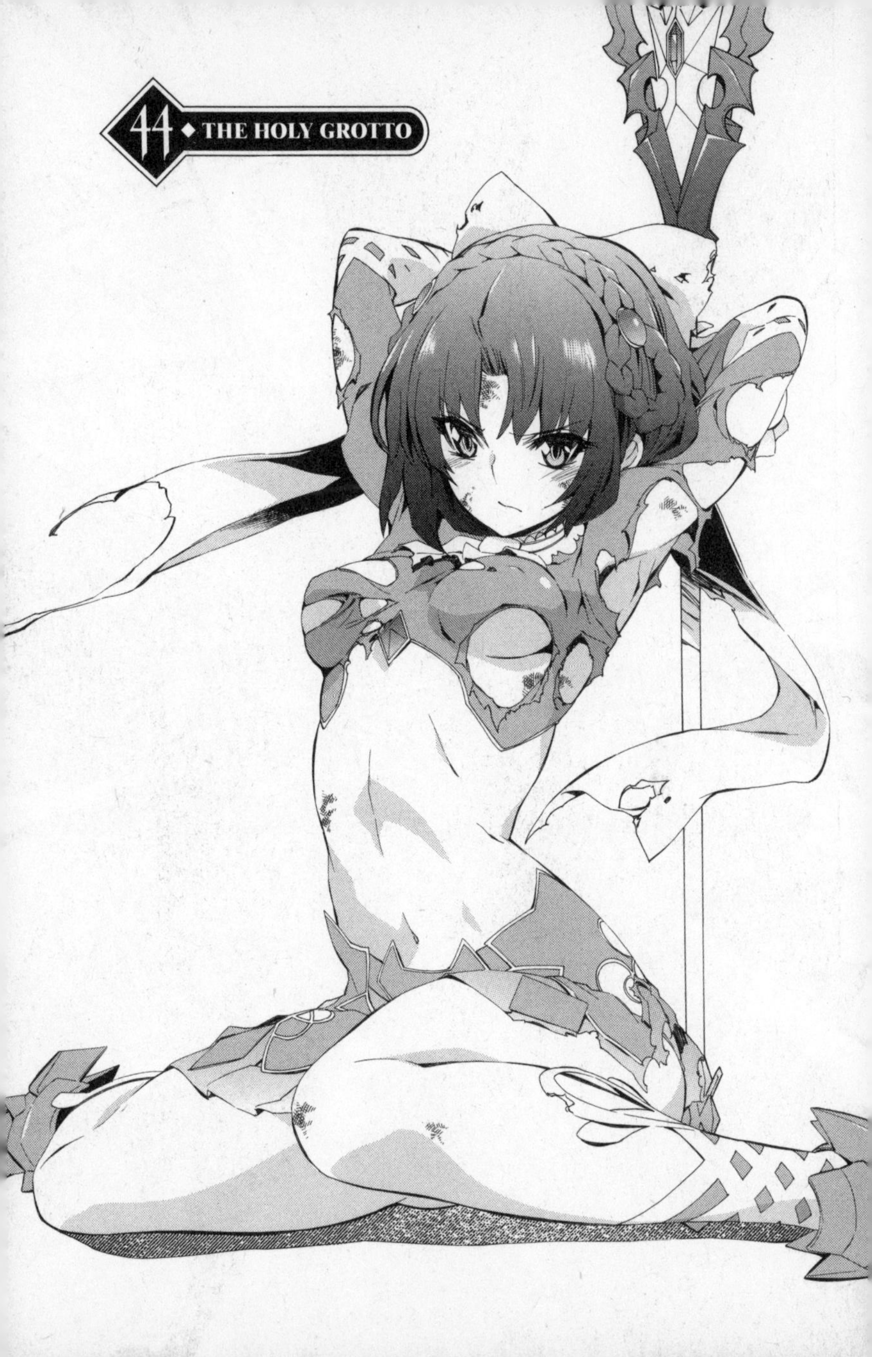

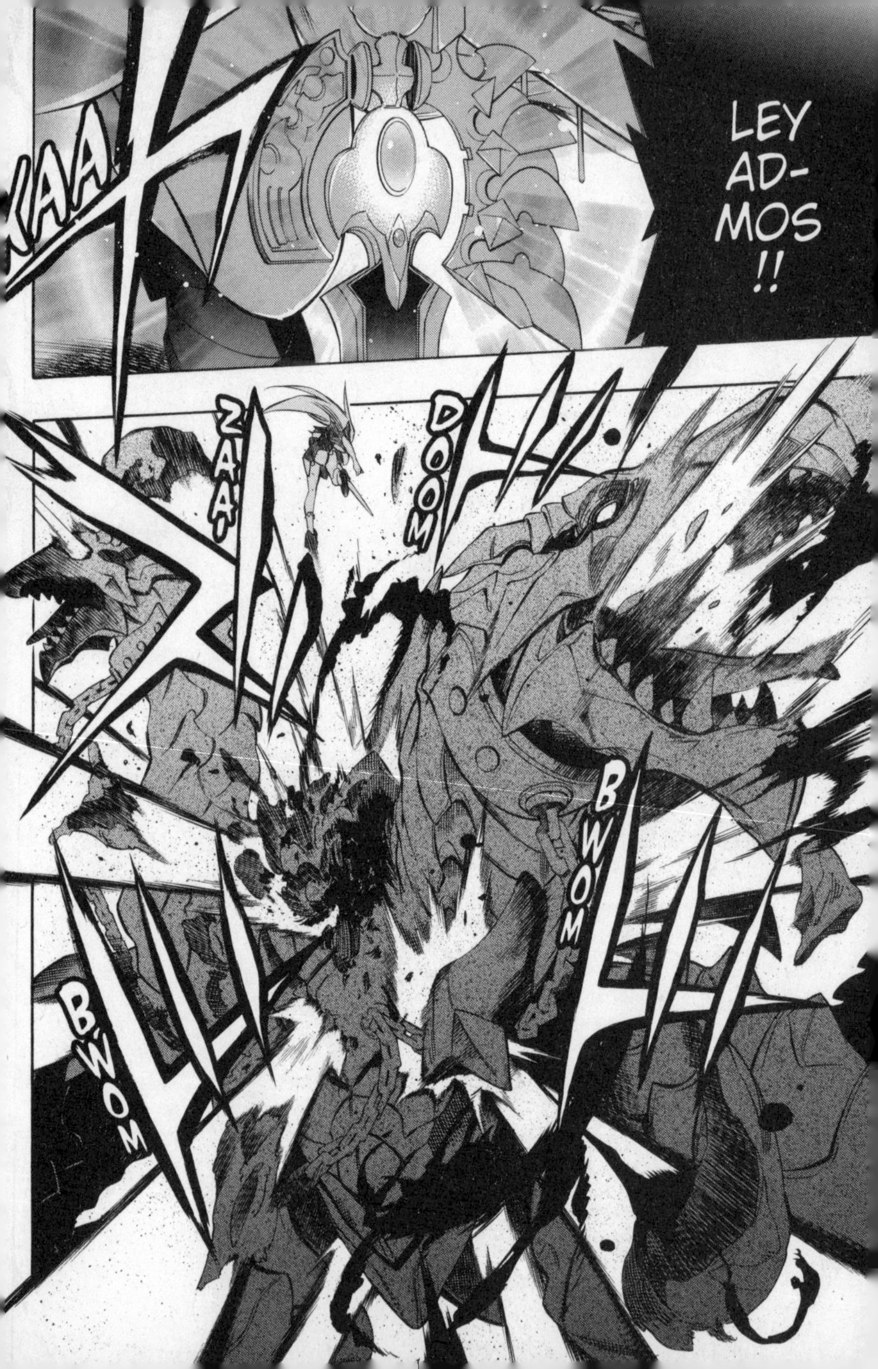
LEY AD-MOS !!
DOOOM
ZAAA
BWOM
BWOM

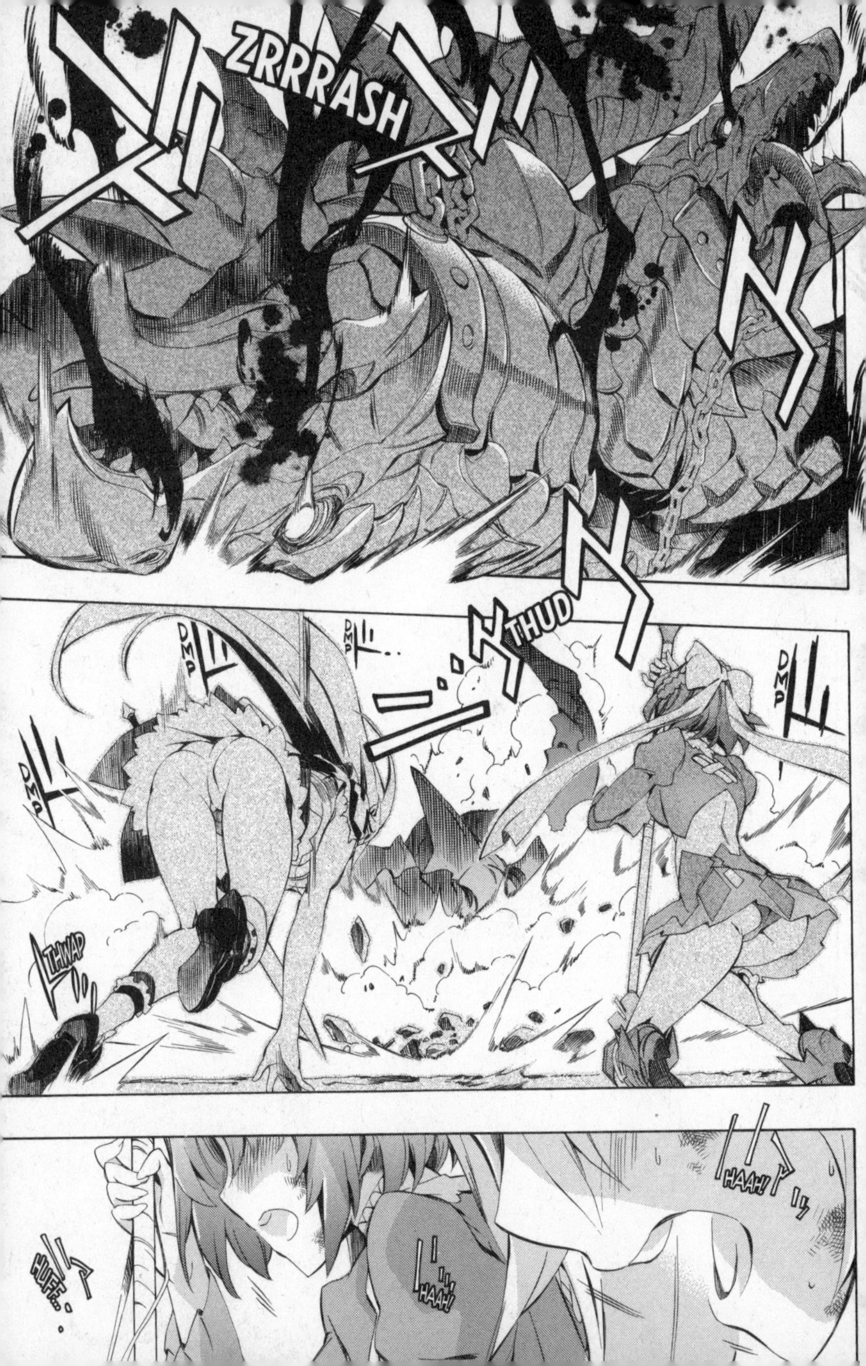
ZRRRASH
THUD
DMP
DMP
DMP
DMP
THWAP
HAAH!
HAAH!
HUFF...

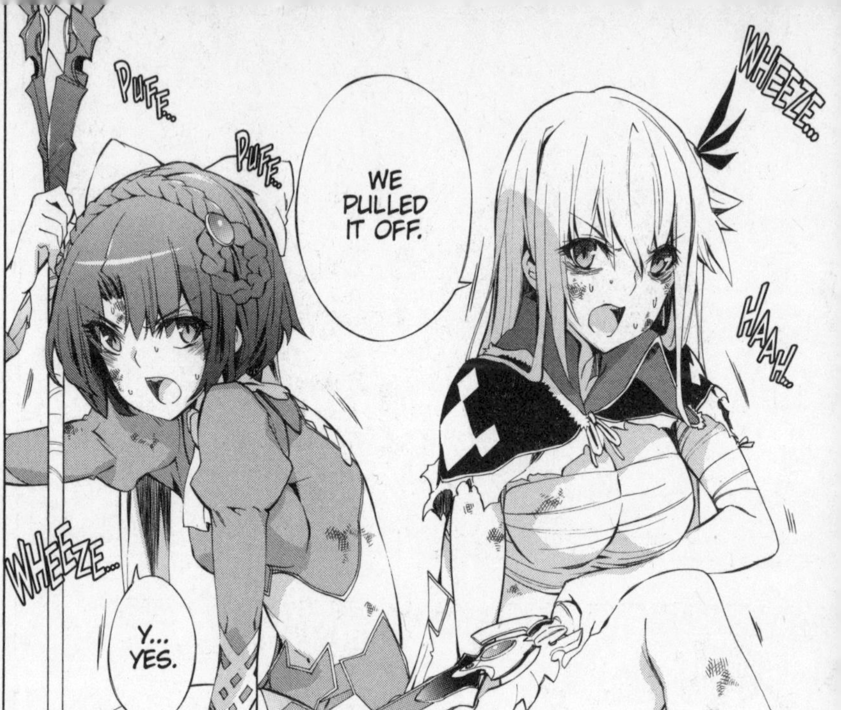
WHEEZE...
HAAH...
WE PULLED IT OFF.
PUFF...
PUFF...
WHEEZE...
Y... YES.
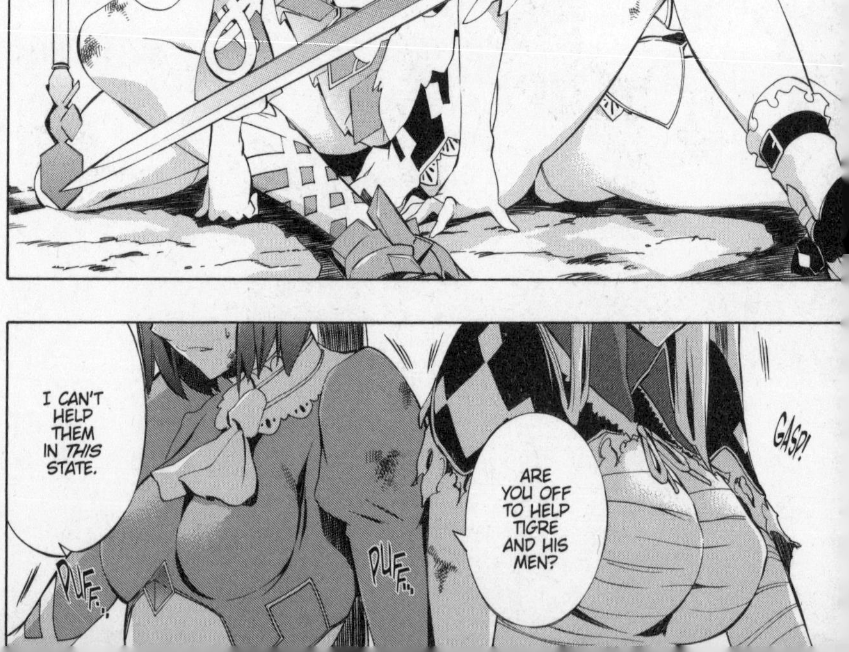
GASP!
ARE YOU OFF TO HELP TIGRE AND HIS MEN?
PUFF...
I CAN'T HELP THEM IN *THIS* STATE.
PUFF...

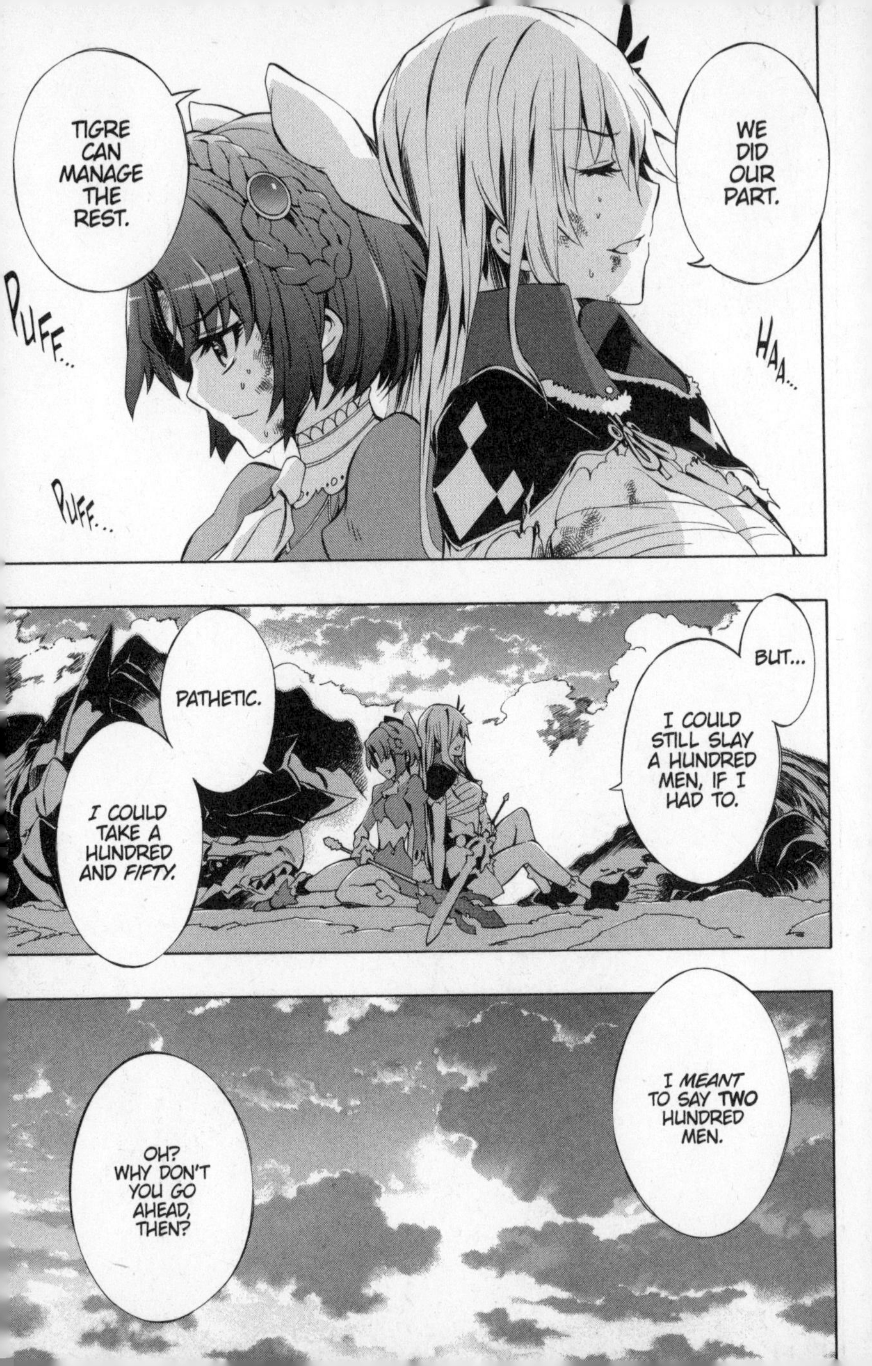
WE DID OUR PART.
TIGRE CAN MANAGE THE REST.
HAA...
PUFF...
PUFF...
BUT...
I COULD STILL SLAY A HUNDRED MEN, IF I HAD TO.
PATHETIC.
I COULD TAKE A HUNDRED AND *FIFTY*.
I *MEANT* TO SAY **TWO** HUNDRED MEN.
OH? WHY DON'T YOU GO AHEAD, THEN?

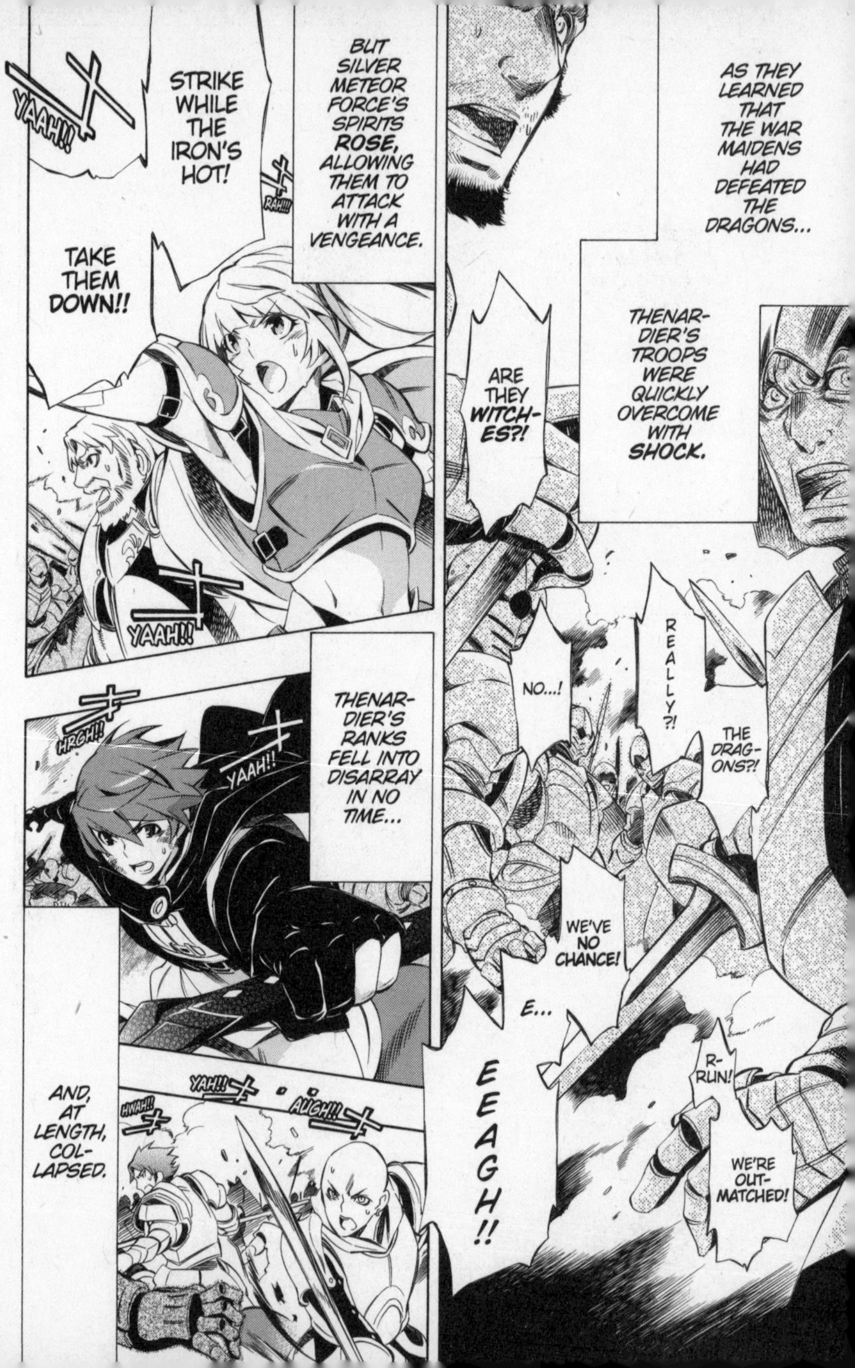
AS THEY LEARNED THAT THE WAR MAIDENS HAD DEFEATED THE DRAGONS...
THENARDIER'S TROOPS WERE QUICKLY OVERCOME WITH SHOCK.
ARE THEY WITCHES?!
REALLY?!
NO...!
THE DRAGONS?!
WE'VE NO CHANCE!
R-RUN!
E...
EEEAGH!!
WE'RE OUTMATCHED!
BUT SILVER METEOR FORCE'S SPIRITS ROSE, ALLOWING THEM TO ATTACK WITH A VENGEANCE.
RAH!!!
STRIKE WHILE THE IRON'S HOT!
YAAH!!
TAKE THEM DOWN!!
YAAH!!
THENARDIER'S RANKS FELL INTO DISARRAY IN NO TIME...
YAAH!!
HRGH!!
YAH!!
AUGH!!
HWAH!!
AND, AT LENGTH, COLLAPSED.

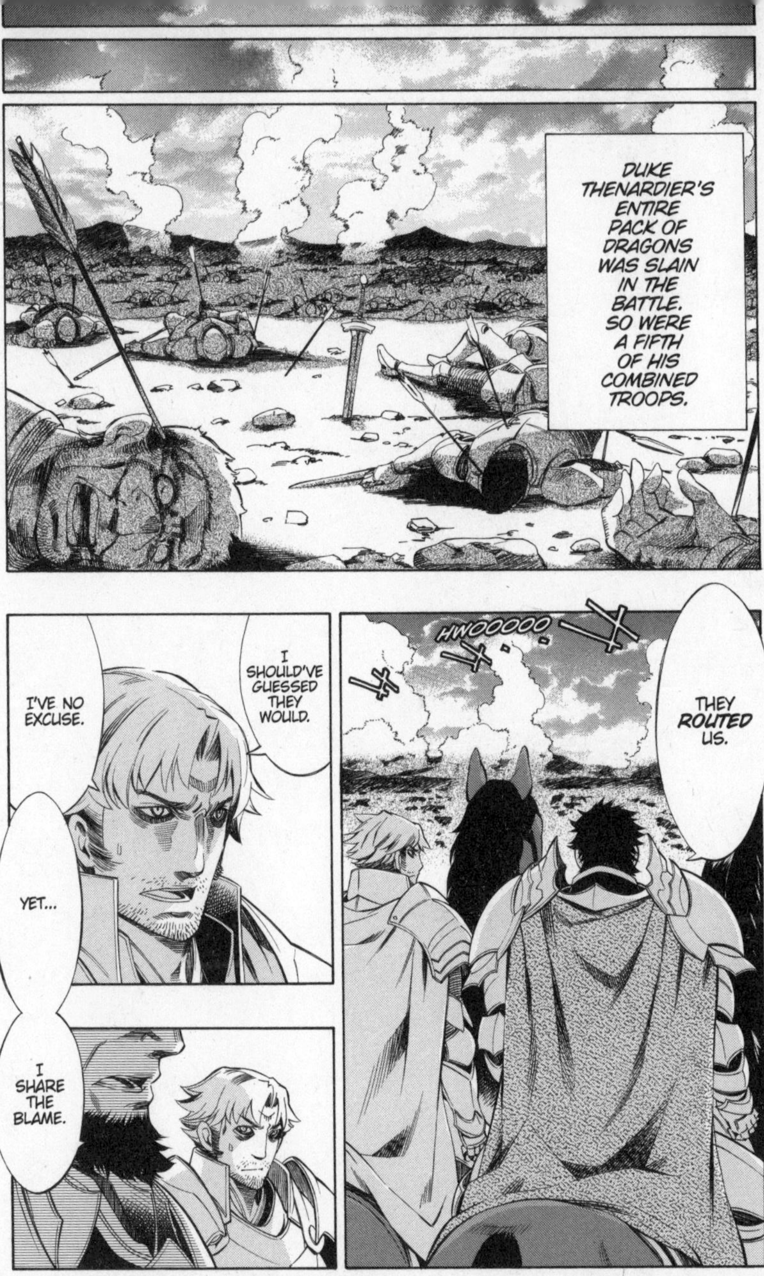
DUKE THENARDIER'S ENTIRE PACK OF DRAGONS WAS SLAIN IN THE BATTLE. SO WERE A FIFTH OF HIS COMBINED TROOPS.
THEY ROUTED US.
HWOOOOO
I SHOULD'VE GUESSED THEY WOULD.
I'VE NO EXCUSE.
YET...
I SHARE THE BLAME.

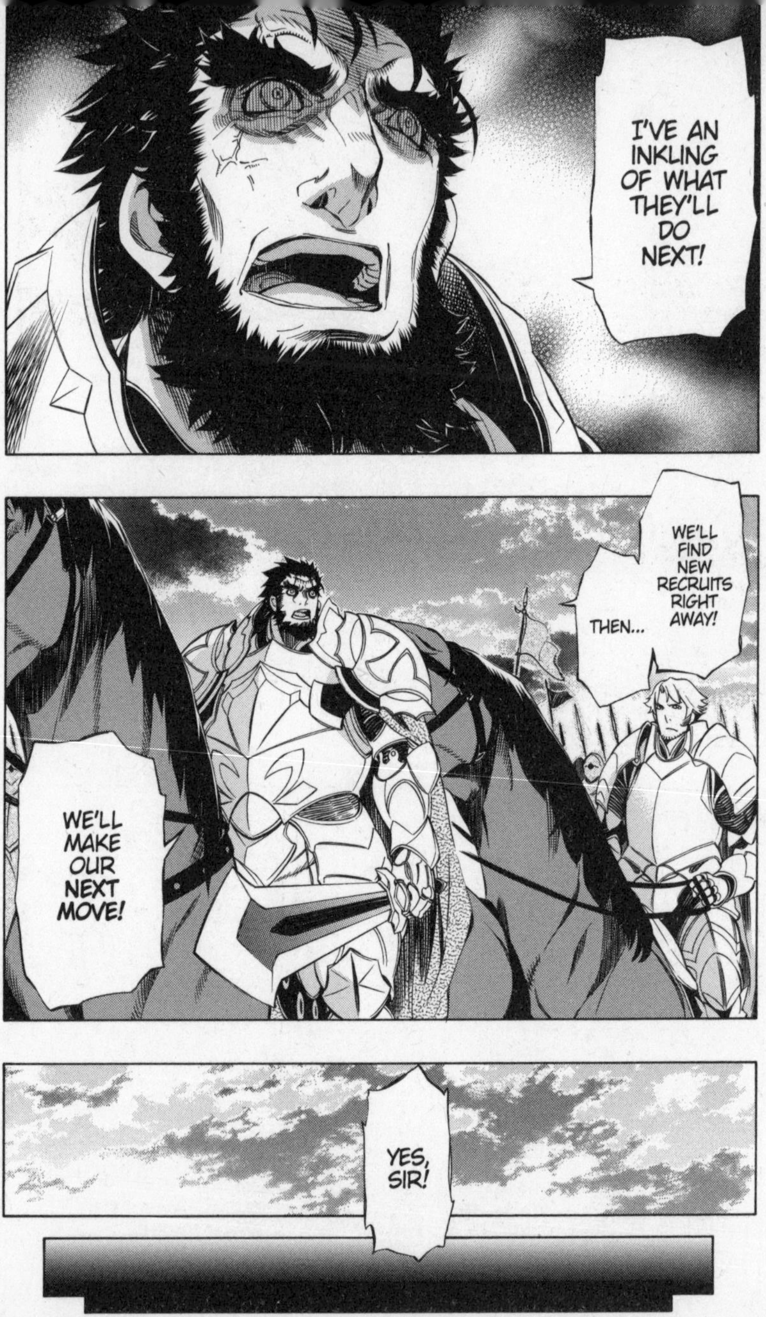
I'VE AN INKLING OF WHAT THEY'LL DO NEXT!
WE'LL FIND NEW RECRUITS RIGHT AWAY!
THEN...
WE'LL MAKE OUR NEXT MOVE!
YES, SIR!

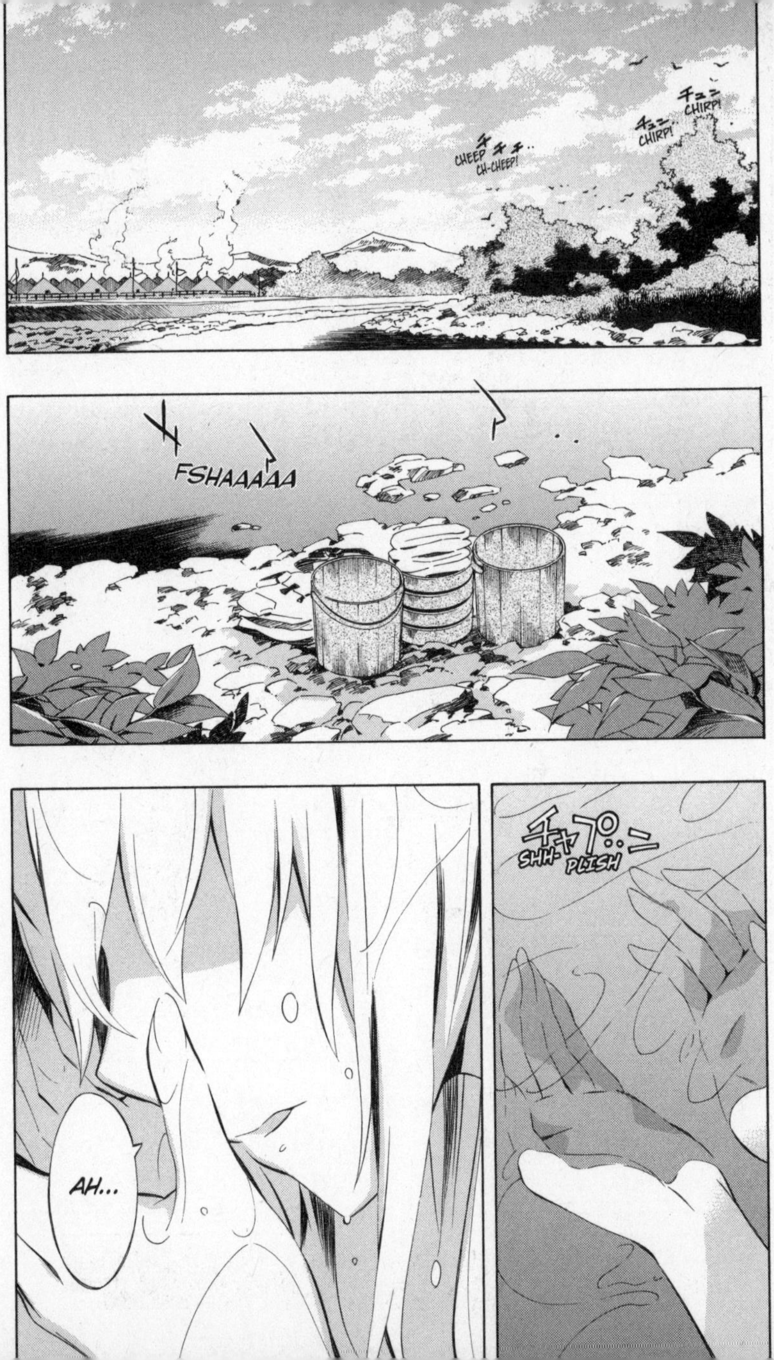
チュン
CHIRP!
チュン..
CHIRP!
チチチ..
CHEEP
CH-CHEEP!
FSHAAAAA
チャプ..ン
SHH-PLISH
AH...

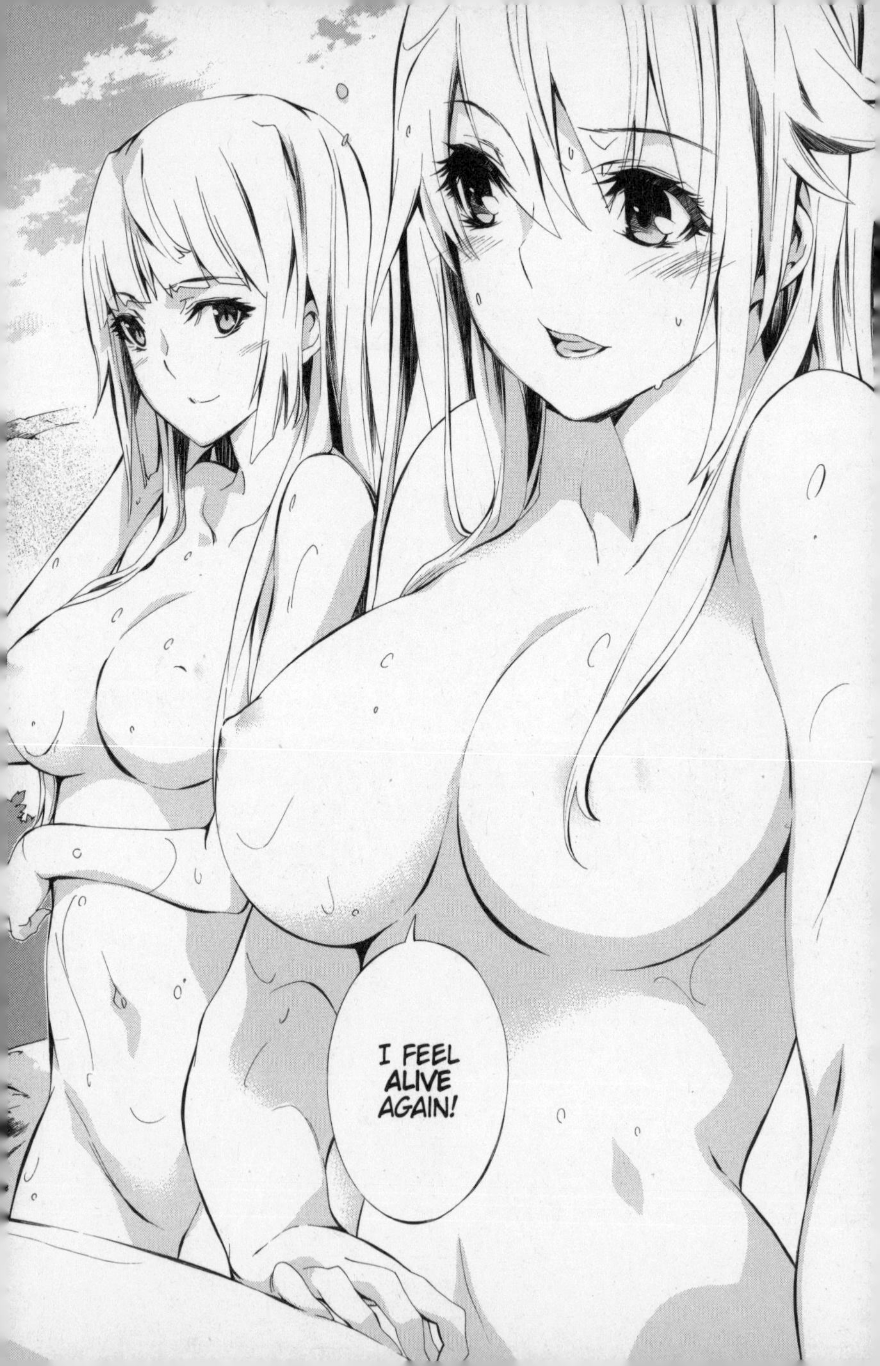
I FEEL ALIVE AGAIN!

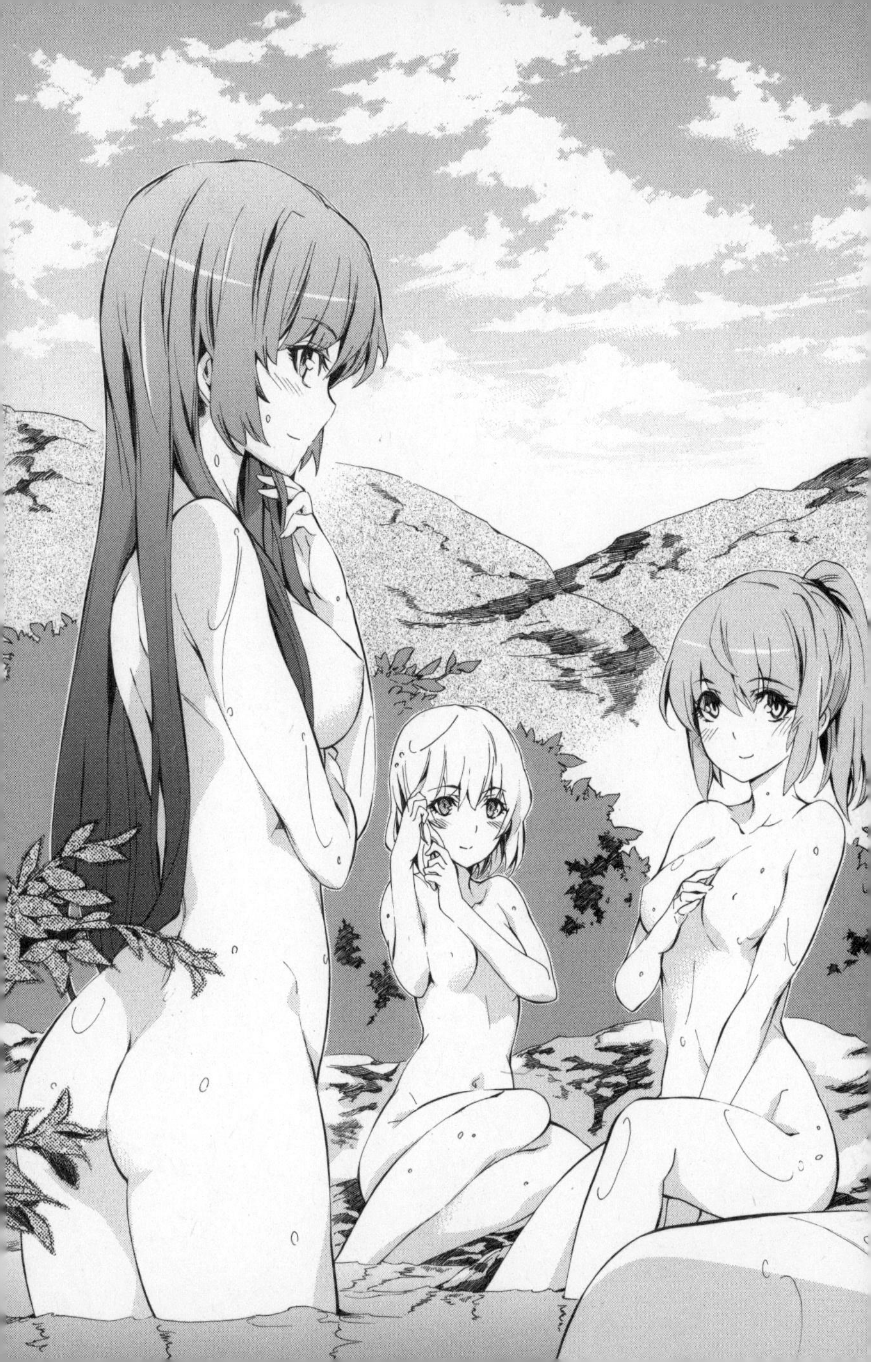

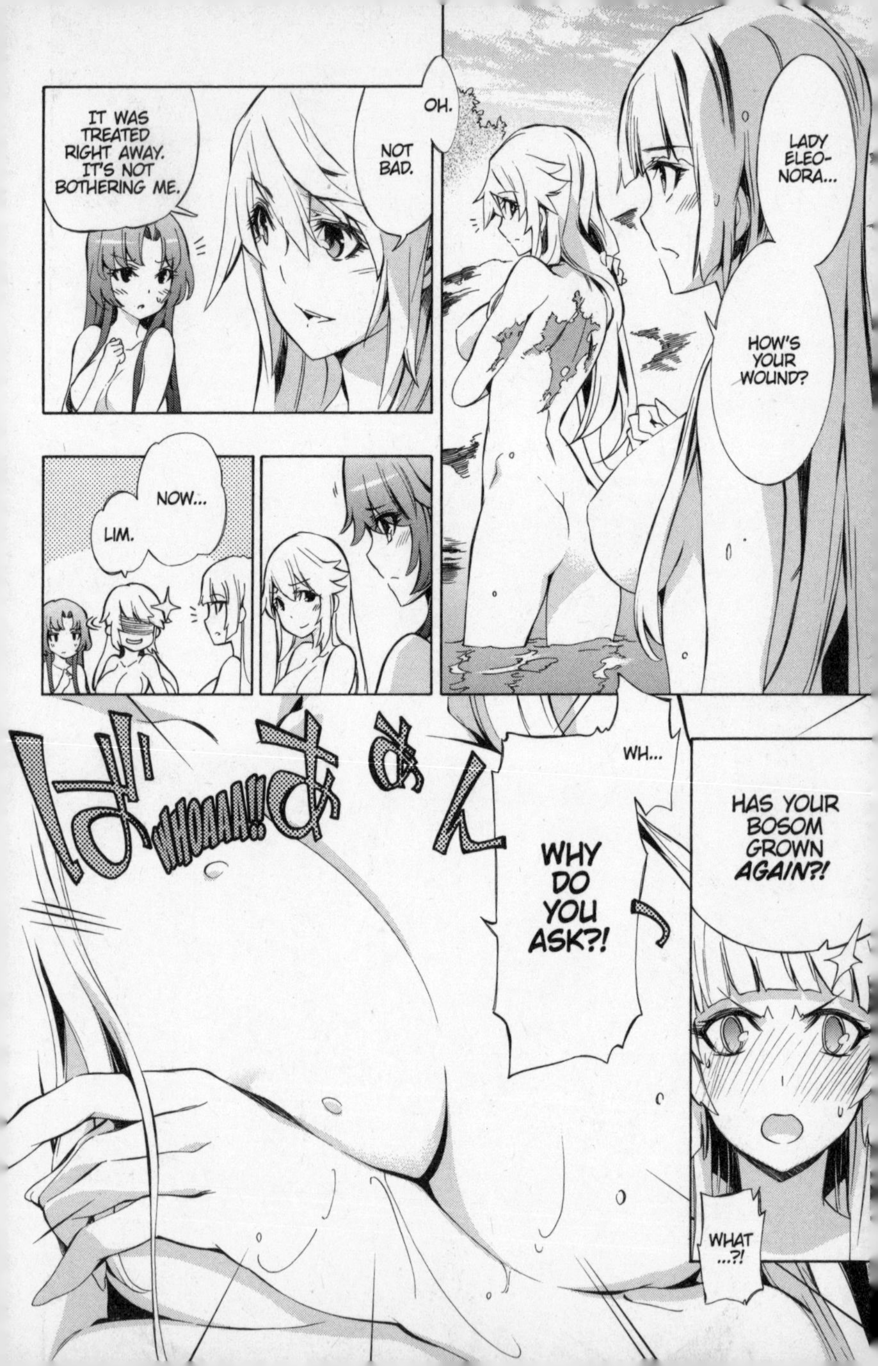

LADY ELEO-NORA...
HOW'S YOUR WOUND?
OH.
NOT BAD.
IT WAS TREATED RIGHT AWAY. IT'S NOT BOTHERING ME.
NOW...
LIM.
HAS YOUR BOSOM GROWN AGAIN?!
WHAT ...?!
WH...
WHY DO YOU ASK?!
ばあん
WHOAAA!!

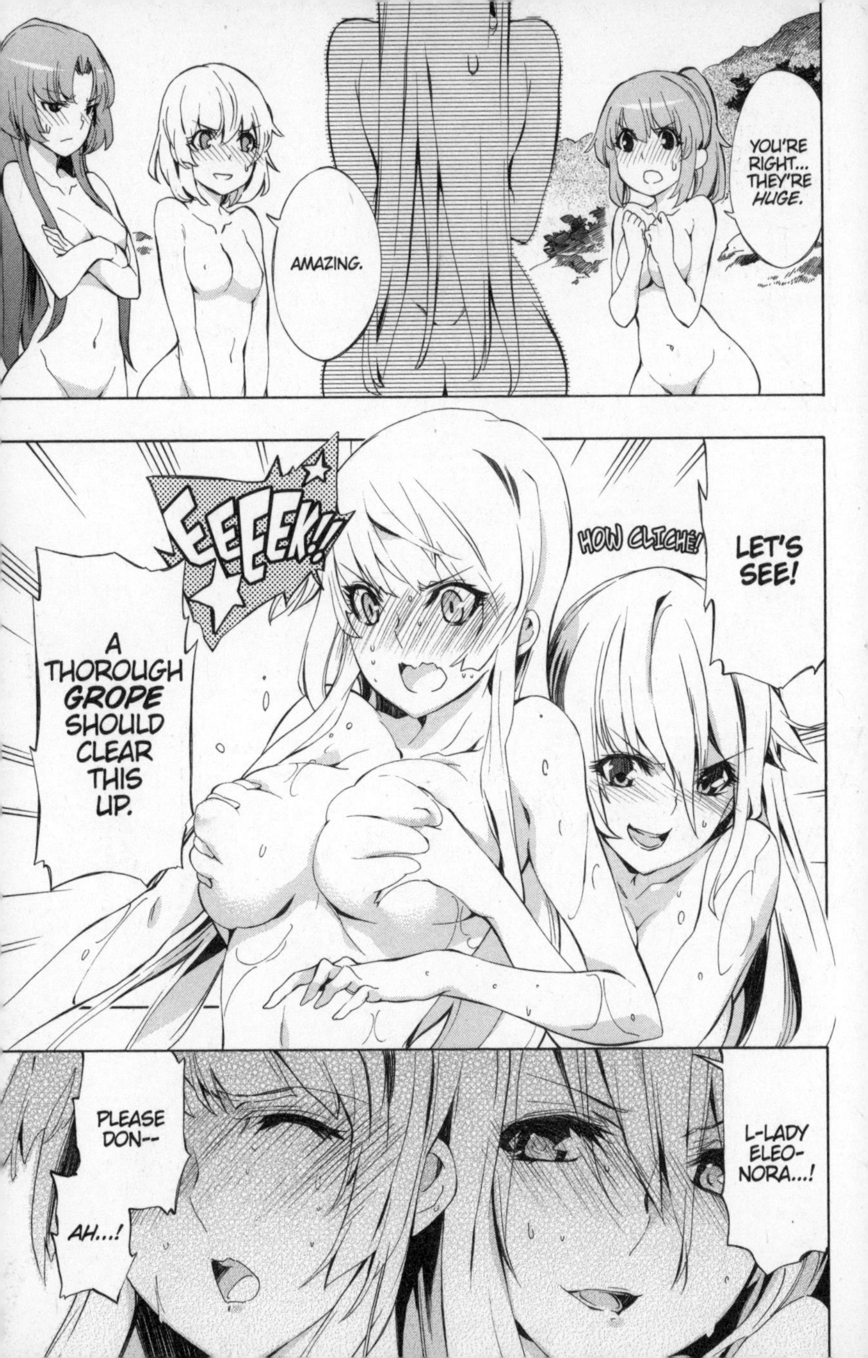
YOU'RE RIGHT... THEY'RE HUGE.
AMAZING.
LET'S SEE!
HOW CLICHÉ!
EEEEK!!
A THOROUGH GROPE SHOULD CLEAR THIS UP.
L-LADY ELEO-NORA...!
PLEASE DON--
AH...!

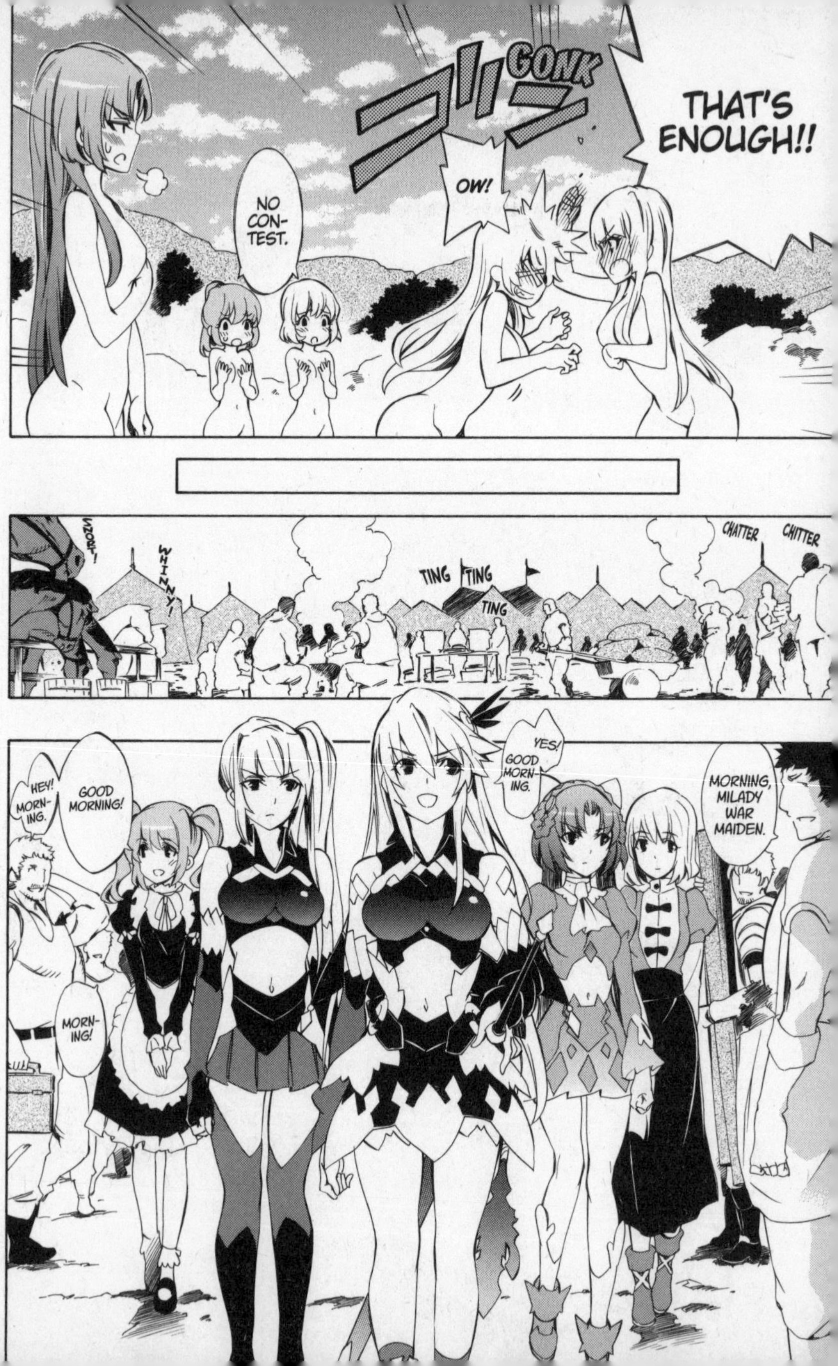
THAT'S ENOUGH!!
GONK
OW!
NO CON-TEST.
CHITTER
CHATTER
TING
TING
TING
WHINNY!
SNORT!
MORNING, MILADY WAR MAIDEN.
YES! GOOD MORN-ING.
GOOD MORNING!
HEY! MORN-ING.
MORN-ING!

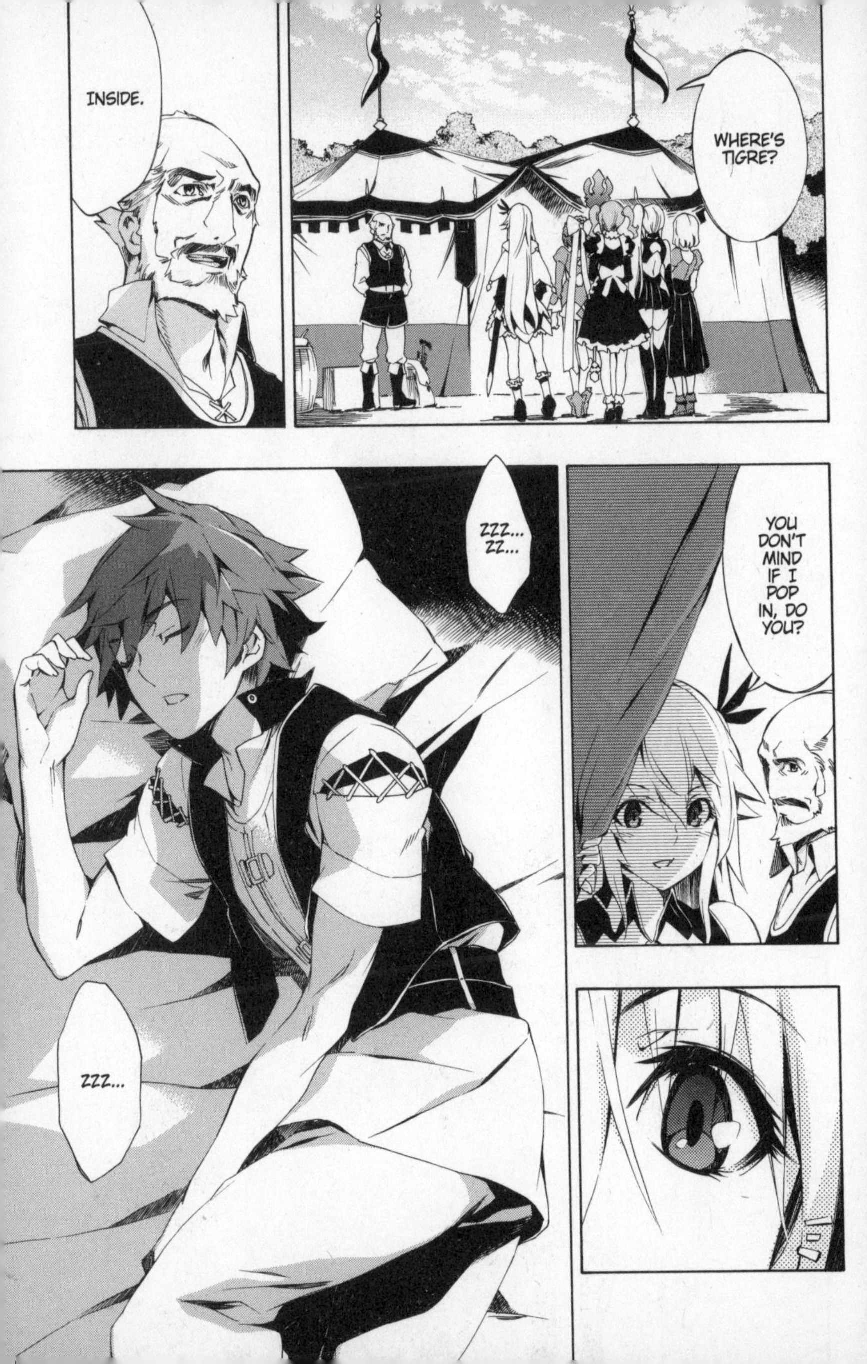
WHERE'S TIGRE?
INSIDE.
YOU DON'T MIND IF I POP IN, DO YOU?
ZZZ... ZZ...
ZZZ...

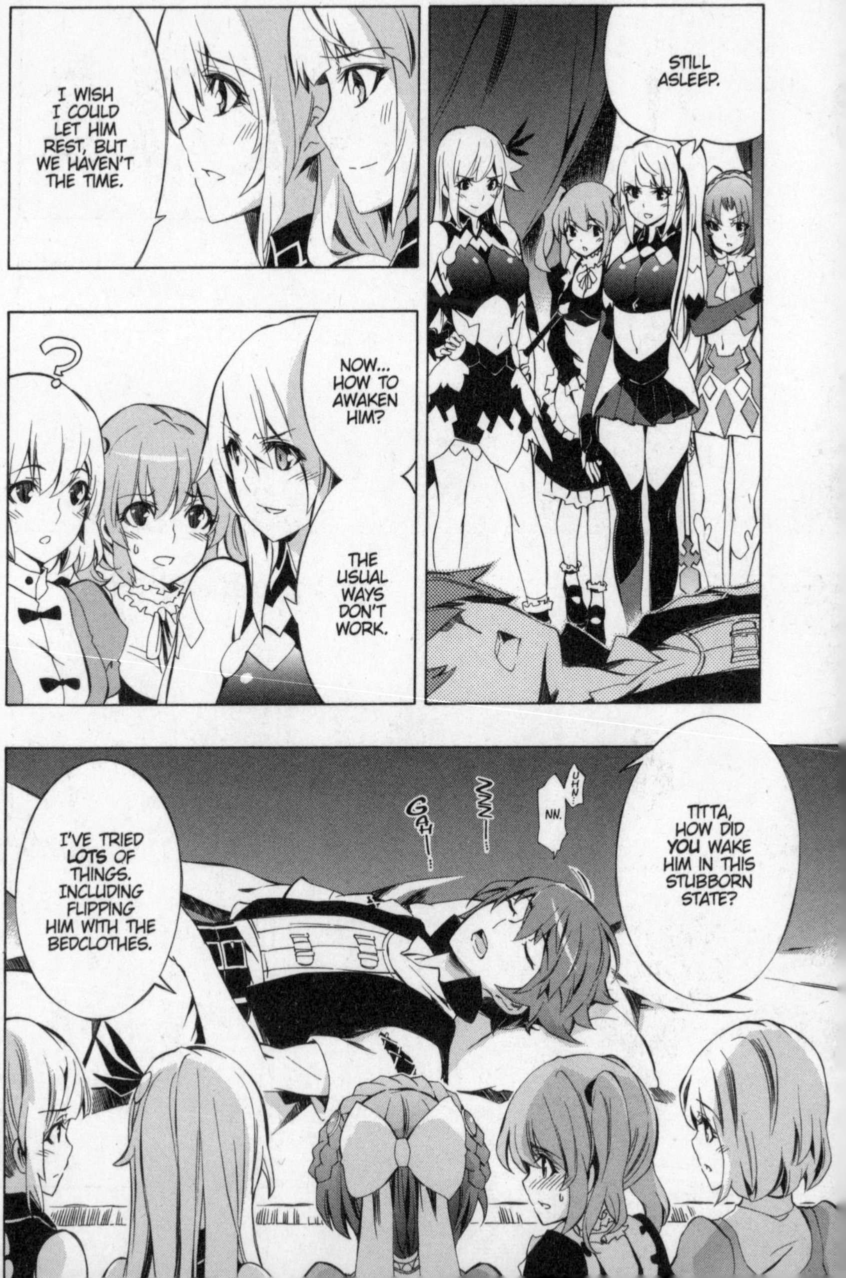
STILL ASLEEP.
I WISH I COULD LET HIM REST, BUT WE HAVEN'T THE TIME.
NOW... HOW TO AWAKEN HIM?
THE USUAL WAYS DON'T WORK.
TITTA, HOW DID YOU WAKE HIM IN THIS STUBBORN STATE?
UHN...
NN.
ZZZ...
GAH...
I'VE TRIED LOTS OF THINGS. INCLUDING FLIPPING HIM WITH THE BEDCLOTHES.

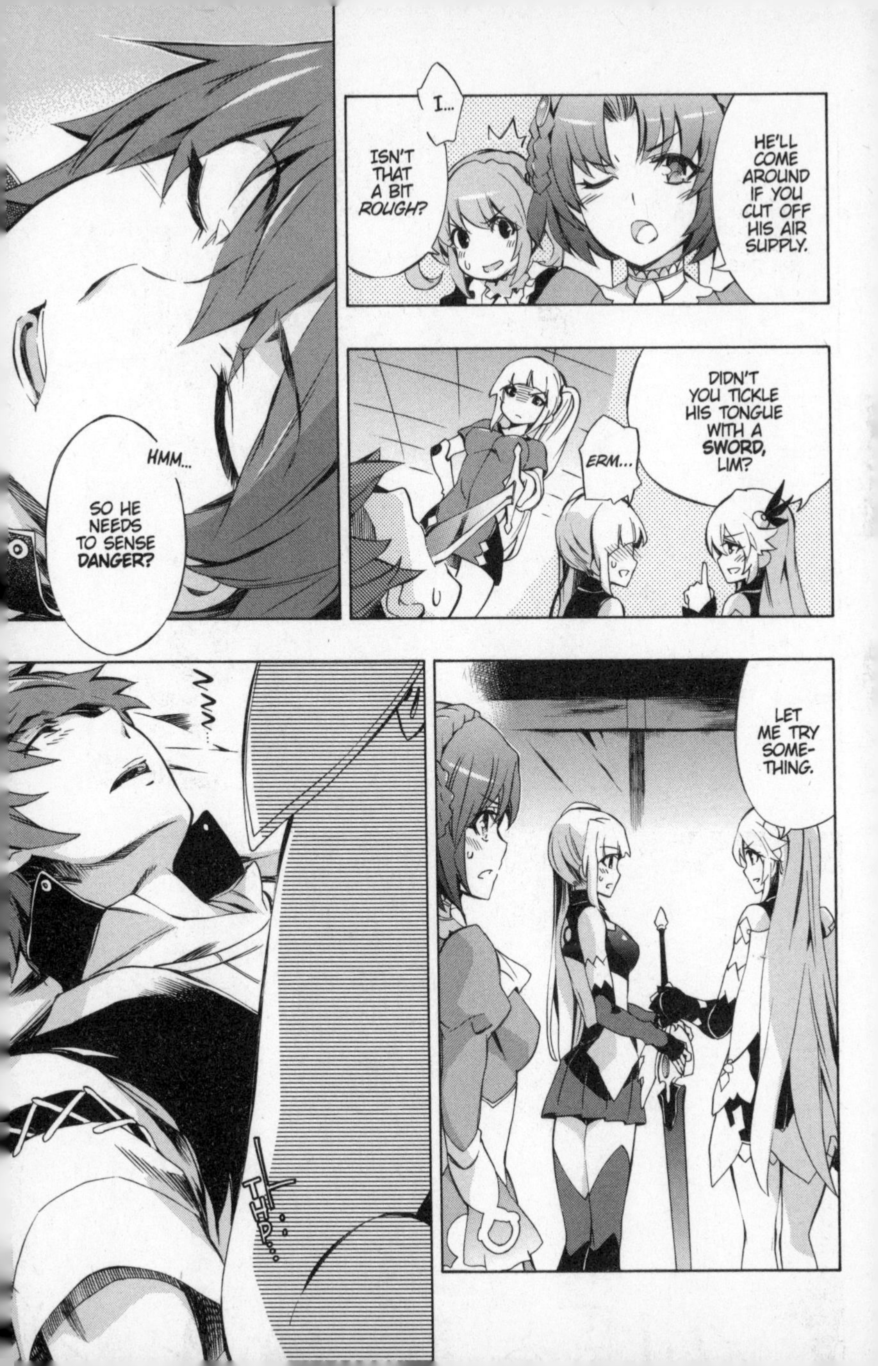
HE'LL COME AROUND IF YOU CUT OFF HIS AIR SUPPLY.
I...
ISN'T THAT A BIT *ROUGH?*
DIDN'T YOU TICKLE HIS TONGUE WITH A **SWORD,** LIM?
ERM...
HMM...
SO HE NEEDS TO SENSE **DANGER?**
LET ME TRY SOME-THING.
NNN...
THUD...

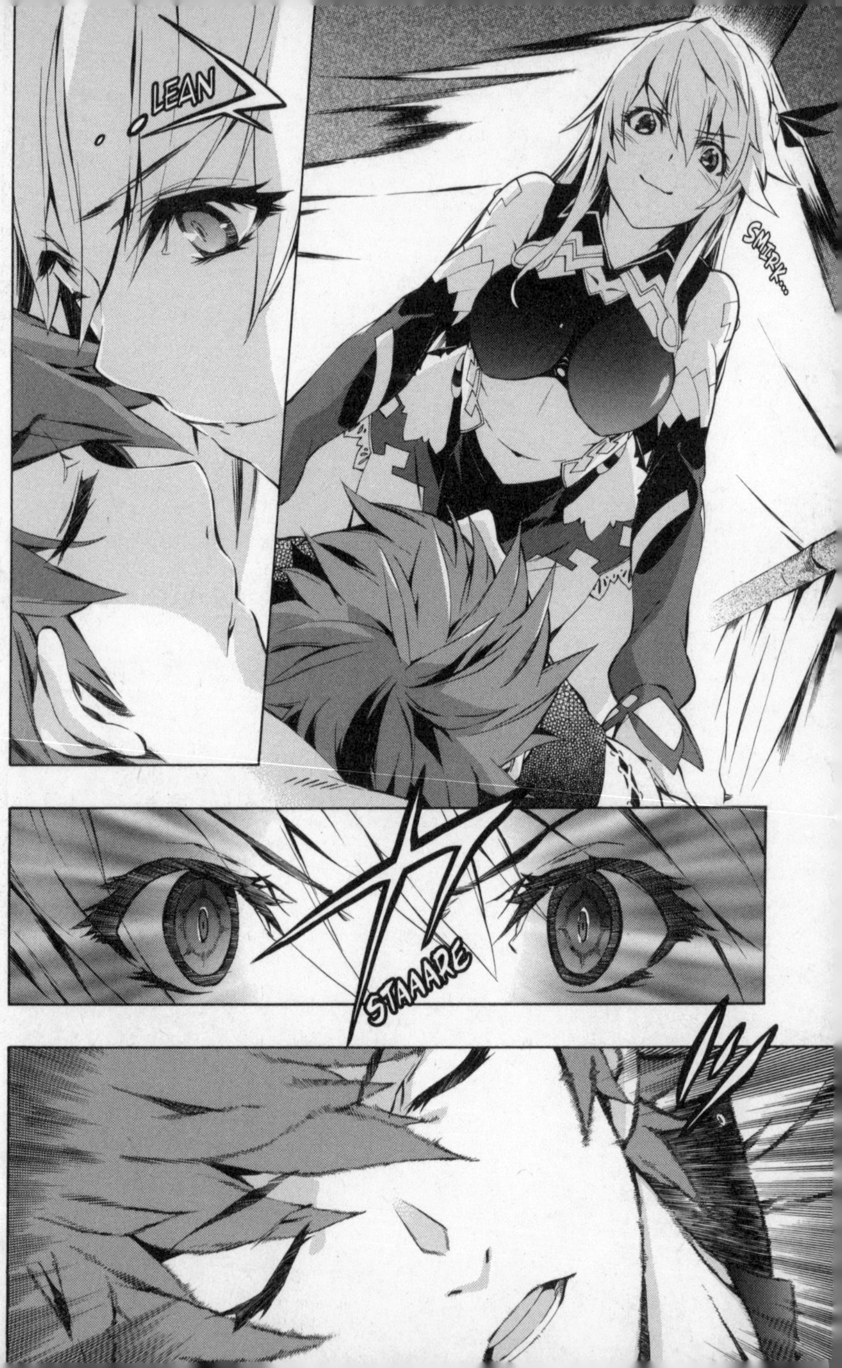
SMIRK...
LEAN
STAAARE

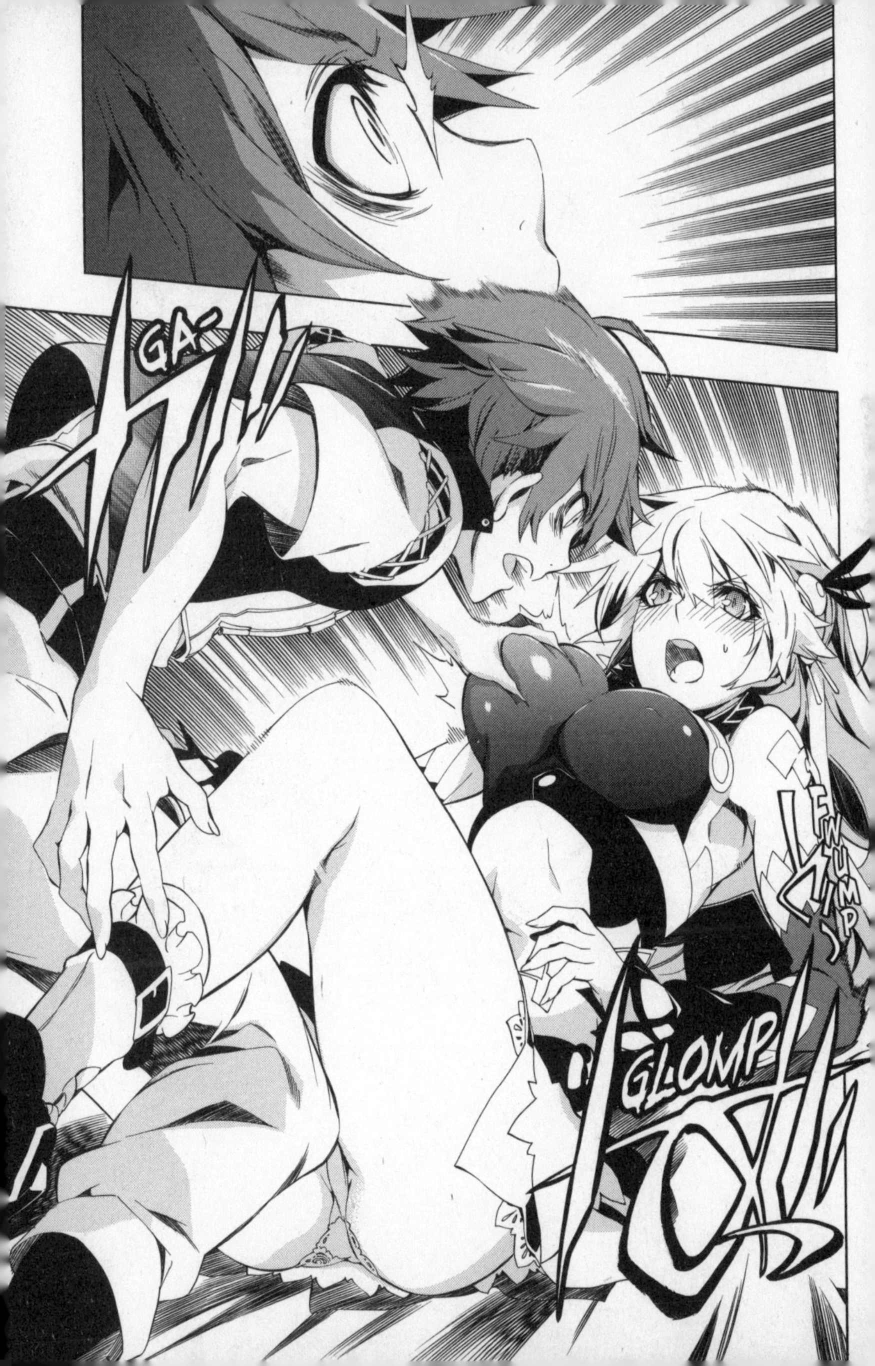
GA-
FWUMP
GLOMP

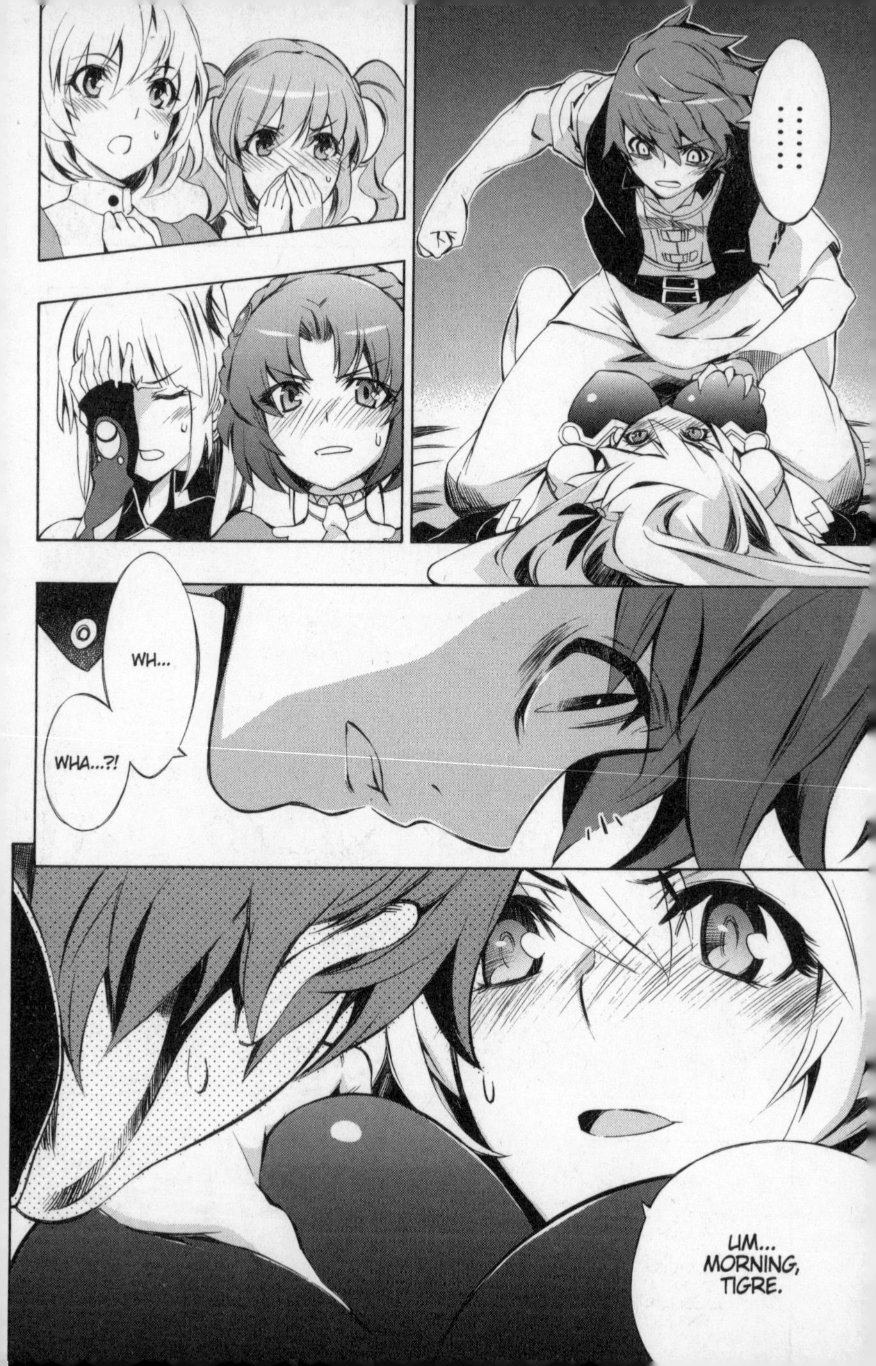
......
WH...
WHA...?!
UM... MORNING, TIGRE.

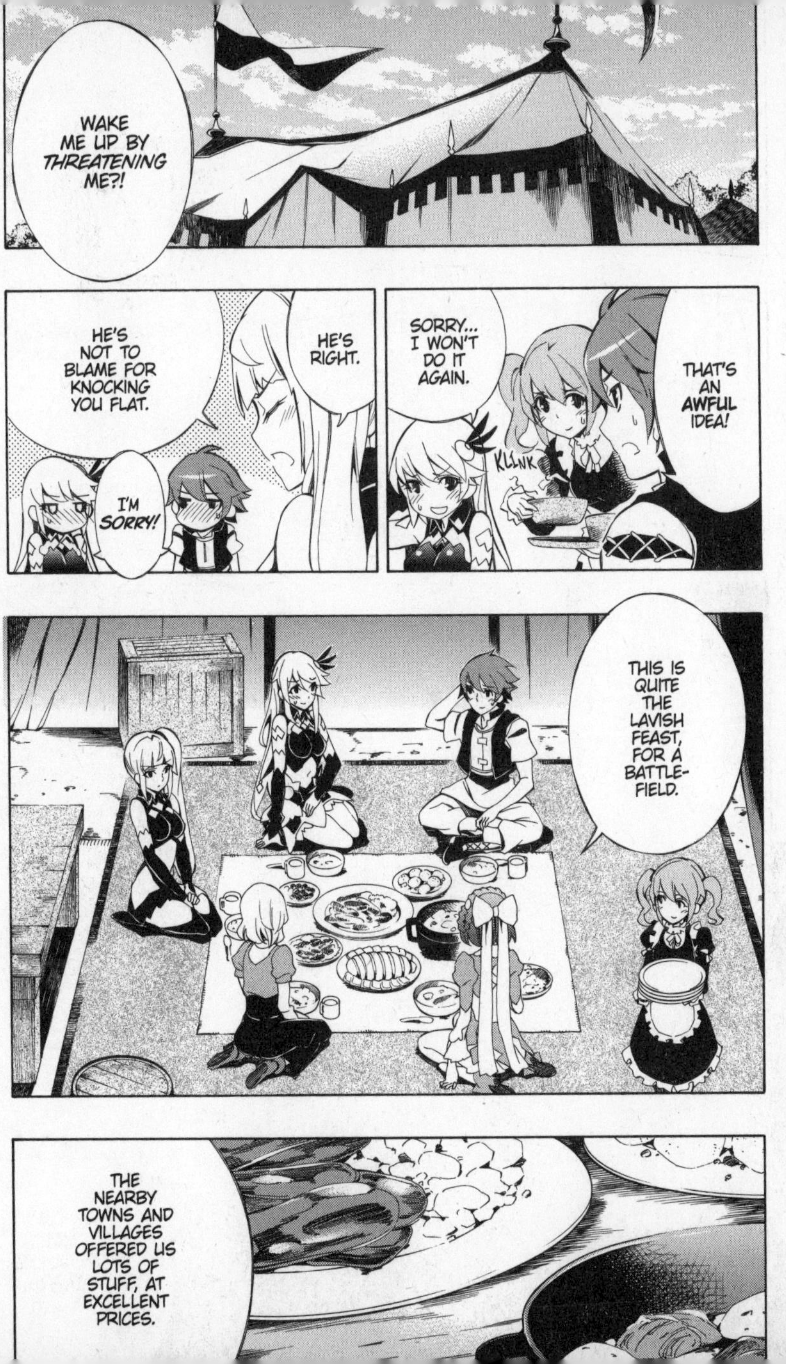
WAKE ME UP BY *THREATENING* ME?!
THAT'S AN **AWFUL** IDEA!
KLINK
SORRY... I WON'T DO IT AGAIN.
HE'S RIGHT.
HE'S NOT TO BLAME FOR KNOCKING YOU FLAT.
I'M *SORRY!*
THIS IS QUITE THE LAVISH FEAST, FOR A BATTLE-FIELD.
THE NEARBY TOWNS AND VILLAGES OFFERED US LOTS OF STUFF, AT EXCELLENT PRICES.

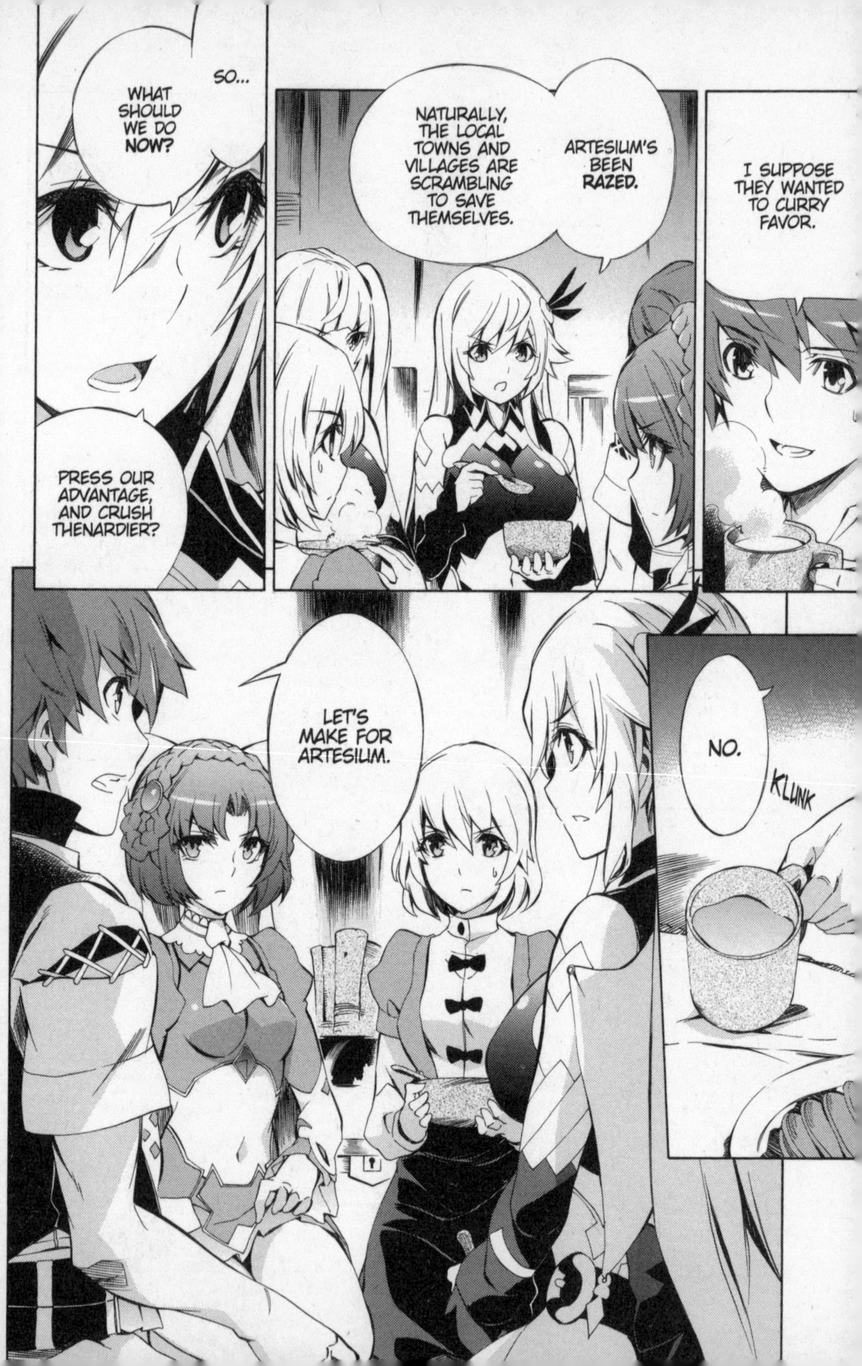
I SUPPOSE THEY WANTED TO CURRY FAVOR.
ARTESIUM'S BEEN RAZED.
NATURALLY, THE LOCAL TOWNS AND VILLAGES ARE SCRAMBLING TO SAVE THEMSELVES.
SO... WHAT SHOULD WE DO NOW?
PRESS OUR ADVANTAGE, AND CRUSH THENARDIER?
NO.
KLUNK
LET'S MAKE FOR ARTESIUM.

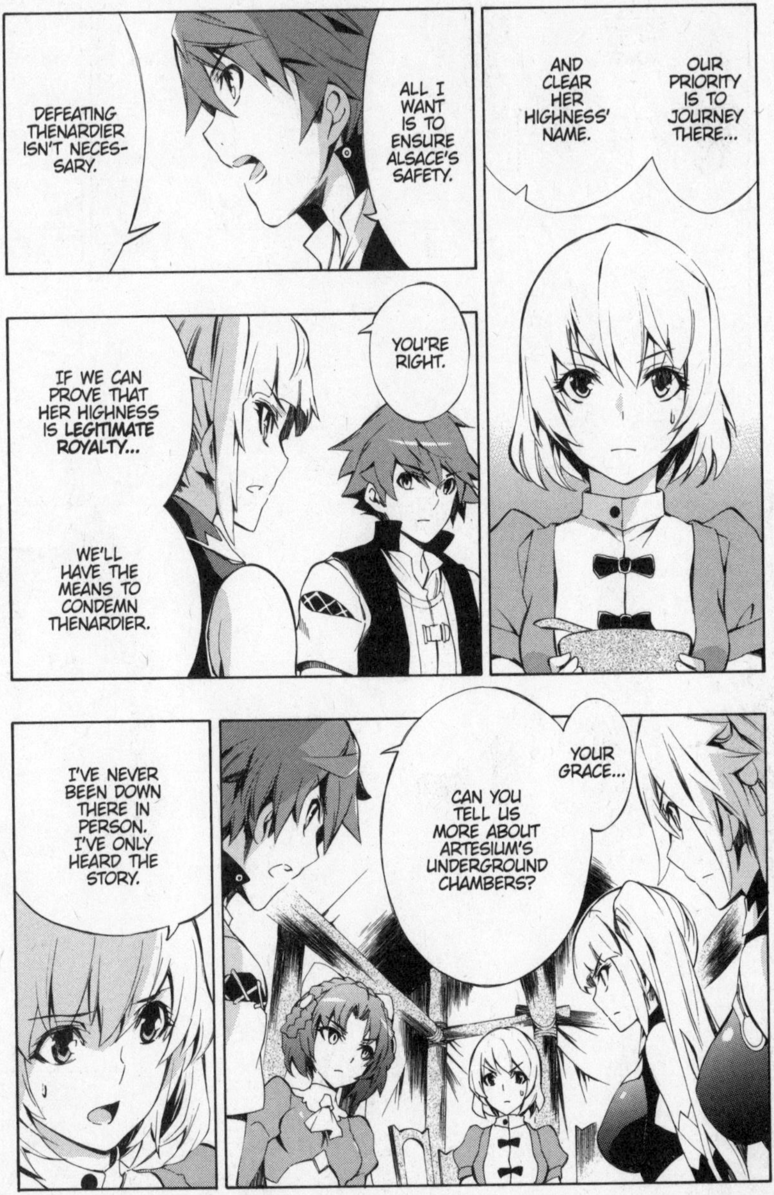
OUR PRIORITY IS TO JOURNEY THERE...
AND CLEAR HER HIGHNESS' NAME.
ALL I WANT IS TO ENSURE ALSACE'S SAFETY.
DEFEATING THENARDIER ISN'T NECES-SARY.
YOU'RE RIGHT.
IF WE CAN PROVE THAT HER HIGHNESS IS LEGITIMATE ROYALTY...
WE'LL HAVE THE MEANS TO CONDEMN THENARDIER.
YOUR GRACE...
CAN YOU TELL US MORE ABOUT ARTESIUM'S UNDERGROUND CHAMBERS?
I'VE NEVER BEEN DOWN THERE IN PERSON. I'VE ONLY HEARD THE STORY.

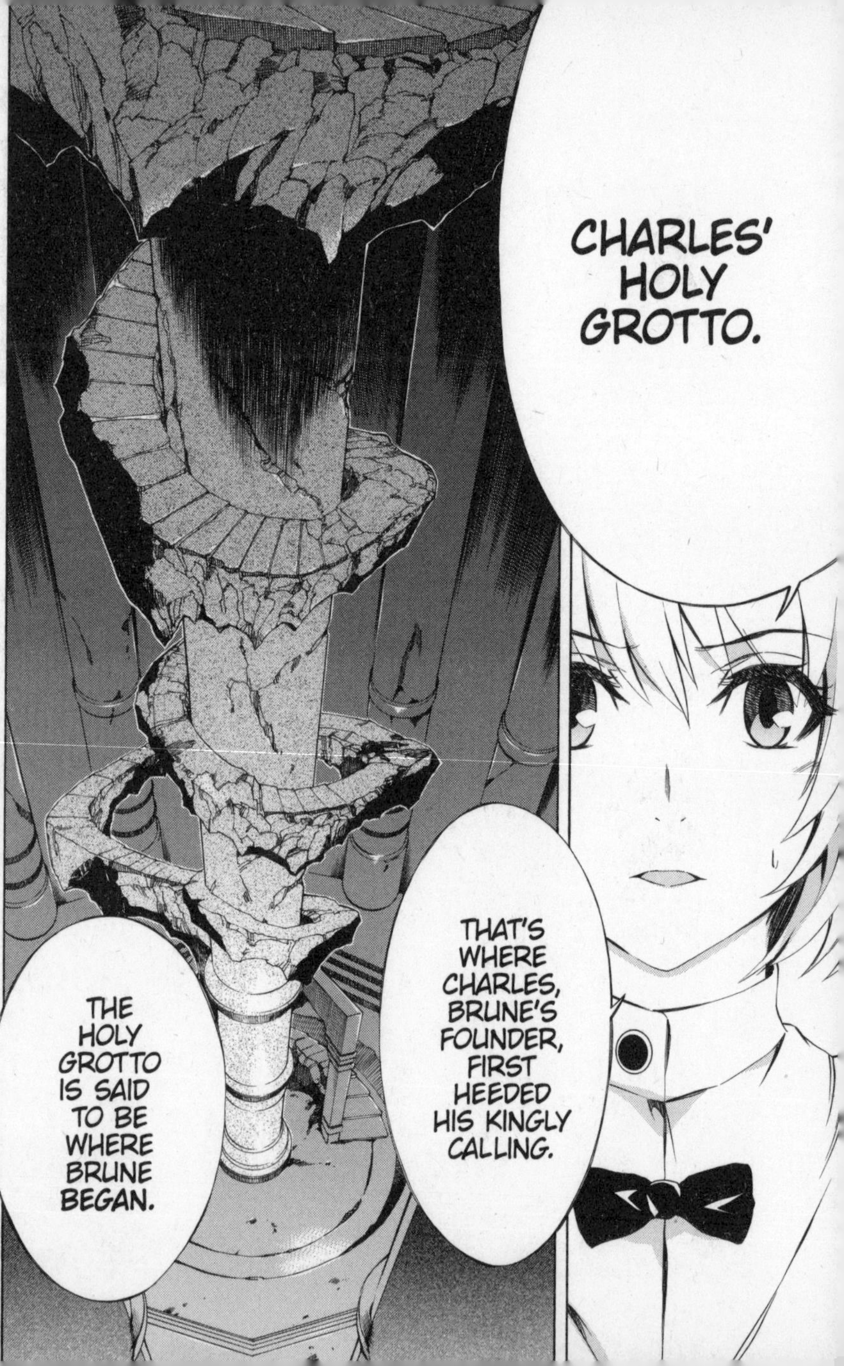
CHARLES' HOLY GROTTO.
THAT'S WHERE CHARLES, BRUNE'S FOUNDER, FIRST HEEDED HIS KINGLY CALLING.
THE HOLY GROTTO IS SAID TO BE WHERE BRUNE BEGAN.

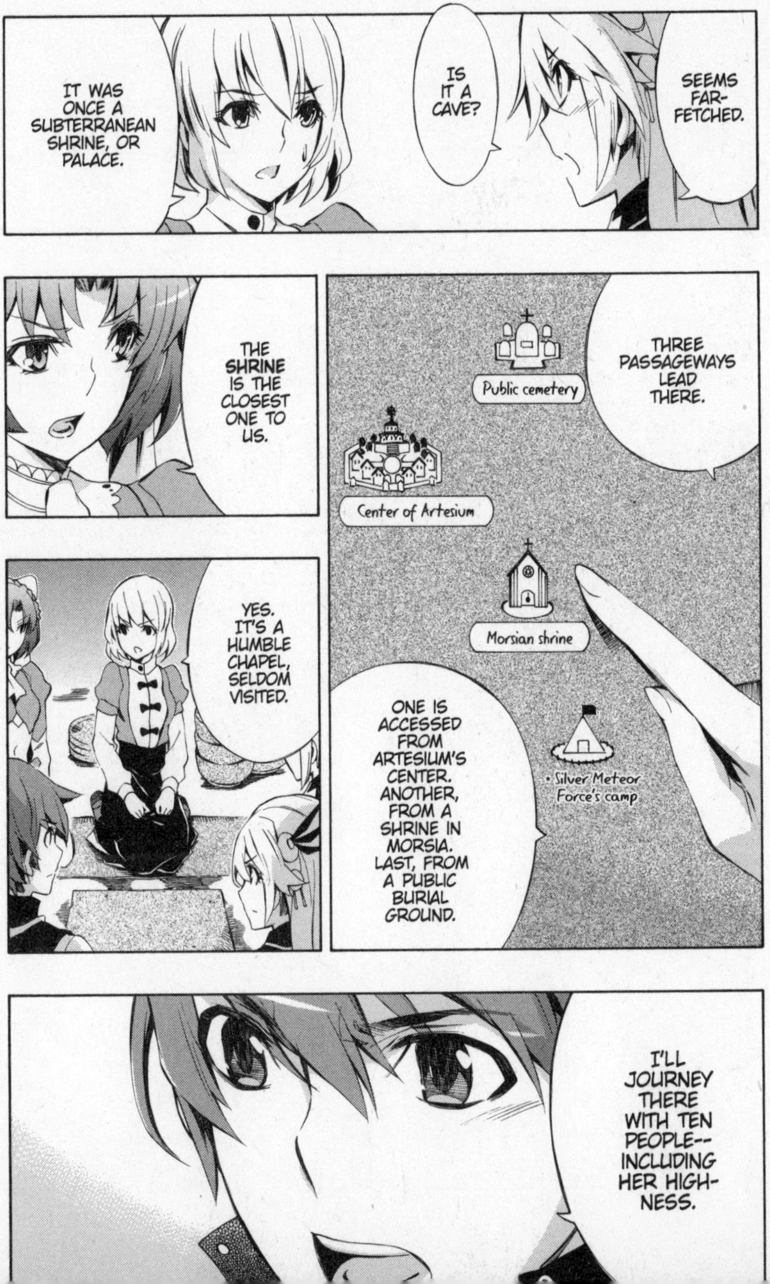
SEEMS FAR-FETCHED.
IS IT A CAVE?
IT WAS ONCE A SUBTERRANEAN SHRINE, OR PALACE.
THREE PASSAGEWAYS LEAD THERE.
Public cemetery
Center of Artesium
Morsian shrine
Silver Meteor Force's camp
ONE IS ACCESSED FROM ARTESIUM'S CENTER. ANOTHER, FROM A SHRINE IN MORSIA. LAST, FROM A PUBLIC BURIAL GROUND.
THE SHRINE IS THE CLOSEST ONE TO US.
YES. IT'S A HUMBLE CHAPEL, SELDOM VISITED.
I'LL JOURNEY THERE WITH TEN PEOPLE--INCLUDING HER HIGHNESS.

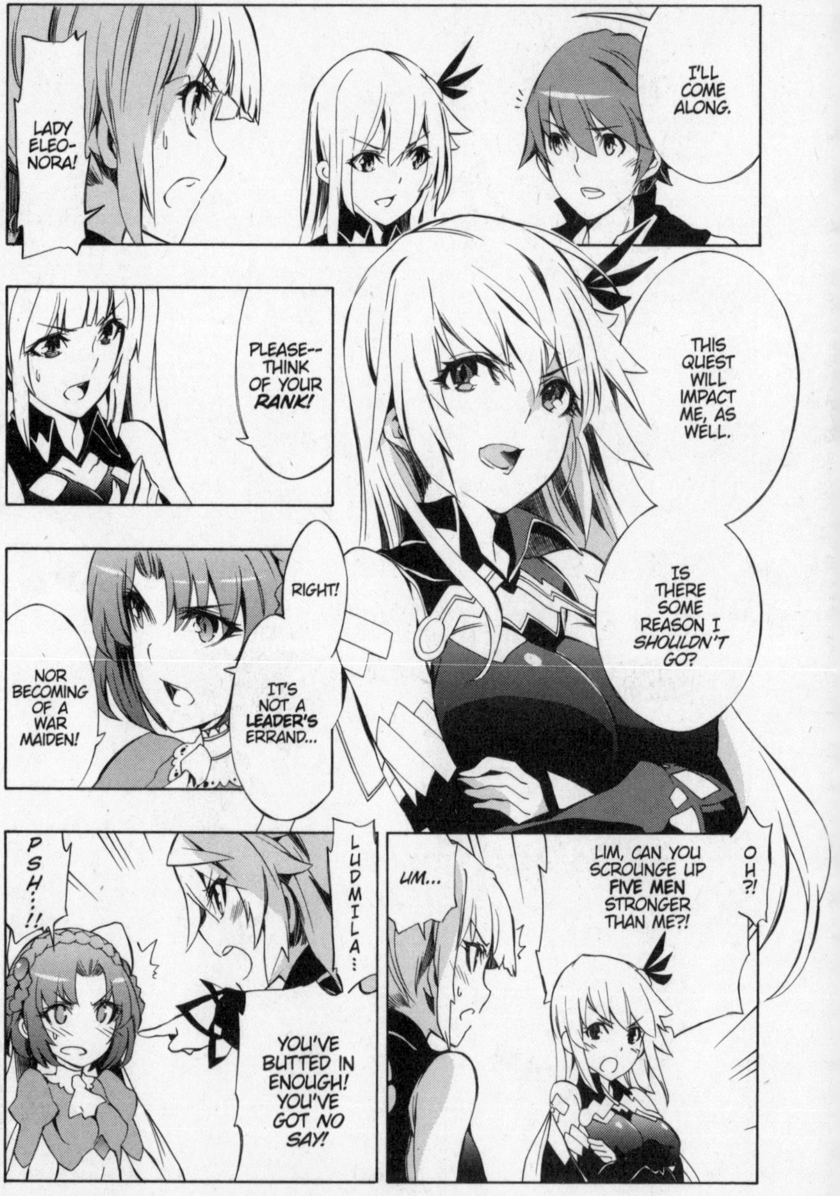
I'LL COME ALONG.
LADY ELEONORA!
THIS QUEST WILL IMPACT ME, AS WELL.
IS THERE SOME REASON I SHOULDN'T GO?
PLEASE-- THINK OF YOUR RANK!
RIGHT!
IT'S NOT A LEADER'S ERRAND...
NOR BECOMING OF A WAR MAIDEN!
OH?!
LIM, CAN YOU SCROUNGE UP FIVE MEN STRONGER THAN ME?!
UM...
LUDMILA...
PSH...!!
YOU'VE BUTTED IN ENOUGH! YOU'VE GOT NO SAY!

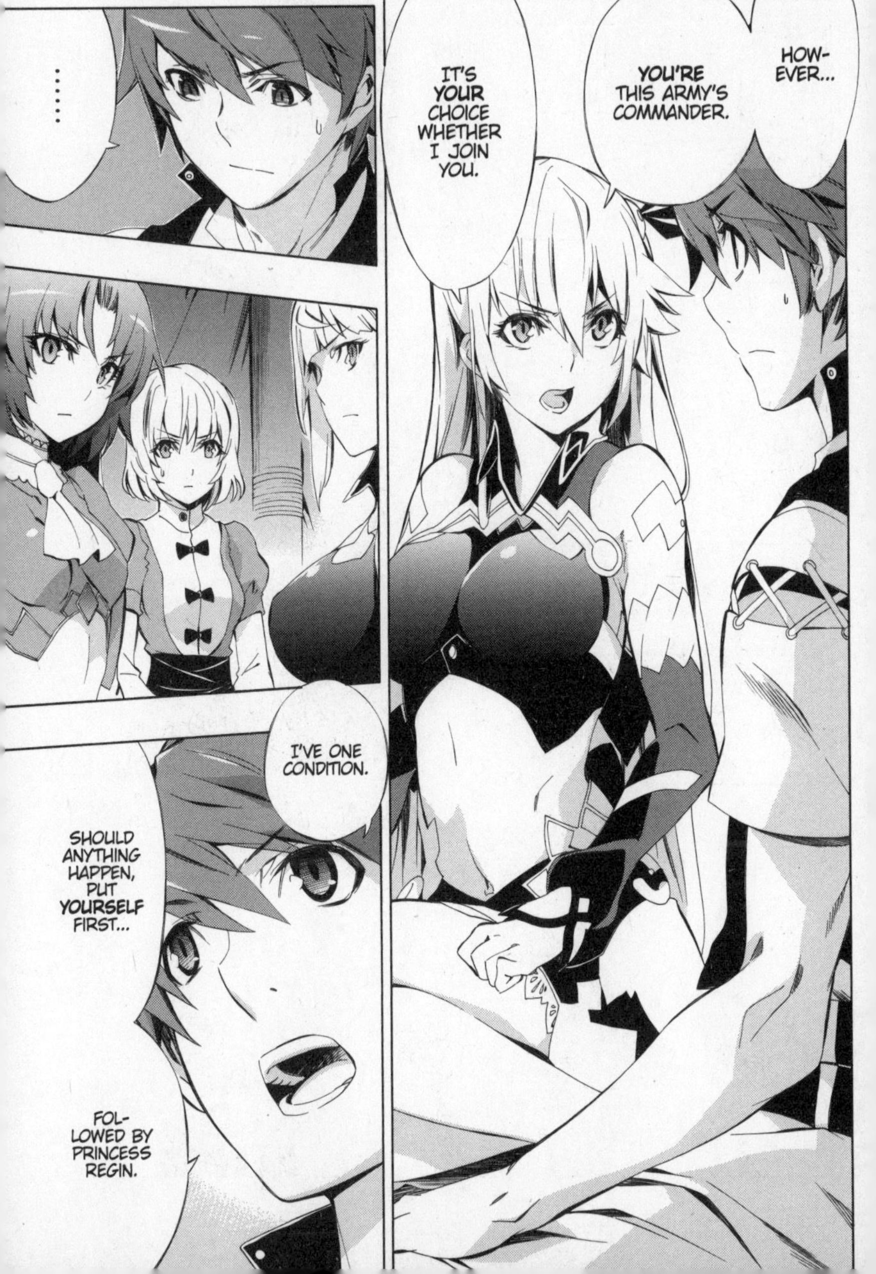
HOW-EVER...
YOU'RE THIS ARMY'S COMMANDER.
IT'S YOUR CHOICE WHETHER I JOIN YOU.
......
I'VE ONE CONDITION.
SHOULD ANYTHING HAPPEN, PUT YOURSELF FIRST...
FOL-LOWED BY PRINCESS REGIN.

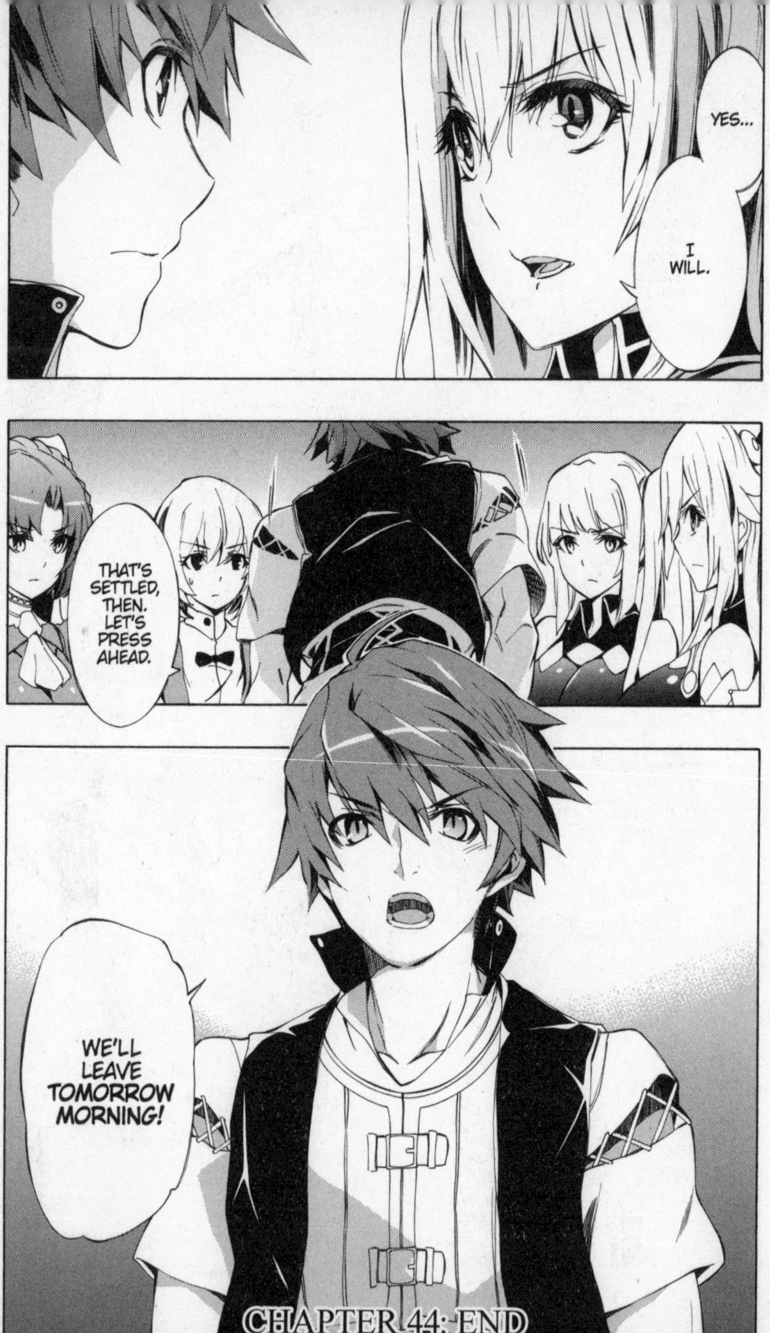
YES...
I WILL.
THAT'S SETTLED, THEN. LET'S PRESS AHEAD.
WE'LL LEAVE TOMORROW MORNING!
CHAPTER 44: END

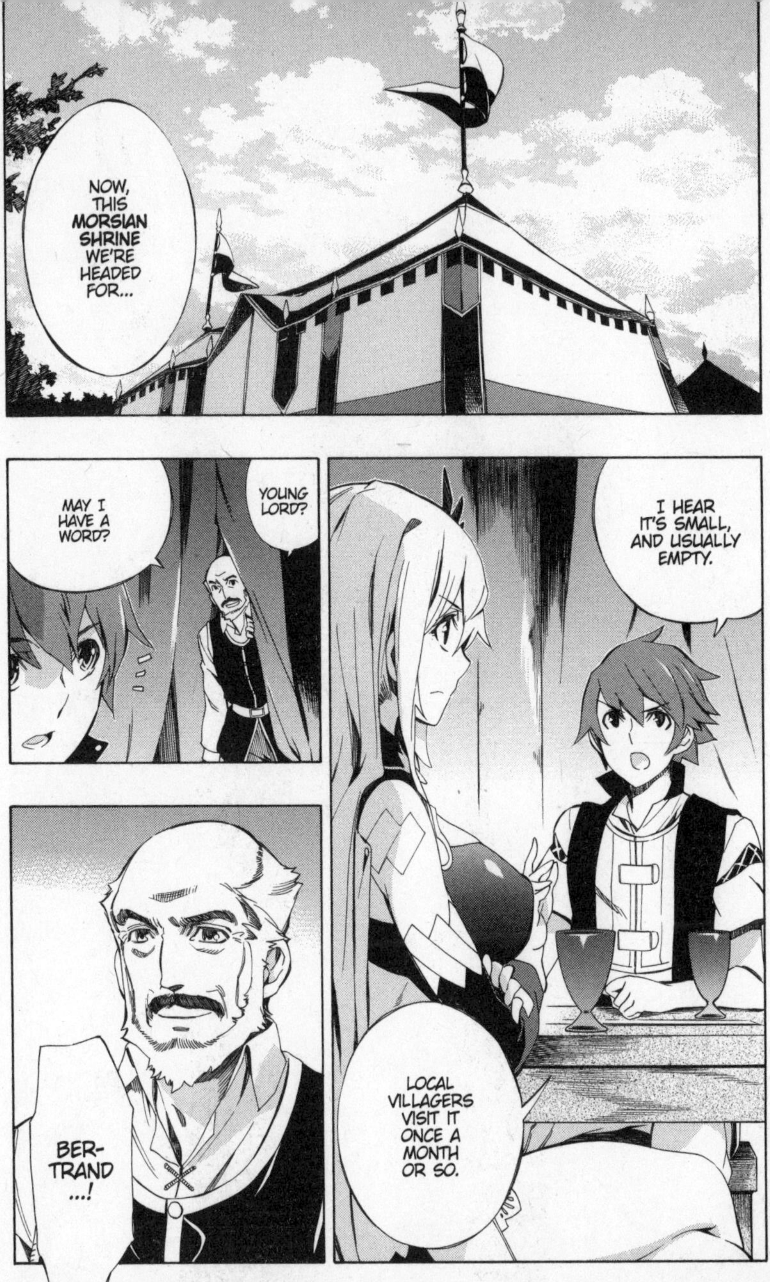
NOW, THIS MORSIAN SHRINE WE'RE HEADED FOR...
I HEAR IT'S SMALL, AND USUALLY EMPTY.
LOCAL VILLAGERS VISIT IT ONCE A MONTH OR SO.
YOUNG LORD?
MAY I HAVE A WORD?
BER-TRAND ...!

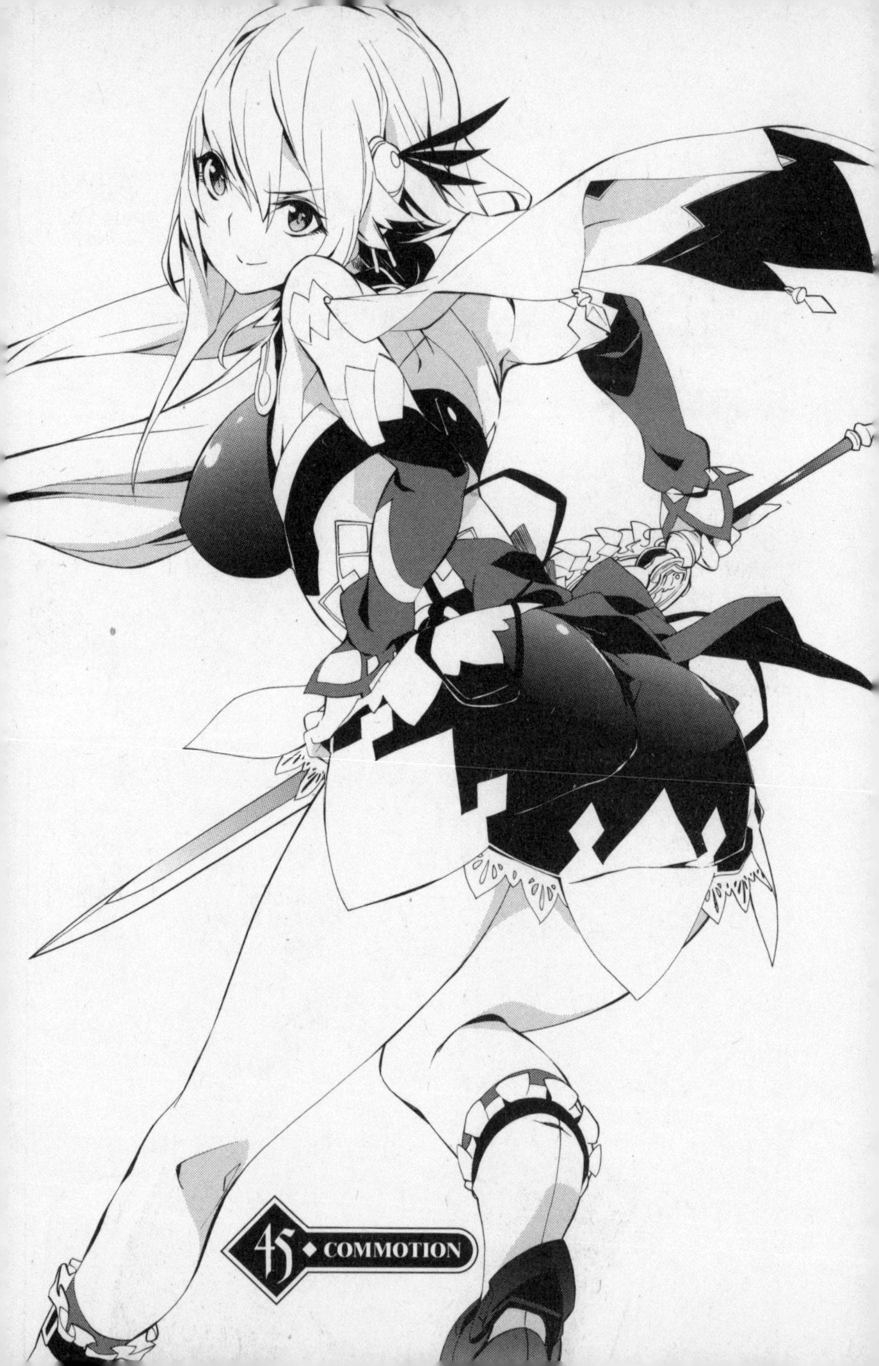
45 ◆ COMMOTION

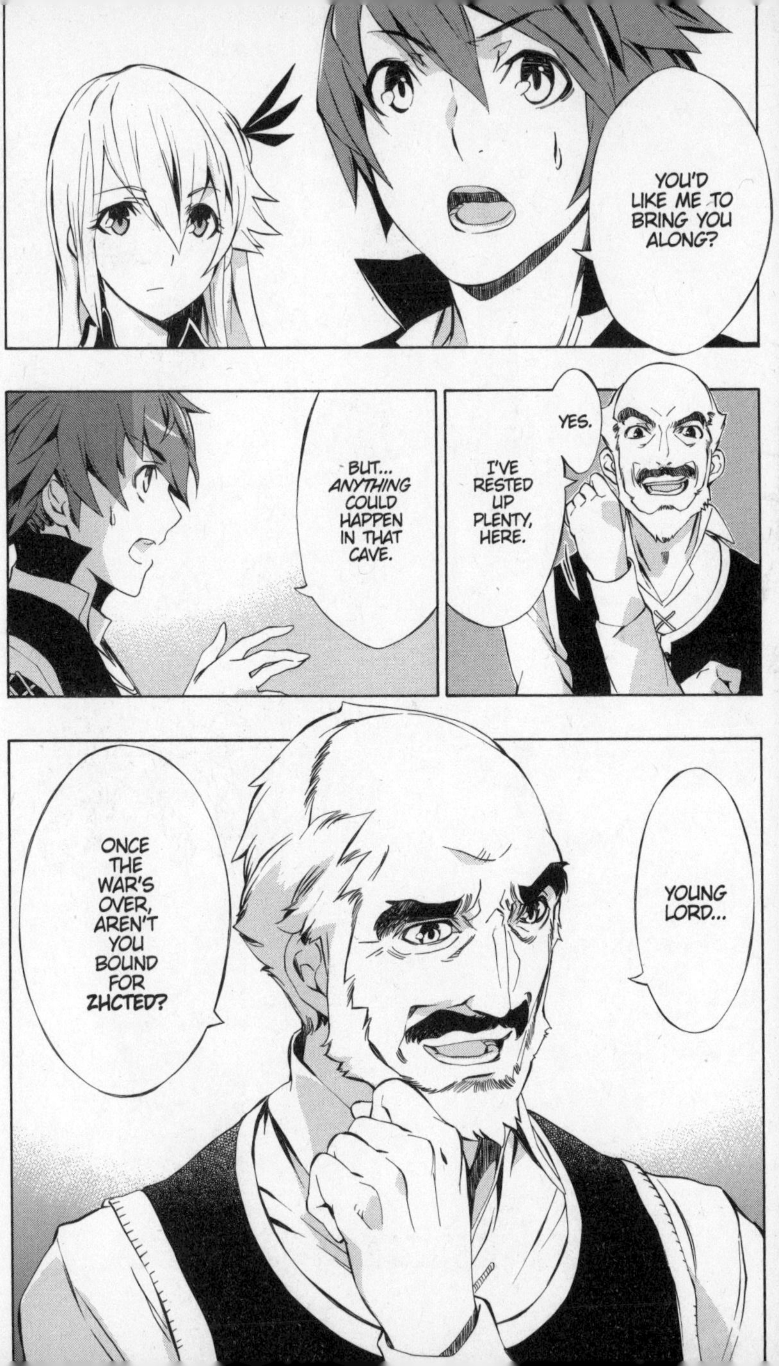
YOU'D LIKE ME TO BRING YOU ALONG?
YES.
I'VE RESTED UP PLENTY, HERE.
BUT... *ANYTHING* COULD HAPPEN IN THAT CAVE.
YOUNG LORD...
ONCE THE WAR'S OVER, AREN'T YOU BOUND FOR ZHCTED?

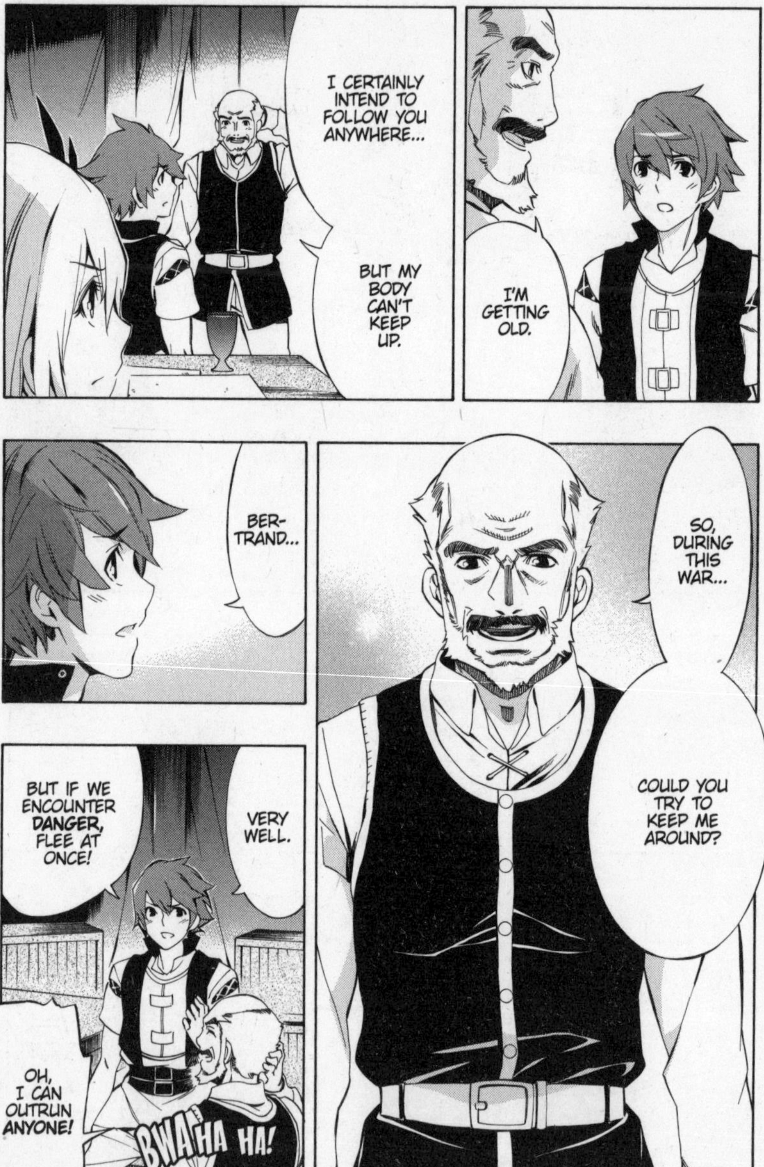
I'M GETTING OLD.
I CERTAINLY INTEND TO FOLLOW YOU ANYWHERE...
BUT MY BODY CAN'T KEEP UP.
SO, DURING THIS WAR...
COULD YOU TRY TO KEEP ME AROUND?
BER-TRAND...
VERY WELL.
BUT IF WE ENCOUNTER DANGER, FLEE AT ONCE!
OH, I CAN OUTRUN ANYONE!
BWAHA HA HA!

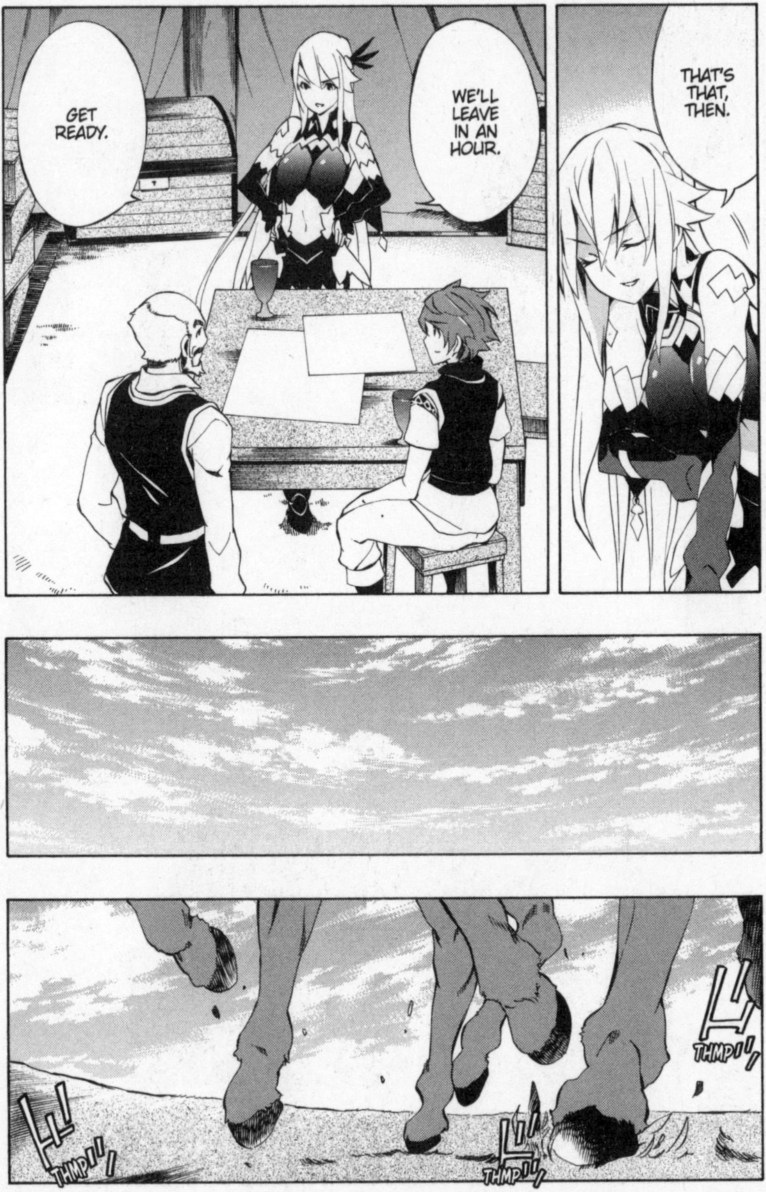
THAT'S THAT, THEN.
WE'LL LEAVE IN AN HOUR.
GET READY.
THMP!
THMP!
THMP!

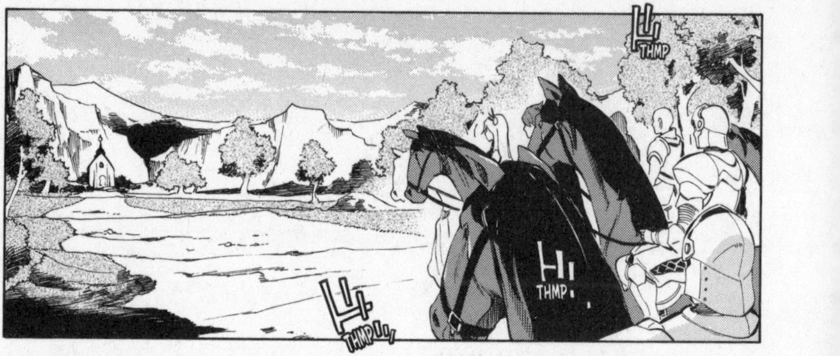
THMP
THMP!
THMP!!
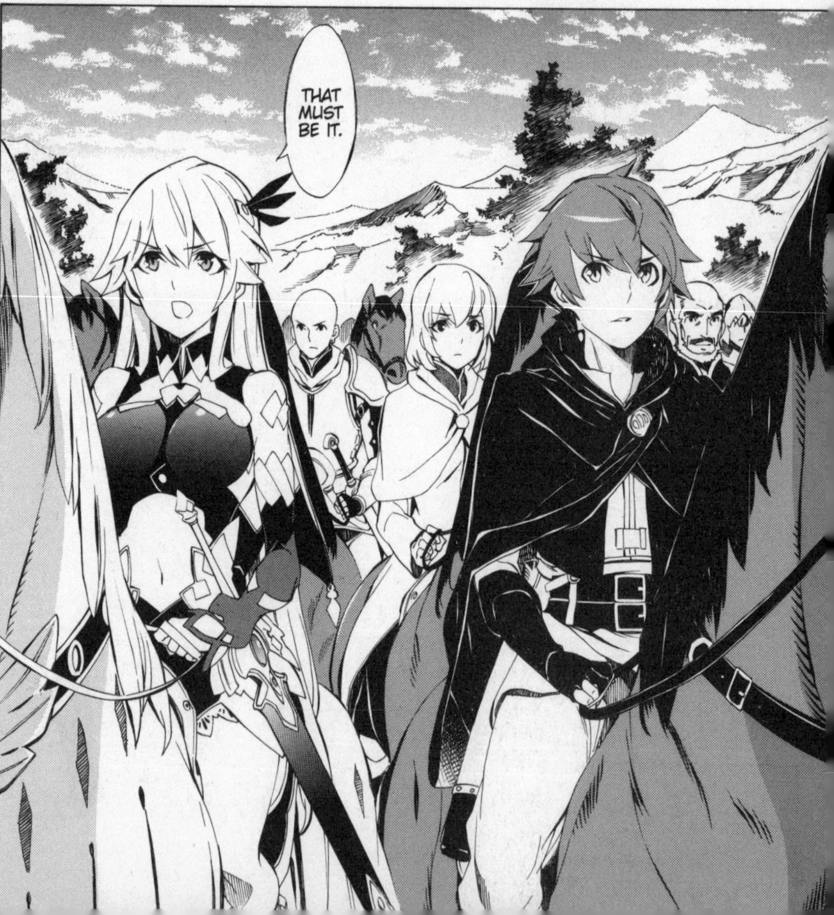
THAT MUST BE IT.

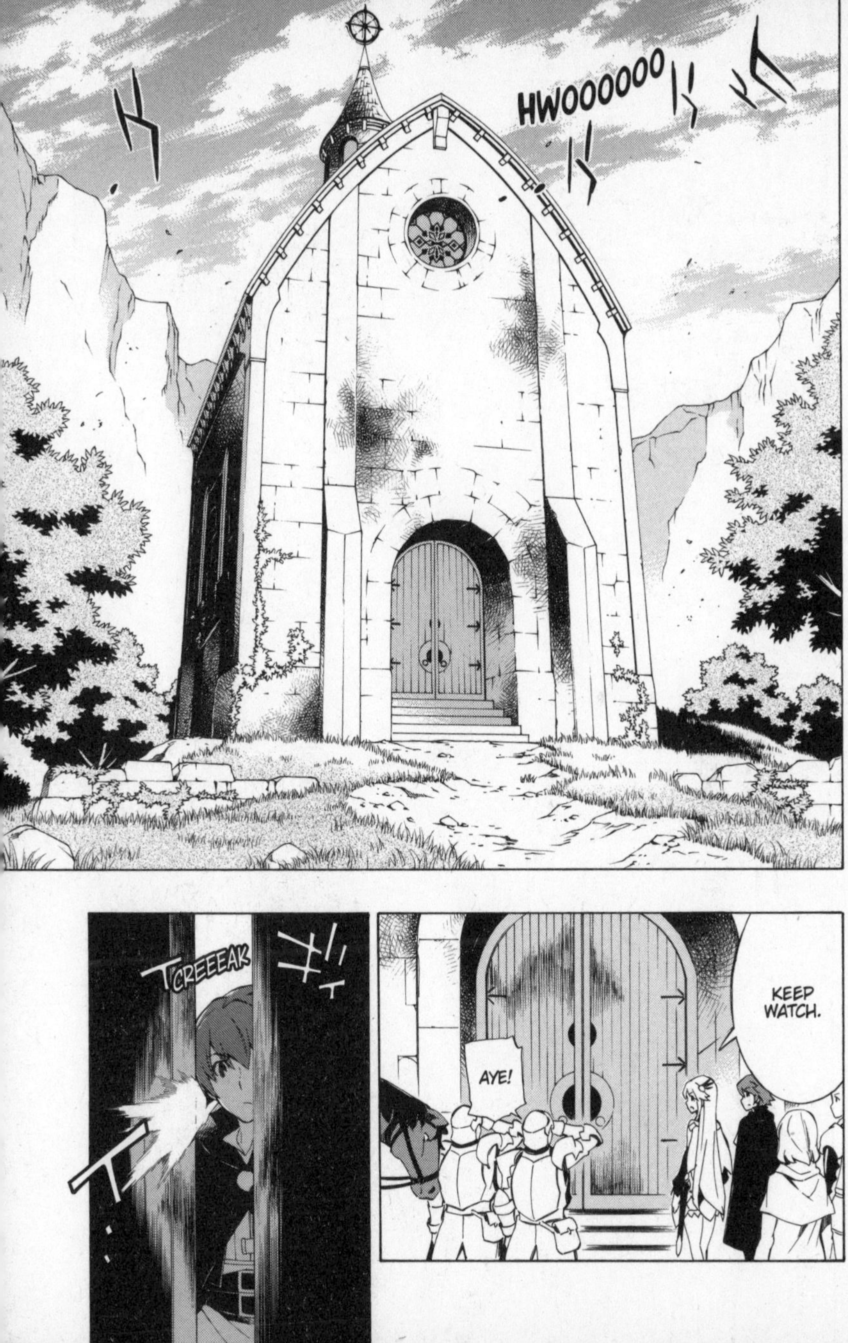
HWOOOOOO
KEEP WATCH.
AYE!
CREEEAK

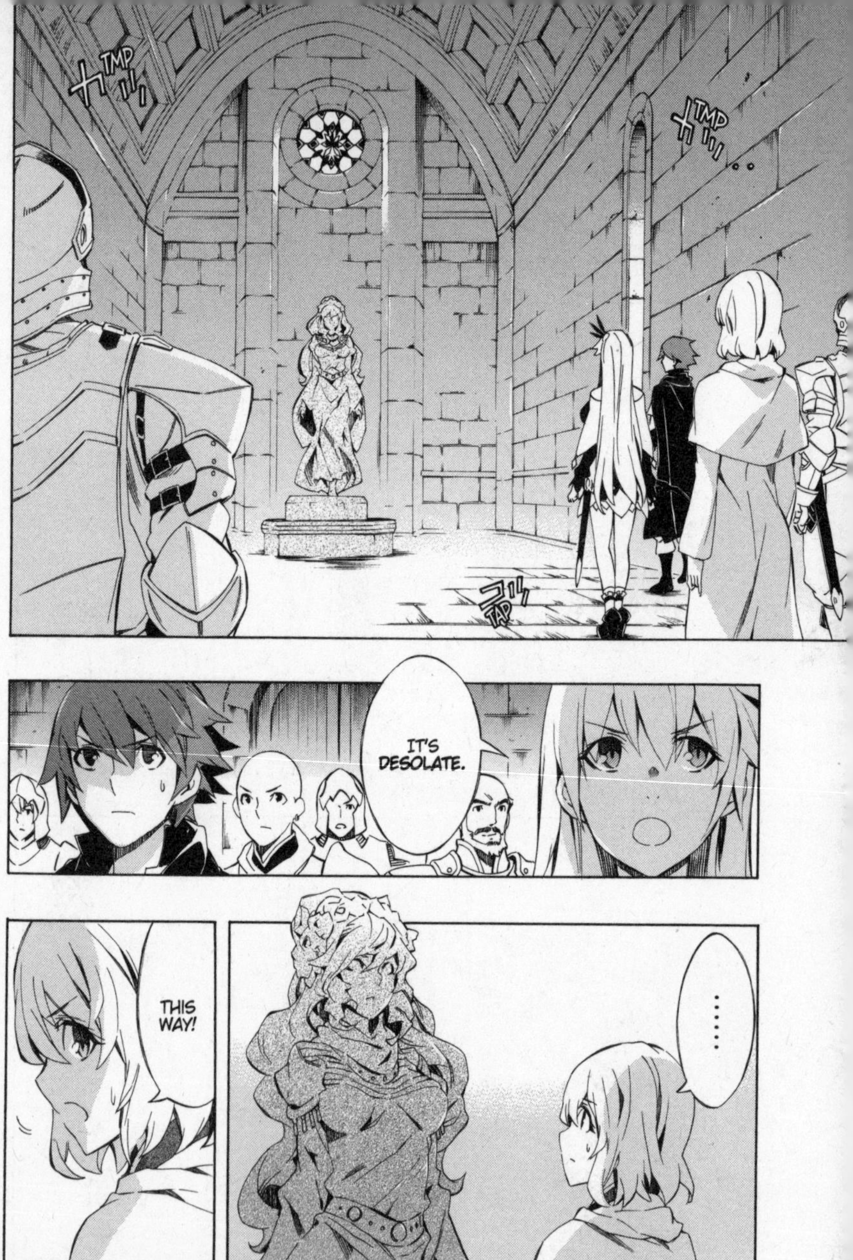
TMP
TMP
TAP
IT'S DESOLATE.
......
THIS WAY!

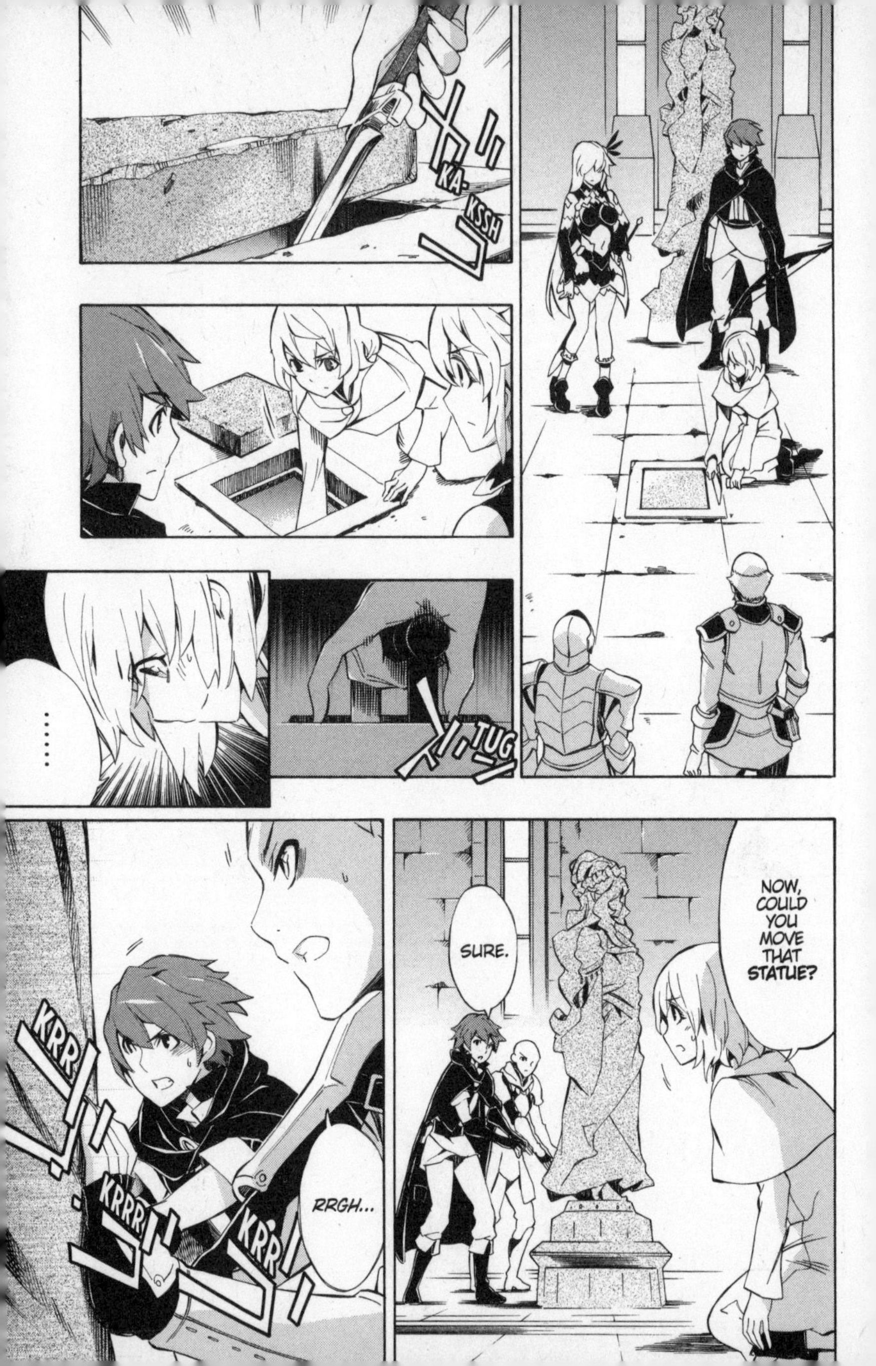
KA-KSSH
TUG
......
NOW, COULD YOU MOVE THAT STATUE?
SURE.
KRR
RRGH...
KRR
KRRR

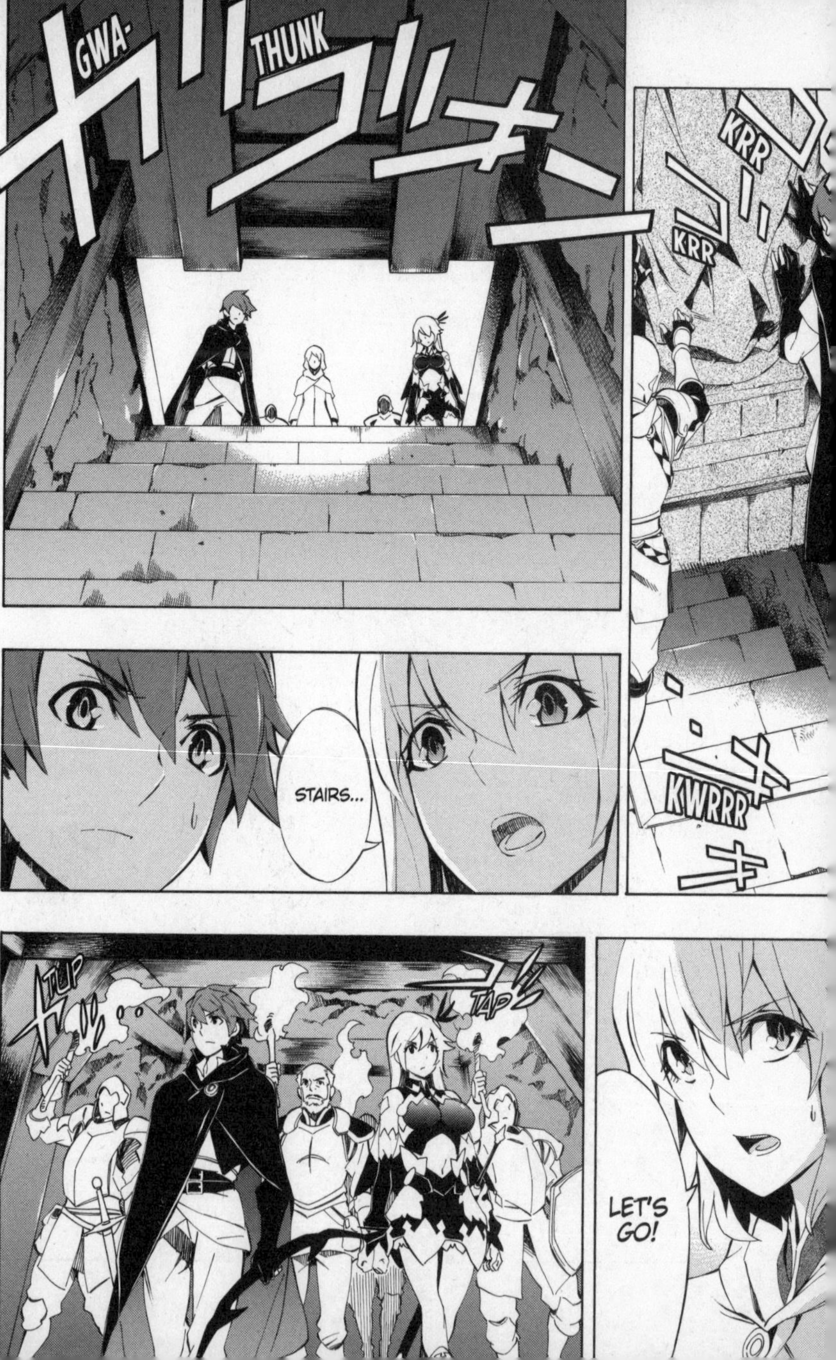
KRR
KRR
KWRRR
GWA-
THUNK
STAIRS...
LET'S GO!
TUP
TAP

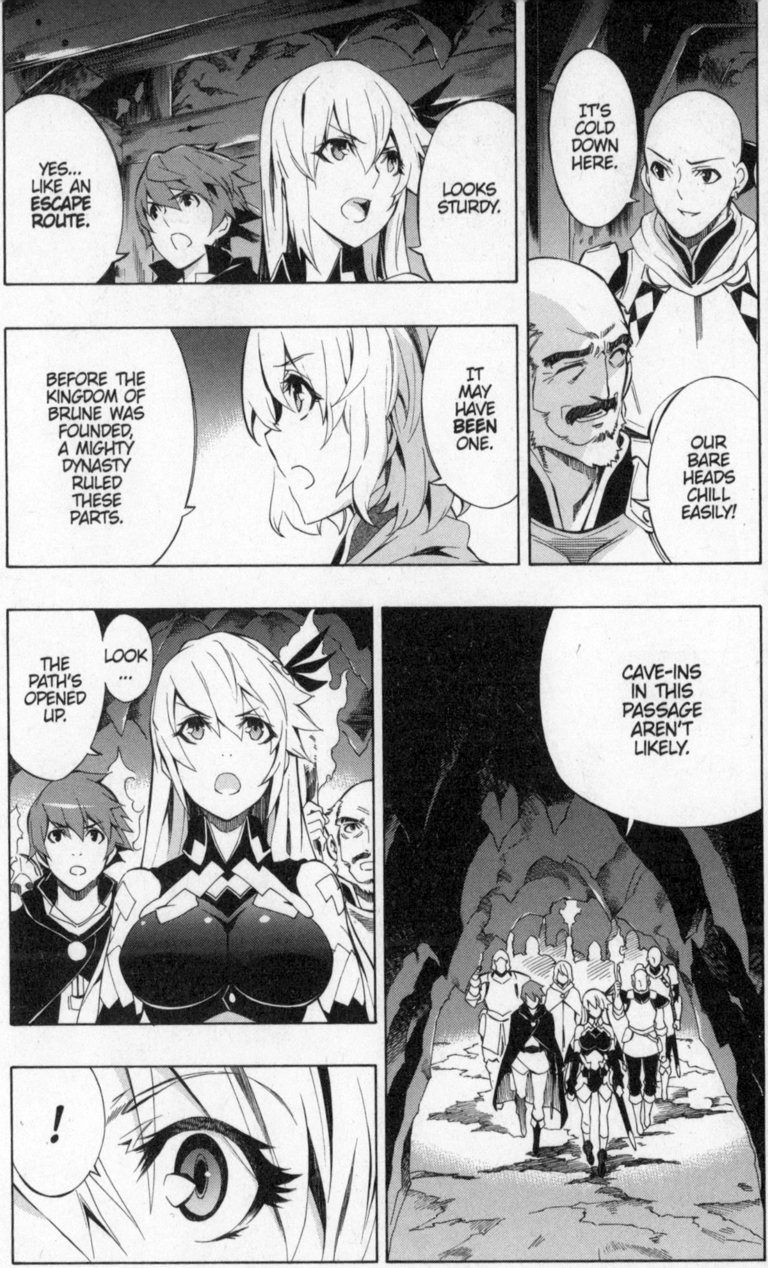
IT'S COLD DOWN HERE.
OUR BARE HEADS CHILL EASILY!
LOOKS STURDY.
YES... LIKE AN ESCAPE ROUTE.
IT MAY HAVE BEEN ONE.
BEFORE THE KINGDOM OF BRUNE WAS FOUNDED, A MIGHTY DYNASTY RULED THESE PARTS.
CAVE-INS IN THIS PASSAGE AREN'T LIKELY.
LOOK...
THE PATH'S OPENED UP.
!

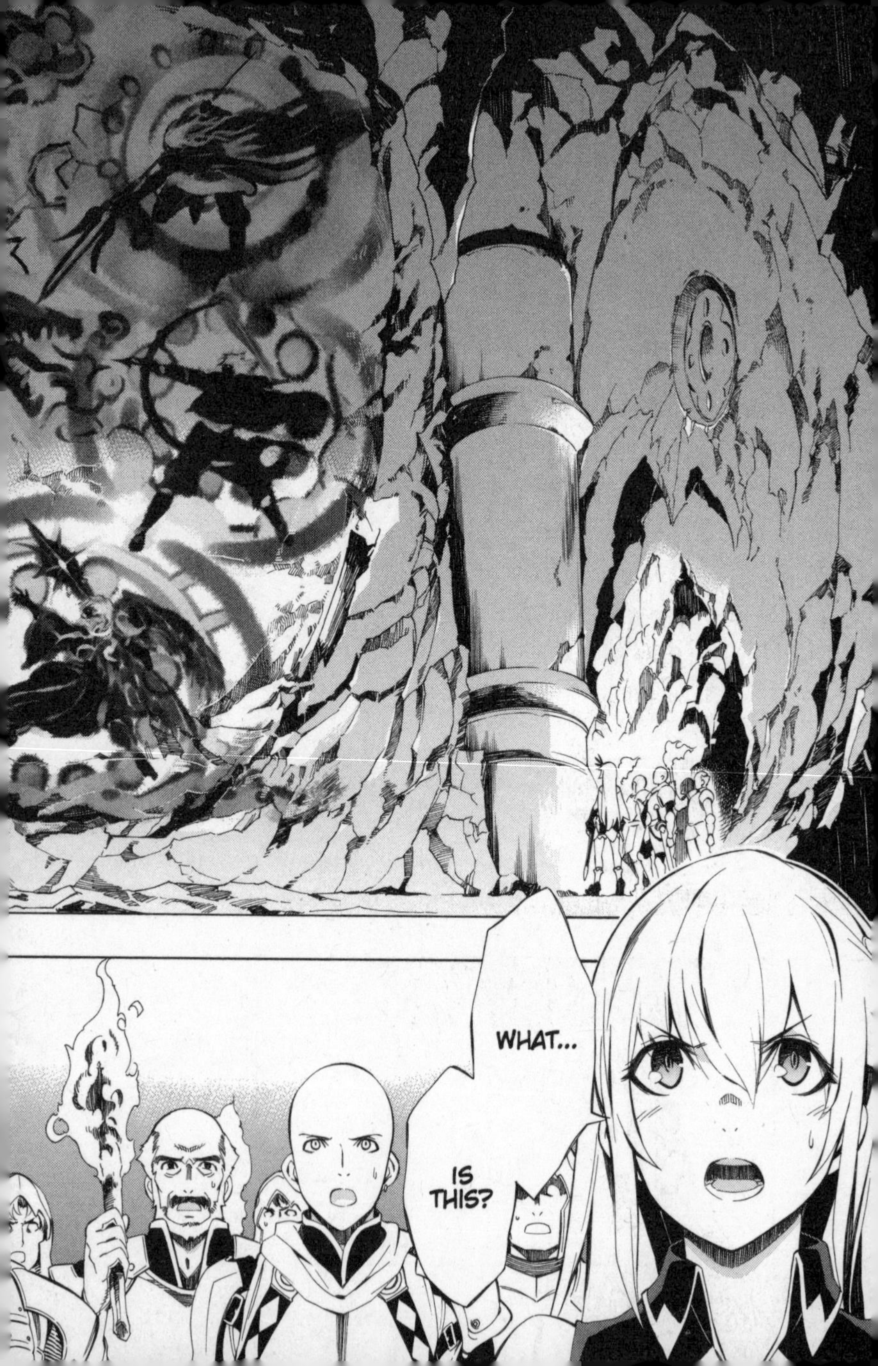
WHAT...
IS THIS?

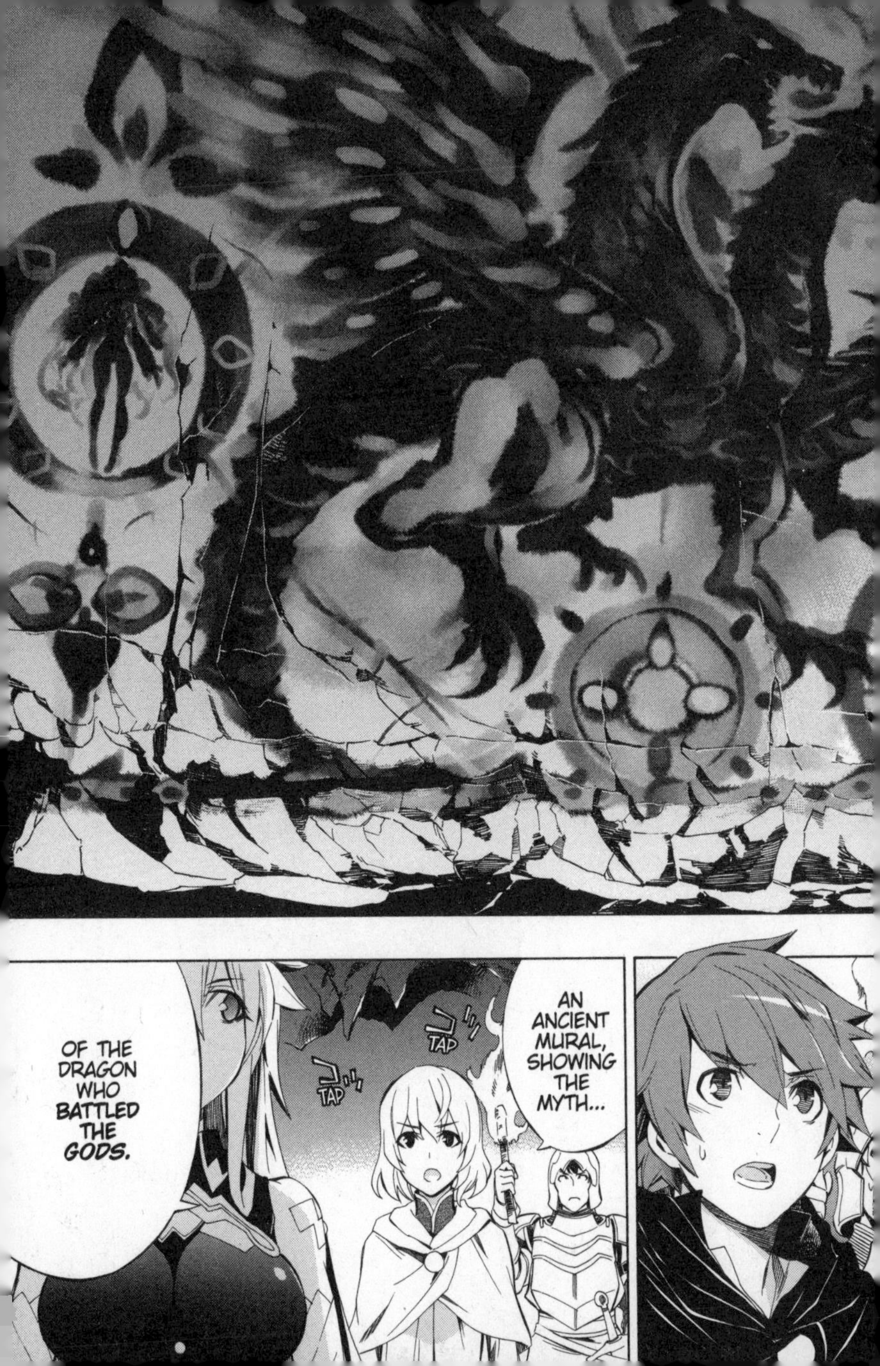
AN ANCIENT MURAL, SHOWING THE MYTH...
TAP
TAP
OF THE DRAGON WHO BATTLED THE GODS.

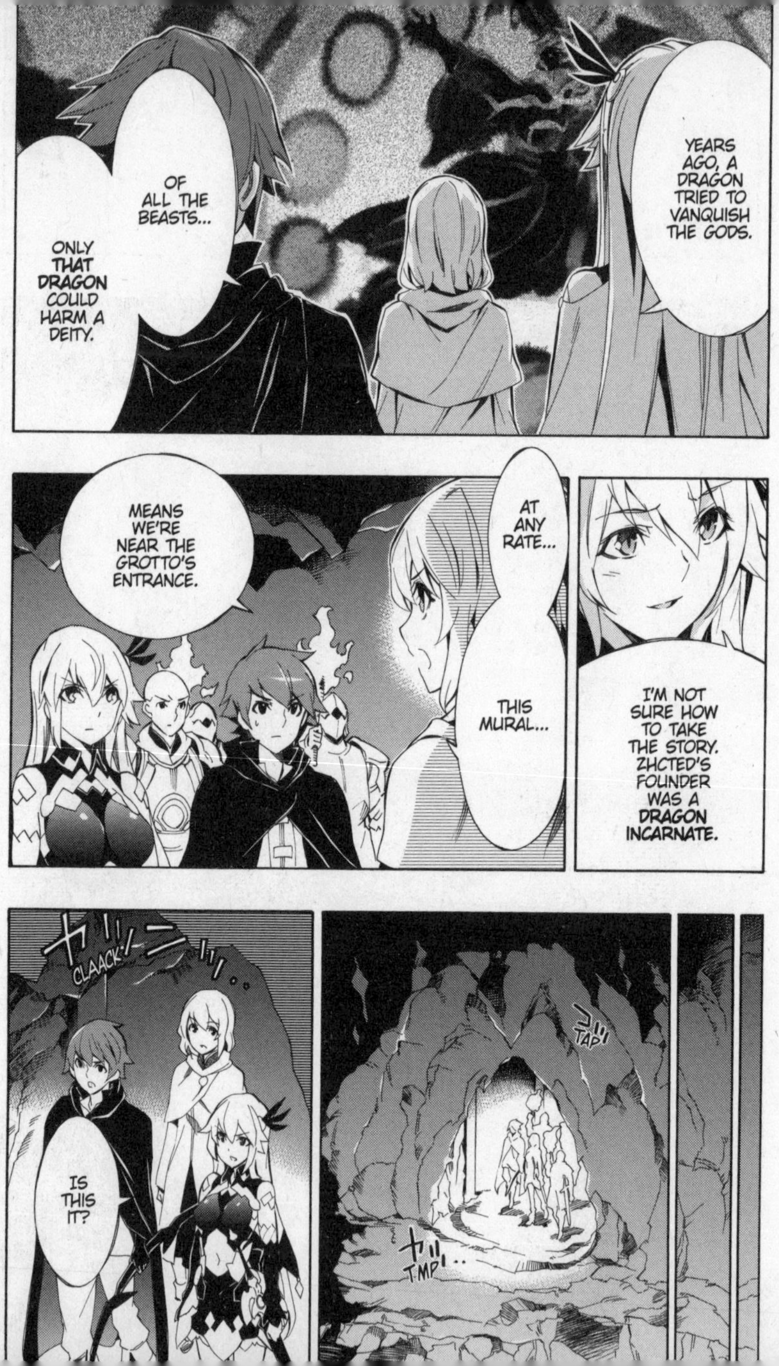
YEARS AGO, A DRAGON TRIED TO VANQUISH THE GODS.
OF ALL THE BEASTS...
ONLY **THAT** DRAGON COULD HARM A DEITY.
I'M NOT SURE HOW TO TAKE THE STORY. ZHCTED'S FOUNDER WAS A **DRAGON INCARNATE.**
AT ANY RATE...
THIS MURAL...
MEANS WE'RE NEAR THE GROTTO'S ENTRANCE.
TAP
TMP..
CLAACK
IS THIS IT?

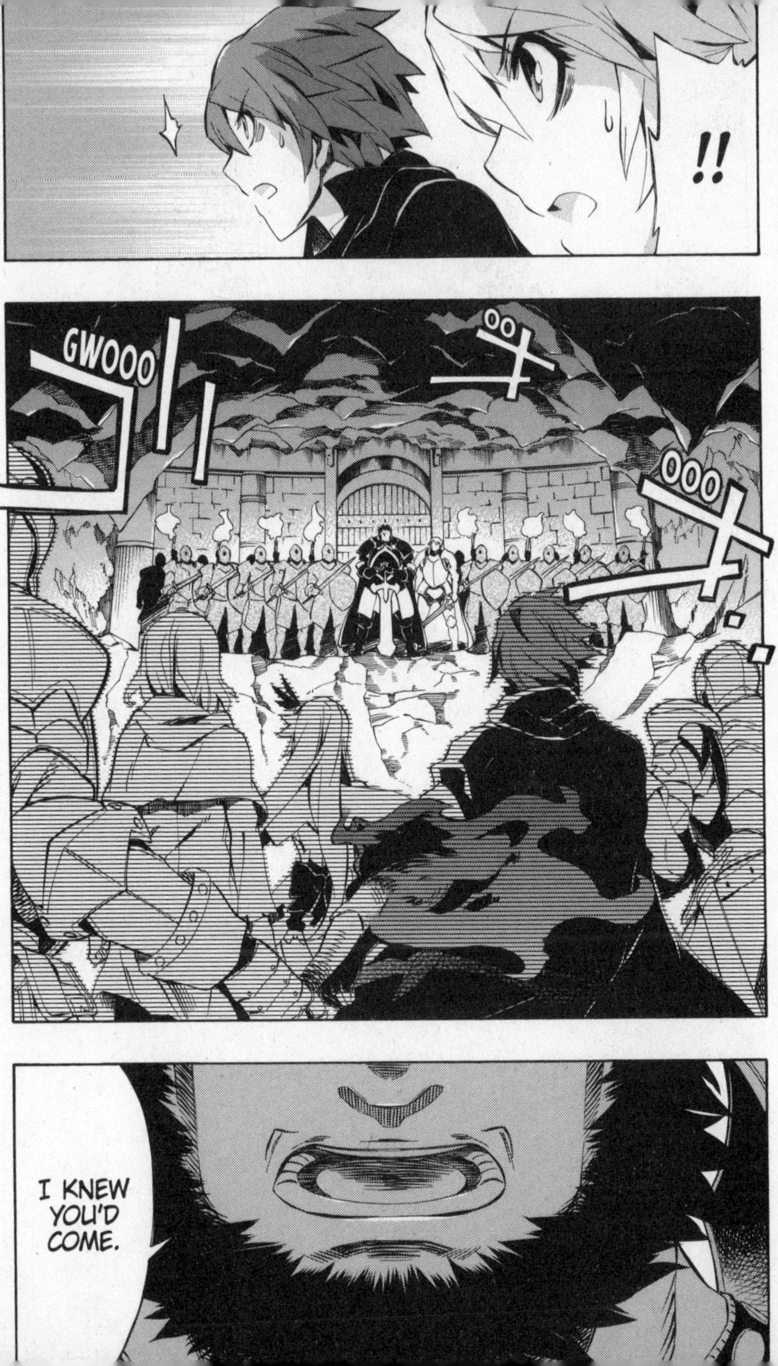
!!
GWOOO
OOO
I KNEW YOU'D COME.

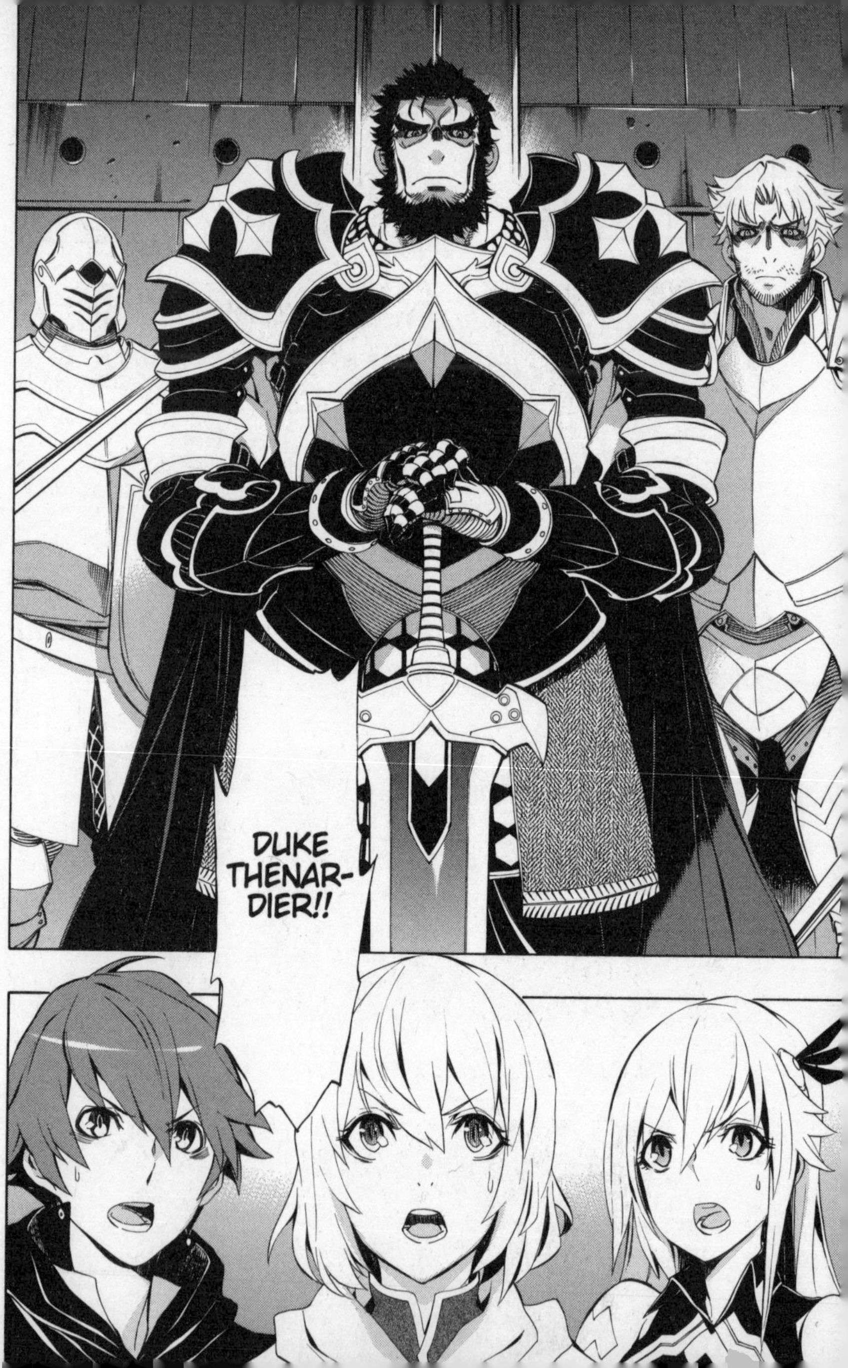
DUKE THENAR-DIER!!

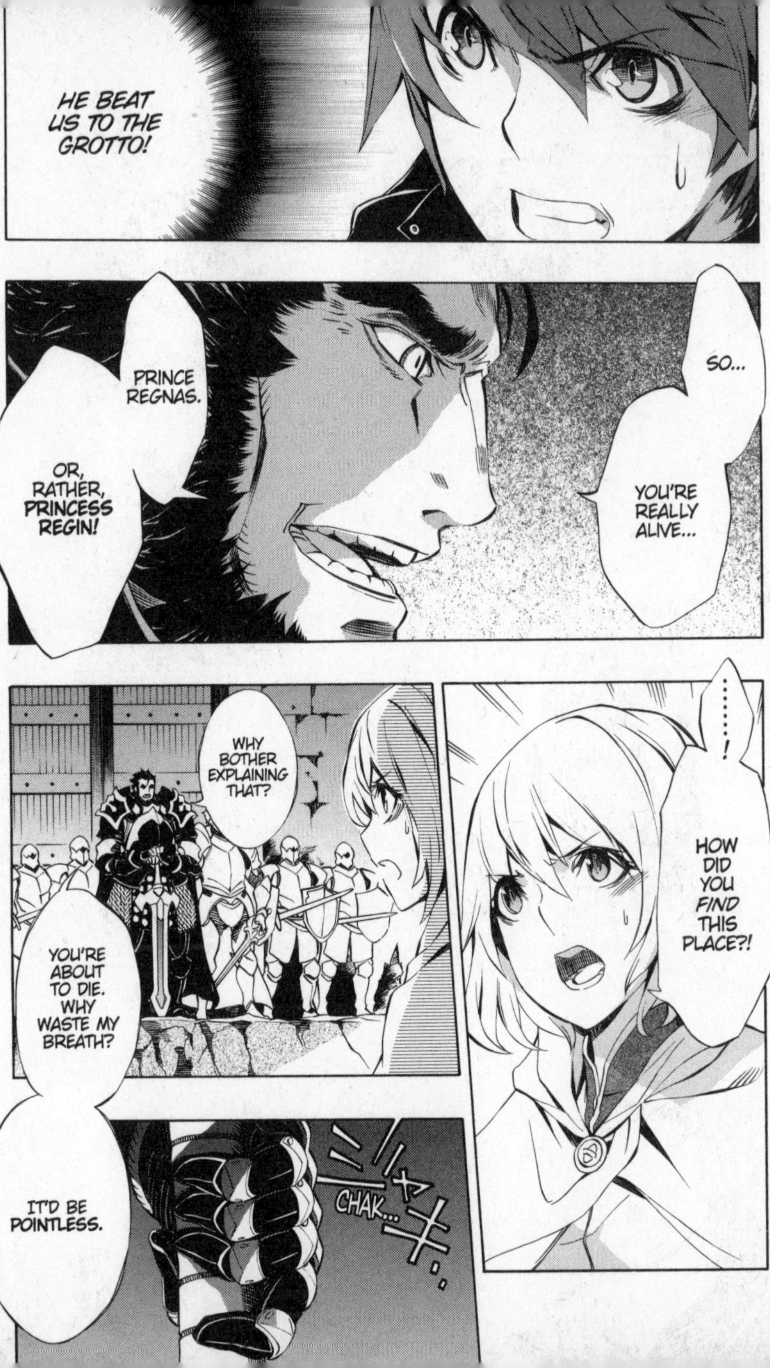
HE BEAT US TO THE GROTTO!
SO... YOU'RE REALLY ALIVE...
PRINCE REGNAS.
OR, RATHER, PRINCESS REGIN!
......!
HOW DID YOU *FIND* THIS PLACE?!
WHY BOTHER EXPLAINING THAT?
YOU'RE ABOUT TO DIE. WHY WASTE MY BREATH?
IT'D BE POINTLESS.
CHAK...

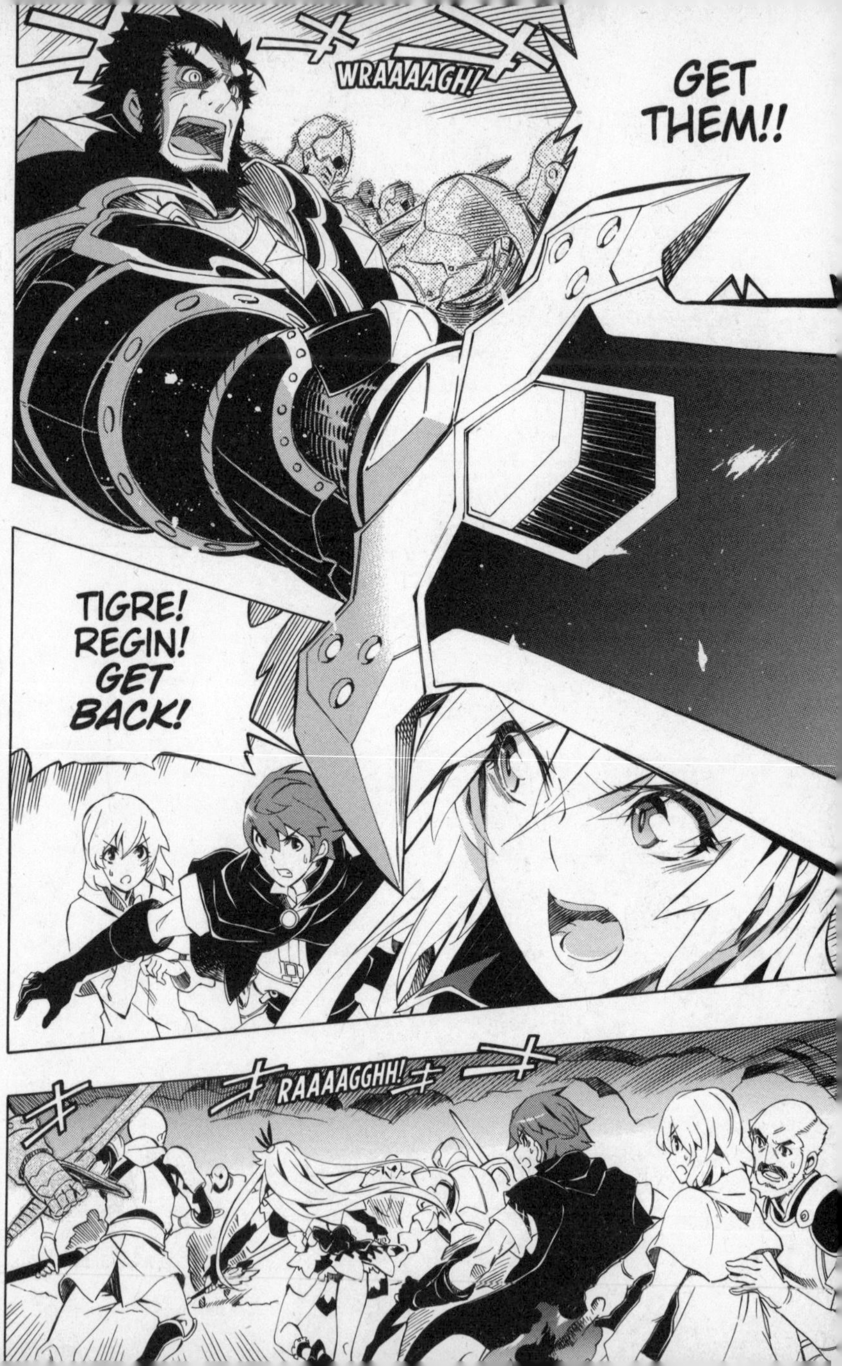
GET THEM!!
WRAAAAGH!
TIGRE! REGIN! GET BACK!
RAAAAGGHH!

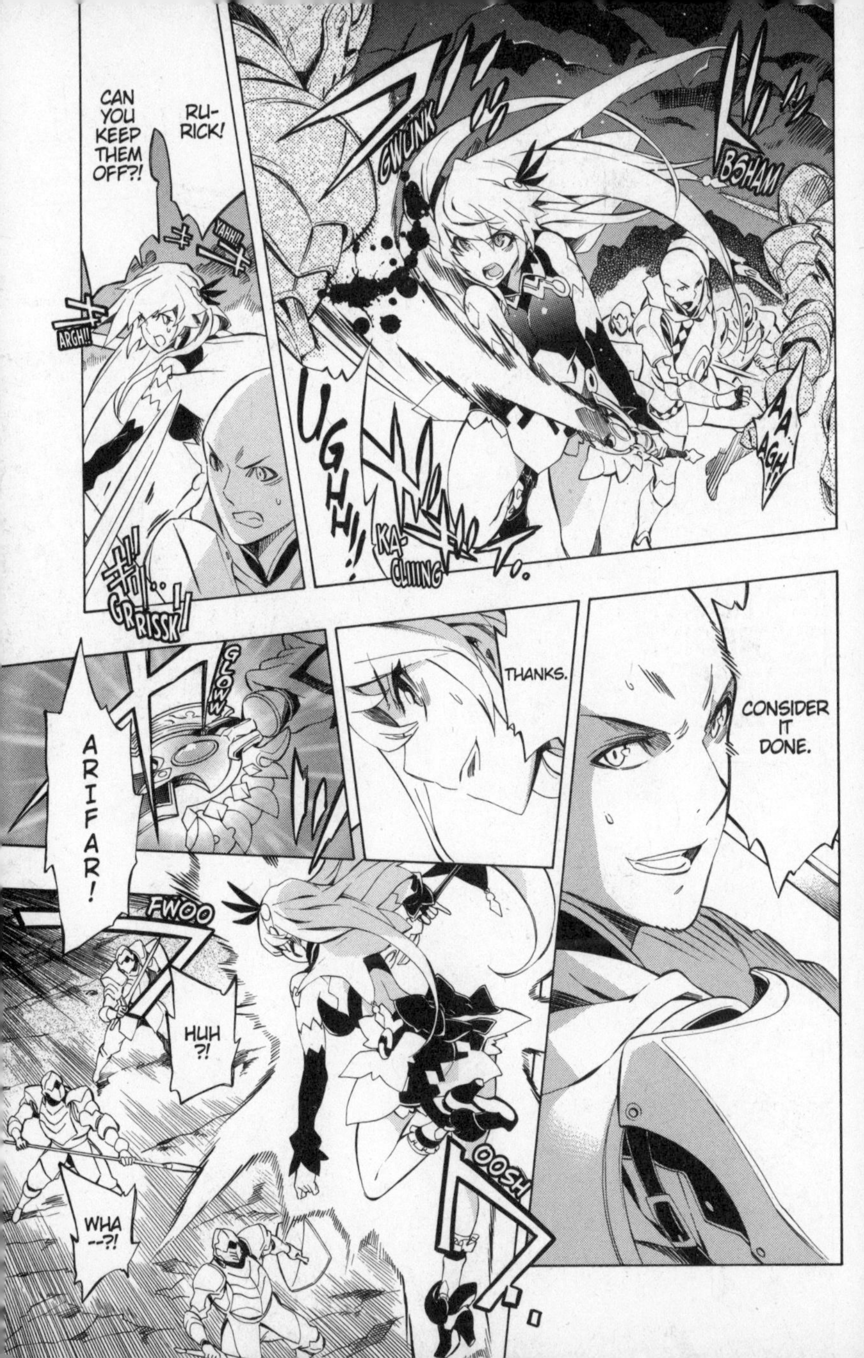
BSHAM
GWUNK
AAAGH!!
UGHH!!
KA-CLIIING
RU-RICK!
CAN YOU KEEP THEM OFF?!
YAHH!!
ARGH!!
GRRISSK
CONSIDER IT DONE.
THANKS.
GLOW
ARIFAR!
FWOO
OOSH
HUH?!
WHA--?!

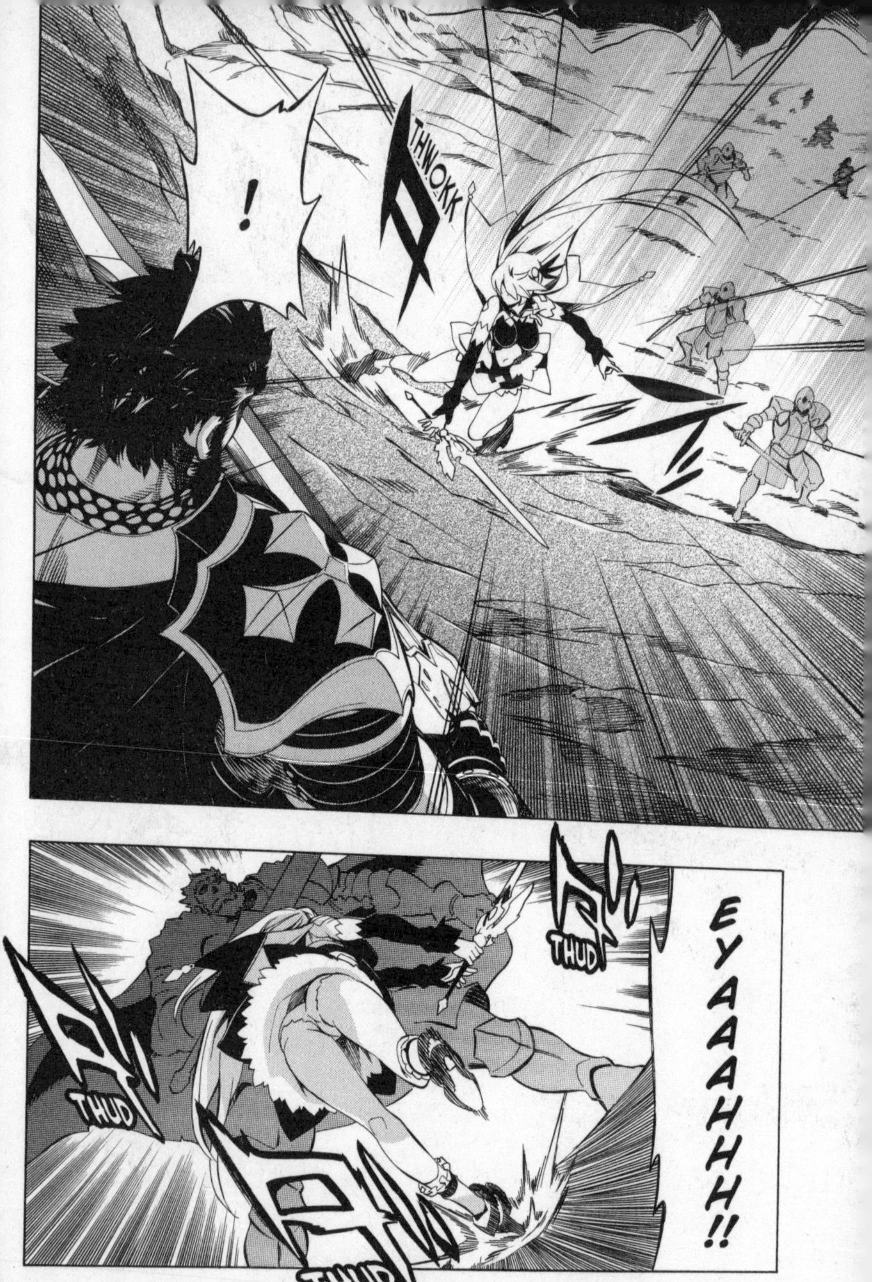
THWOKK
!
EYAAAAHHH!!
THUD
THUD
THUD

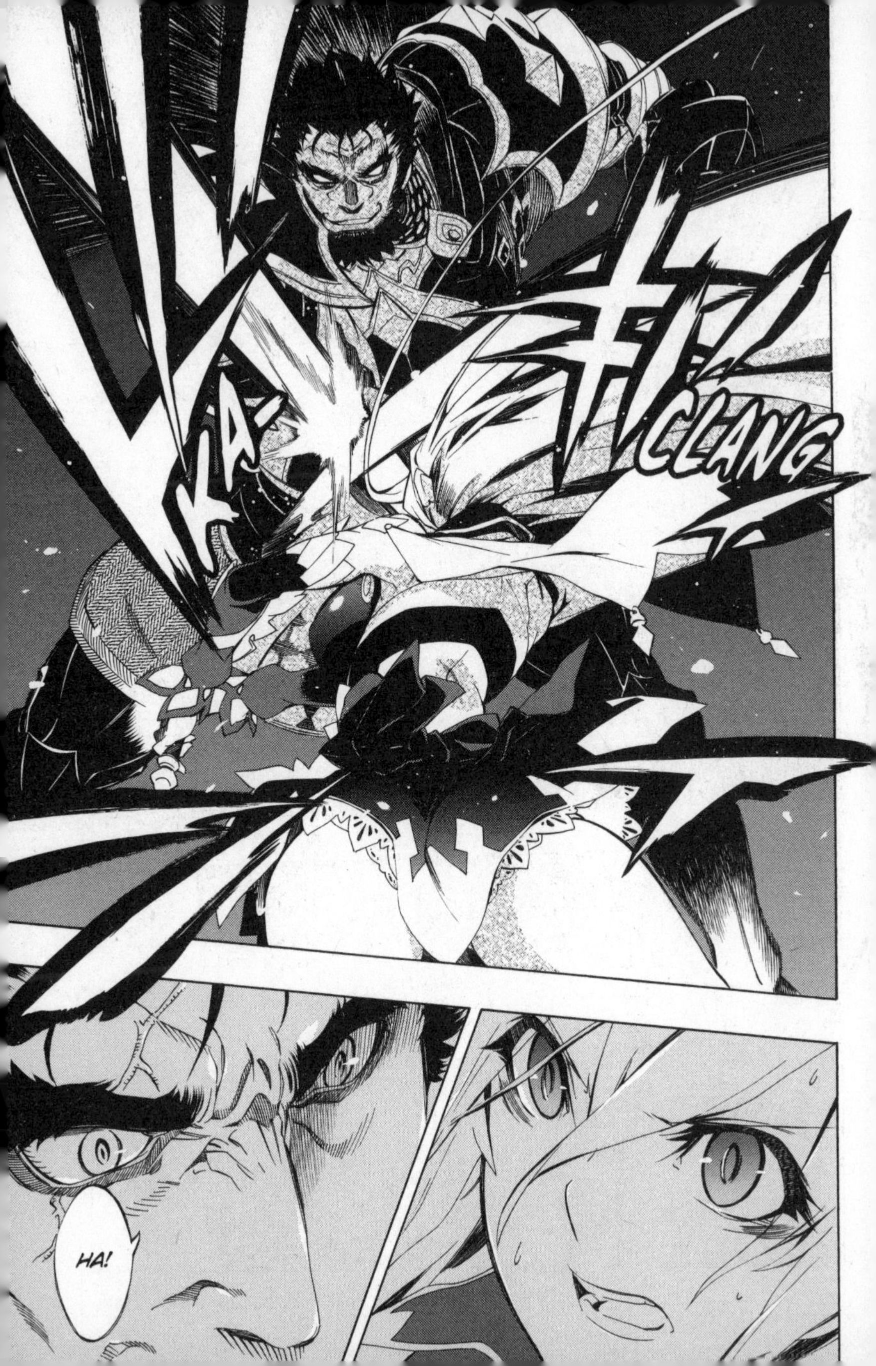
CLANG
KA!
HA!

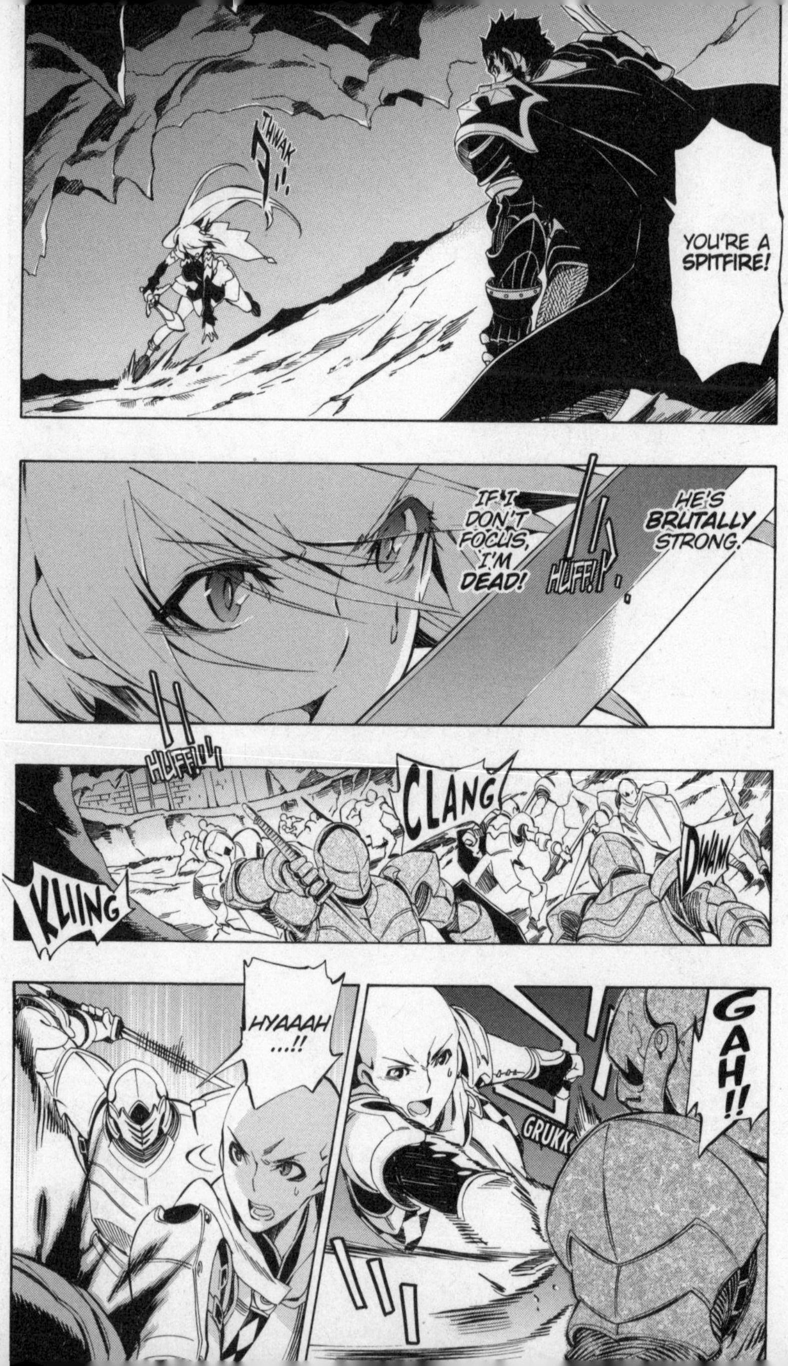
YOU'RE A SPITFIRE!
THWAK!!
HE'S BRUTALLY STRONG.
HUFF!!
IF I DON'T FOCUS, I'M DEAD!
HUFF!!
DWAM
CLANG
KLIING
GAH!!
GRUKK
HYAAAH ...!!

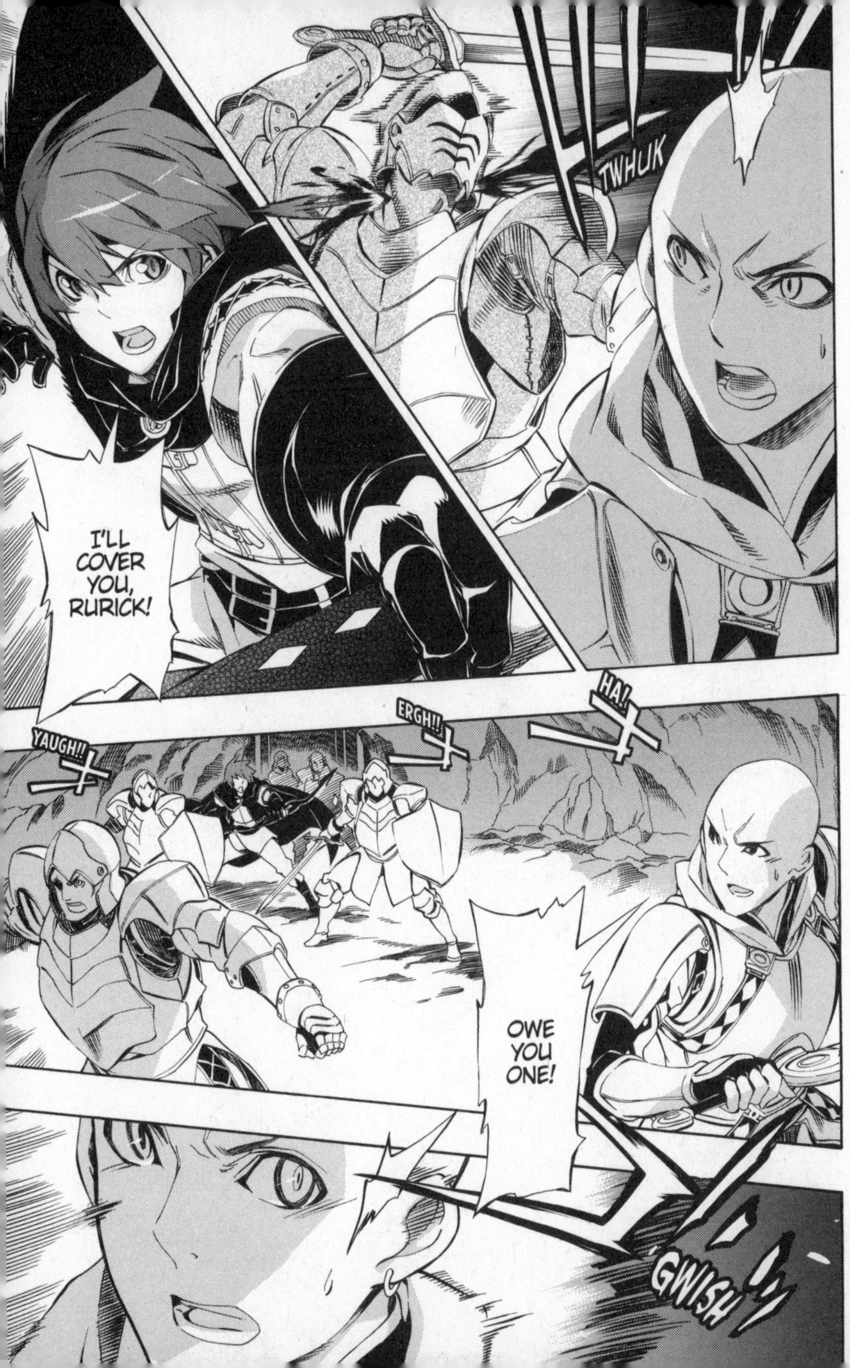
TWHUK
I'LL COVER YOU, RURICK!
HA!
ERGH!!
YAUGH!!
OWE YOU ONE!
GWISH

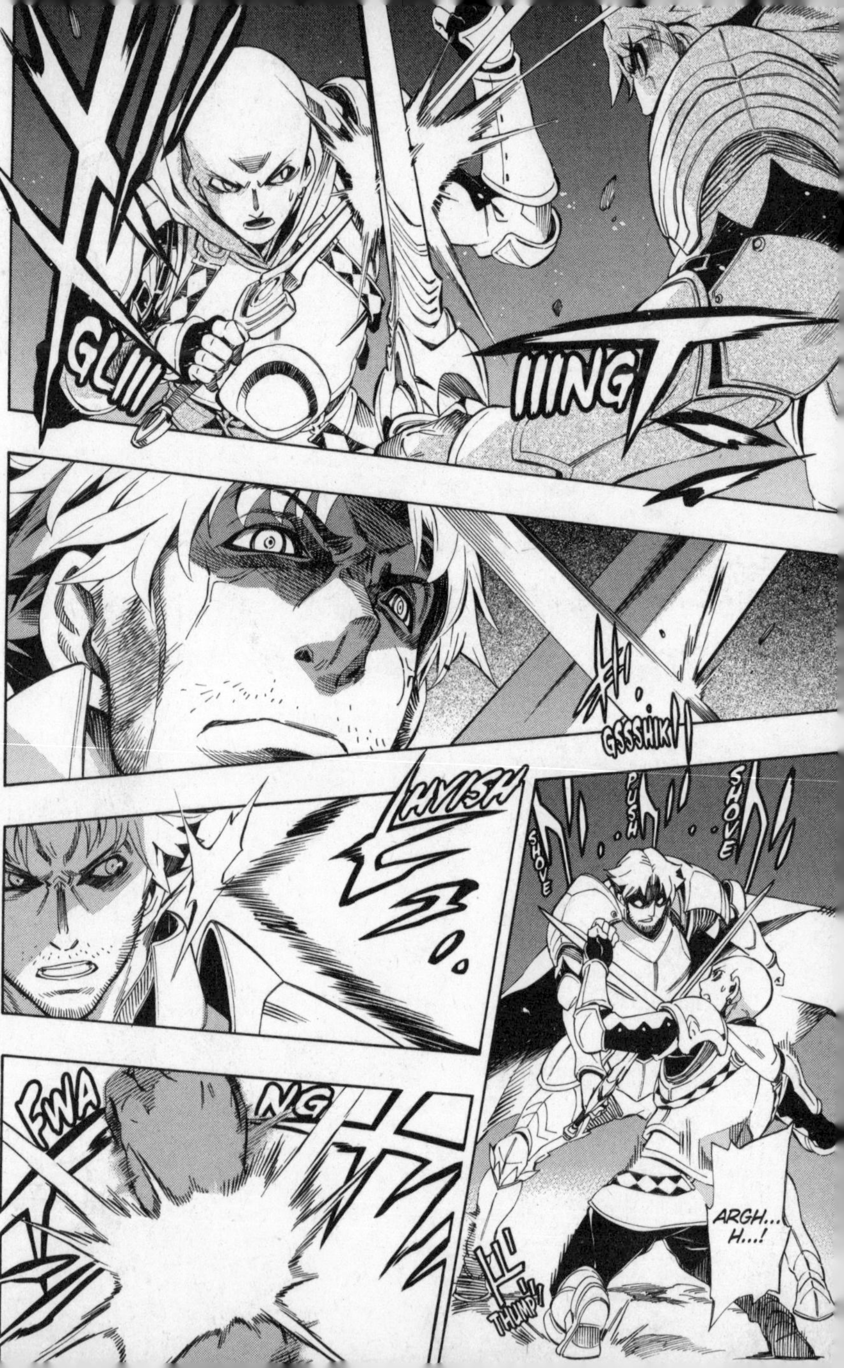
IIING
GLIII
GSSSHIK
SHOVE
PUSH
SHOVE
HWISH
ARGH... H...!
THUMP
FWA NG

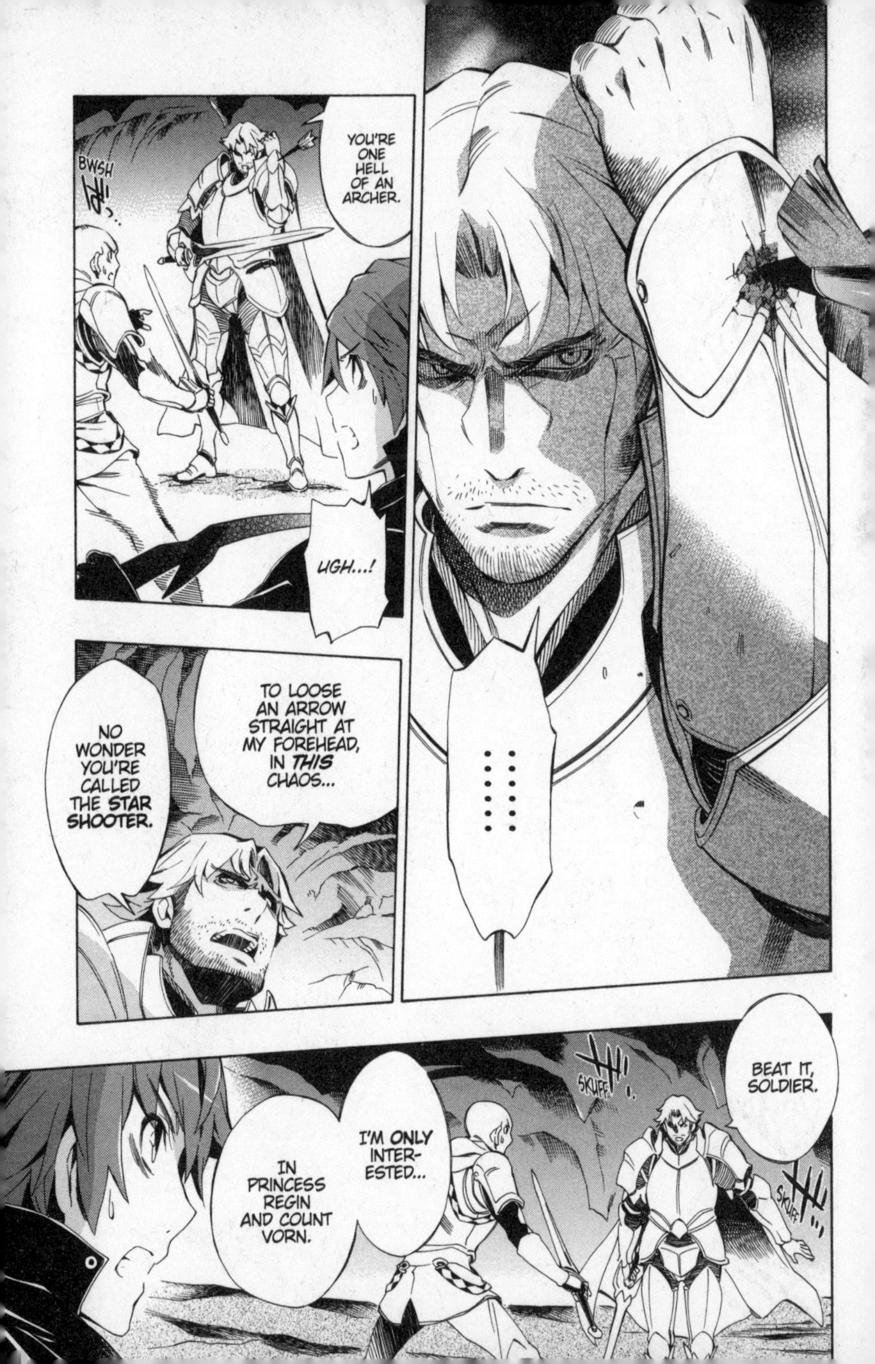
YOU'RE ONE HELL OF AN ARCHER.
BWSH
UGH...!
TO LOOSE AN ARROW STRAIGHT AT MY FOREHEAD, IN *THIS* CHAOS...
NO WONDER YOU'RE CALLED THE **STAR SHOOTER.**
BEAT IT, SOLDIER.
SKUFF
SKUFF
I'M **ONLY** INTER-ESTED...
IN PRINCESS REGIN AND COUNT VORN.

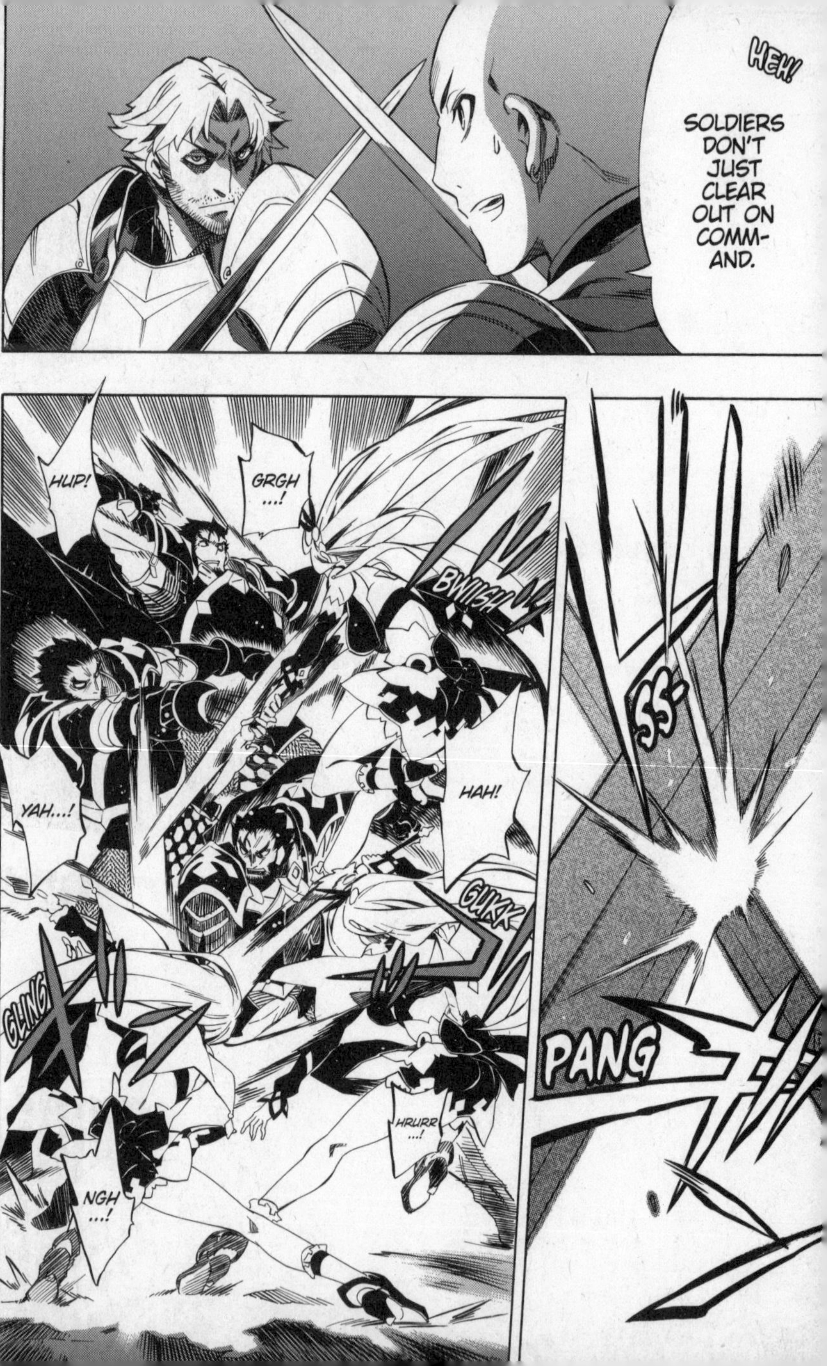
HEH!
SOLDIERS DON'T JUST CLEAR OUT ON COMM-AND.
SS-
PANG
GRGH ...!
BWISH
HUP!
HAH!
GUKK
YAH...!
GLING
HRURR ...!
NGH ...!

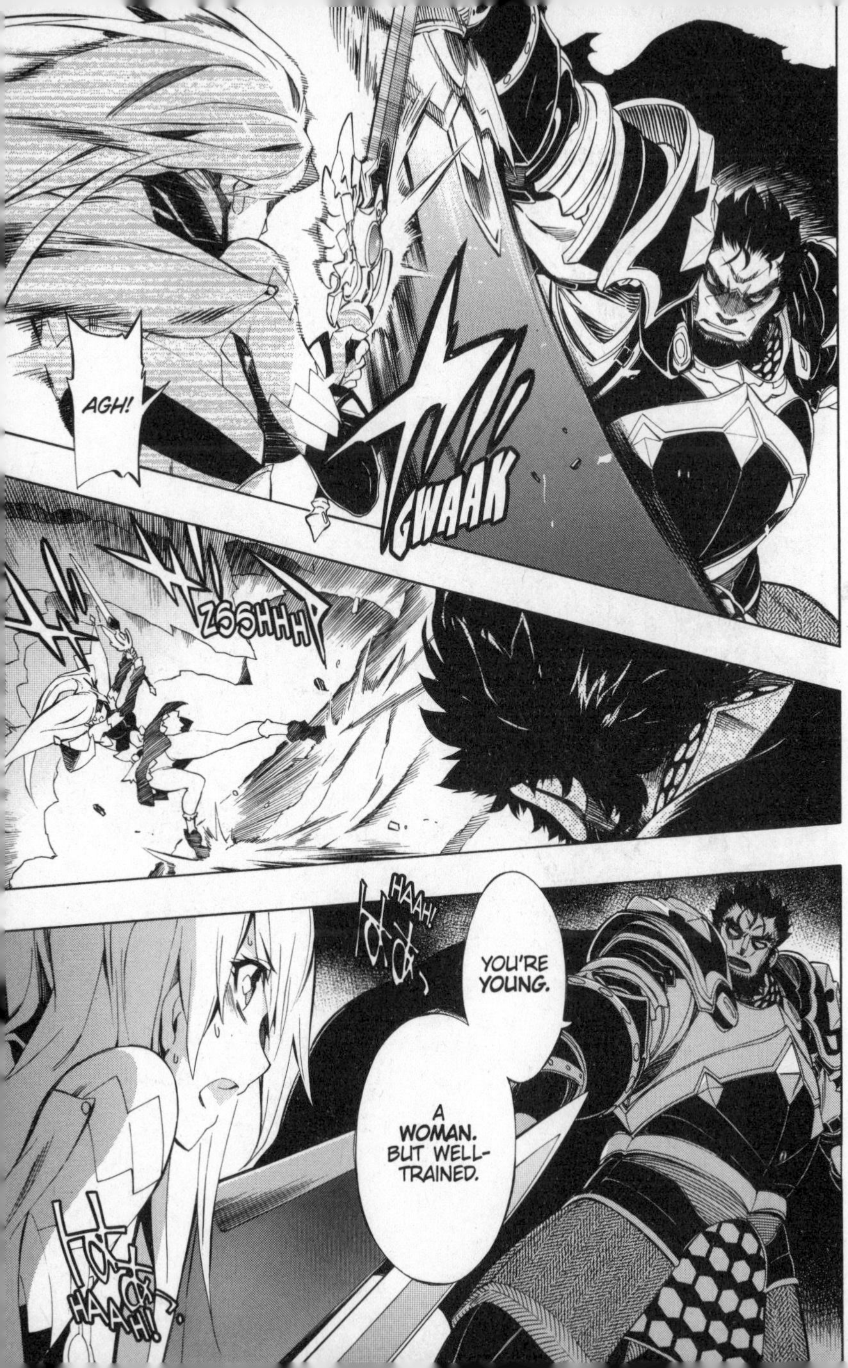
GWAAK
AGH!
ZSSHHHP
HAAH!
YOU'RE YOUNG.
A WOMAN. BUT WELL-TRAINED.
HAAAH!

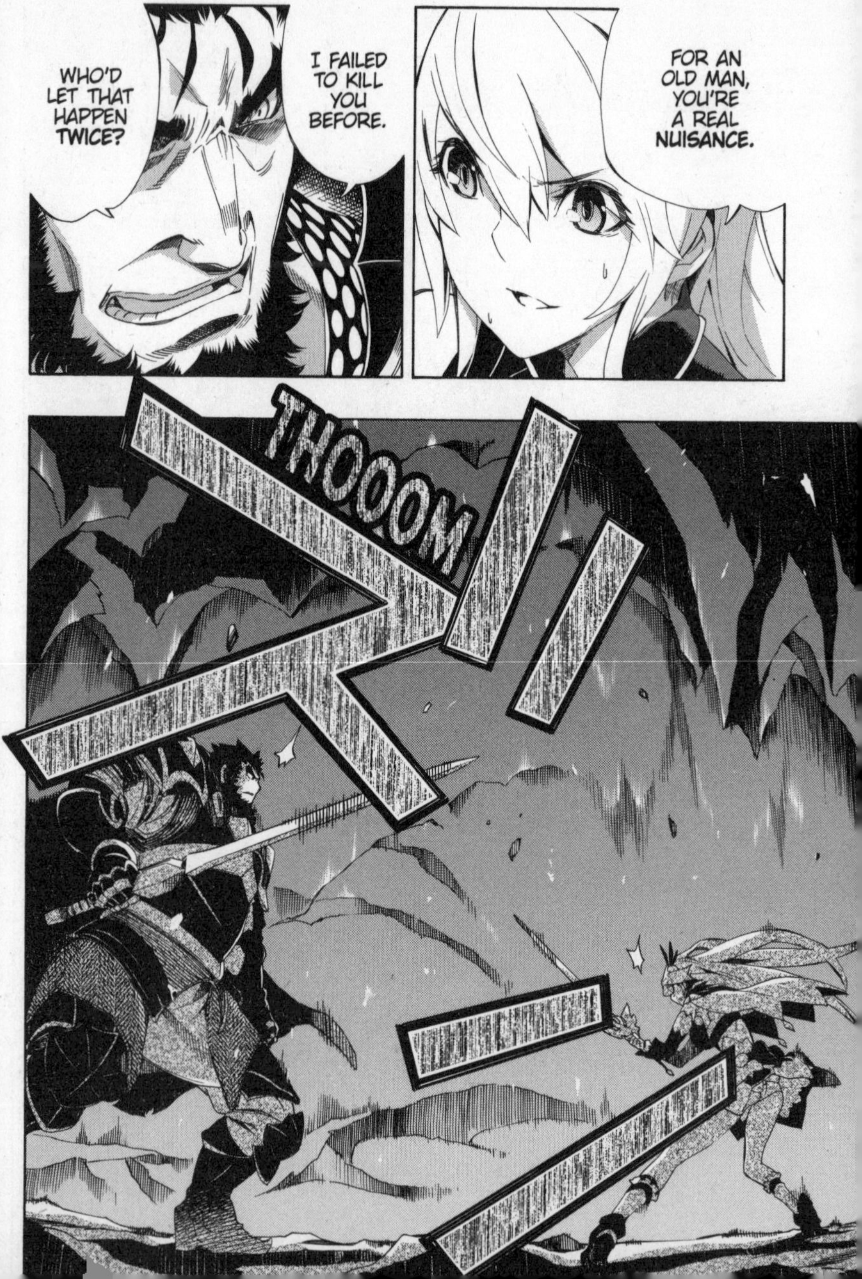
FOR AN OLD MAN, YOU'RE A REAL NUISANCE.
I FAILED TO KILL YOU BEFORE.
WHO'D LET THAT HAPPEN TWICE?
THOOOM

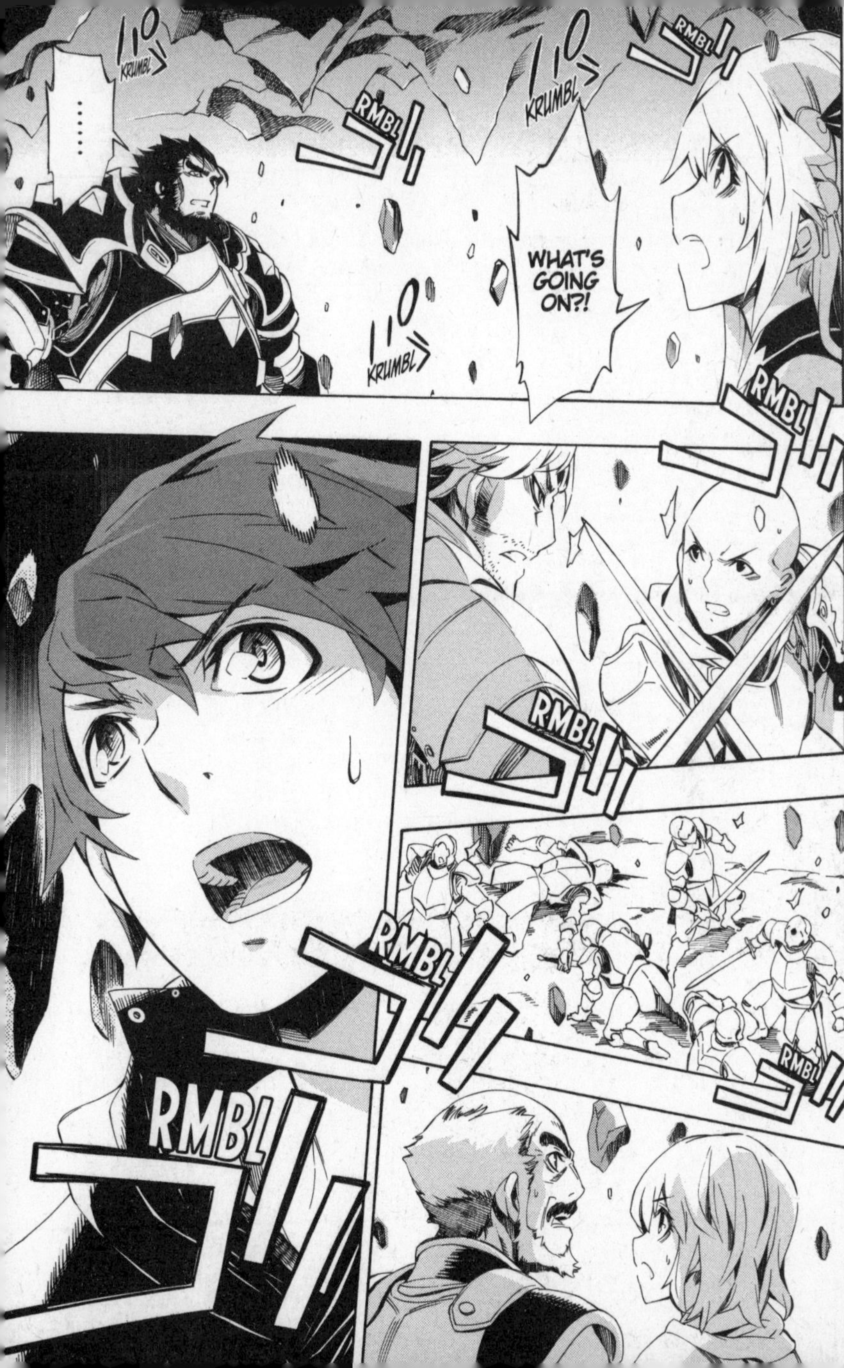
RMBL
KRUMBL
WHAT'S GOING ON?!
RMBL
KRUMBL
KRUMBL
......
KRUMBL
RMBL
RMBL
RMBL
RMBL
RMBL

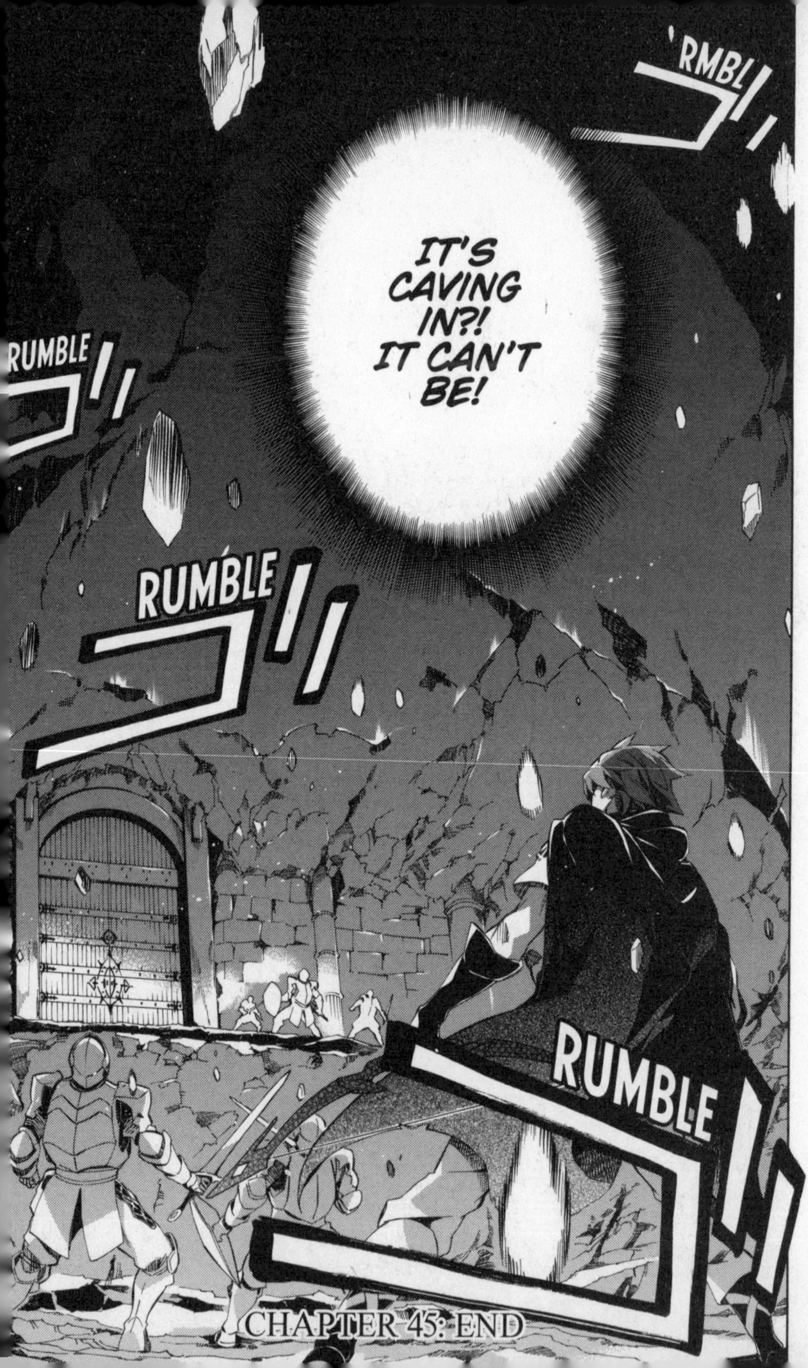
RMBL
IT'S CAVING IN?! IT CAN'T BE!
RUMBLE
RUMBLE
RUMBLE
CHAPTER 45: END

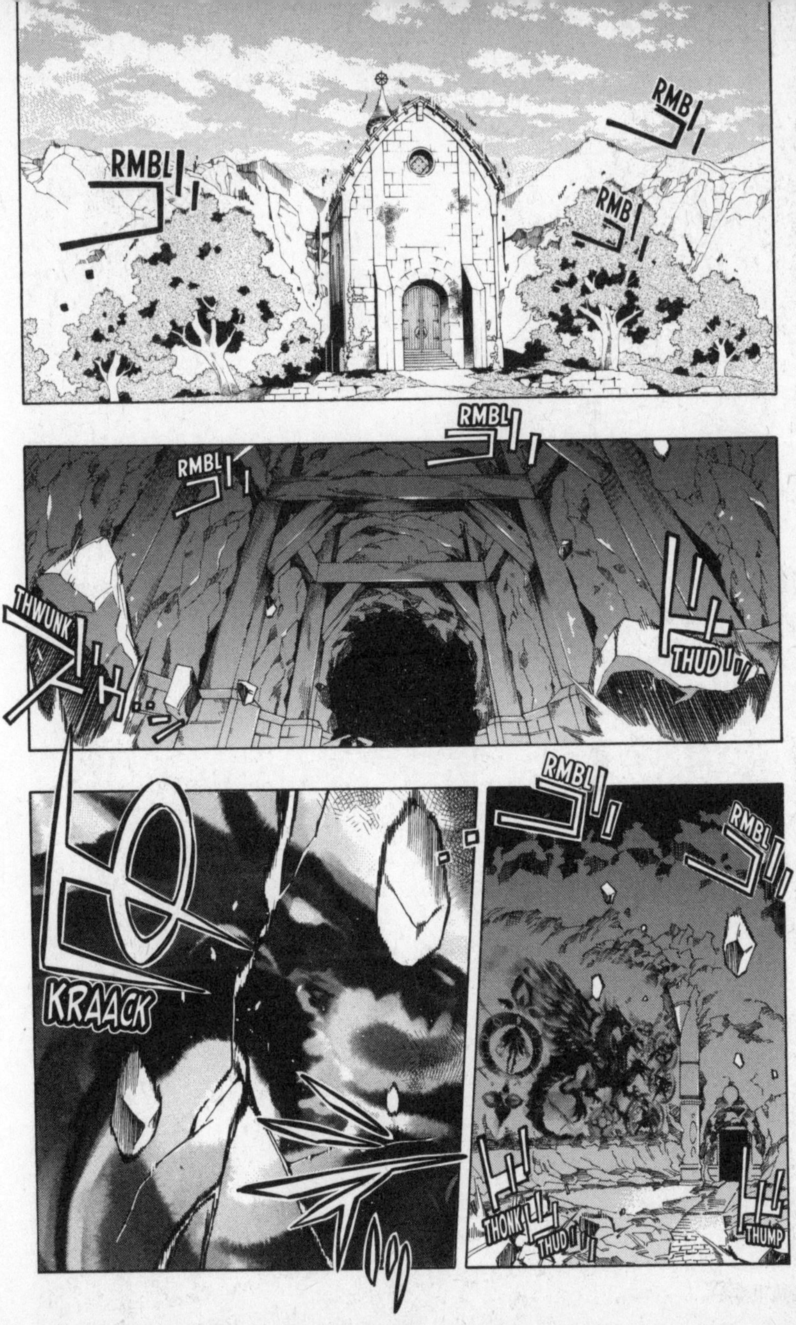
RMB
RMB
RMBL
RMBL
RMBL
THUD
THWUNK
RMBL
RMBL
THUMP
THUD
THONK
KRAACK

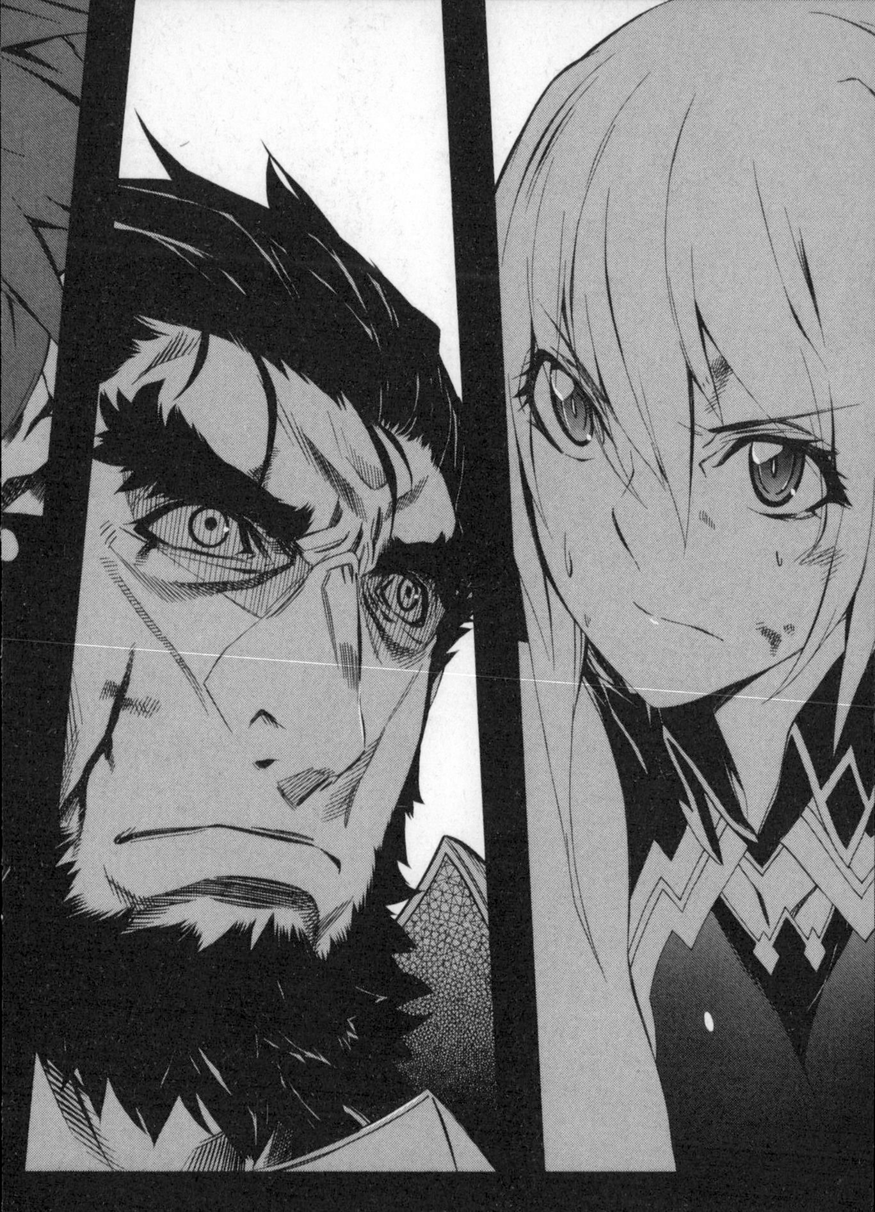

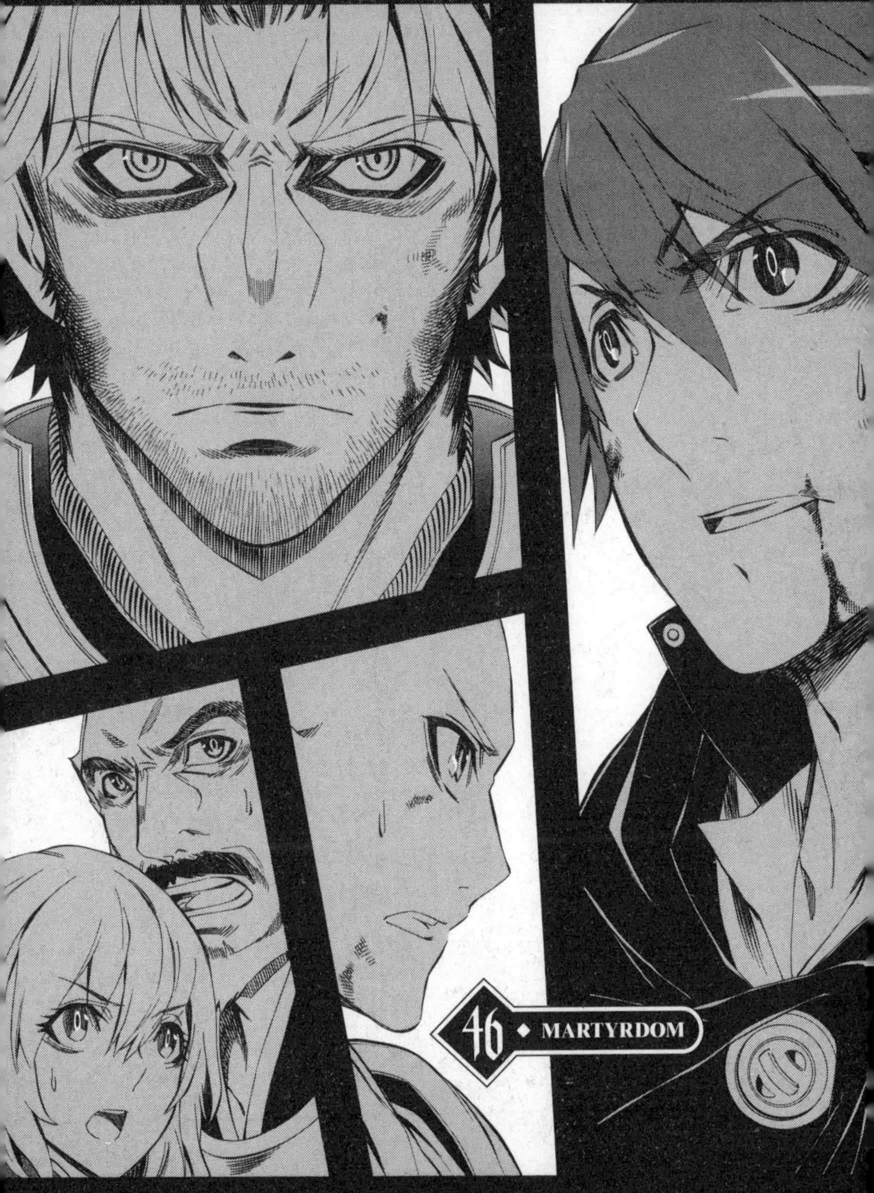
46 ◆ MARTYRDOM

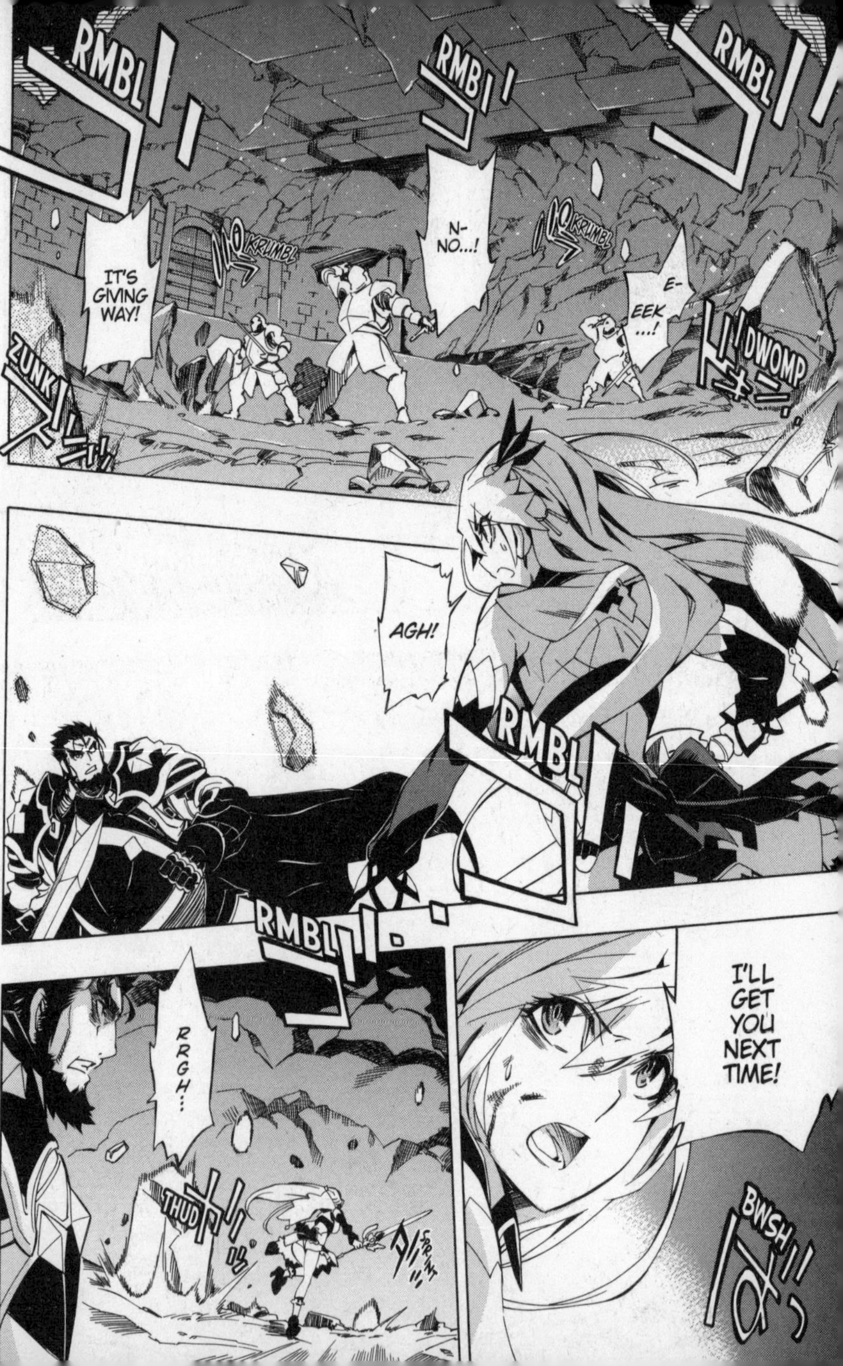
RMBL
RMBL
RMBL
KRUMBL
N-NO...!
E-EEK...!
DWOMP
KRUMBL
IT'S GIVING WAY!
ZUNK
AGH!
RMBL
RMBL
I'LL GET YOU NEXT TIME!
BWSH
RRGH...
THUD
SPRINT

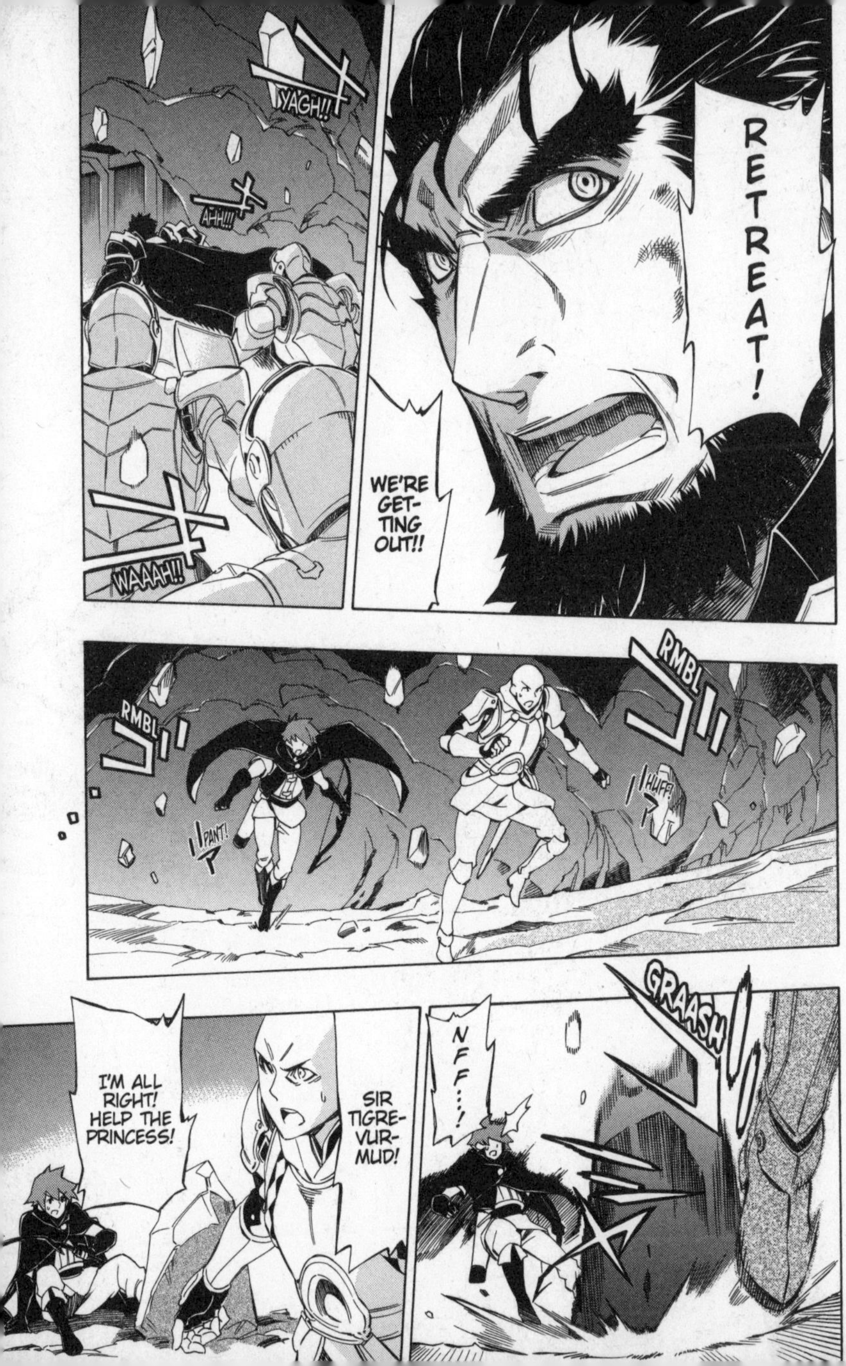
RETREAT!
WE'RE GET-TING OUT!!
YAGH!!
AHH!!!
WAAAH!!
RMBL
HUFF!
RMBL
PANT!
GRAASH
NFF...!
SIR TIGRE-VUR-MUD!
I'M ALL RIGHT! HELP THE PRINCESS!

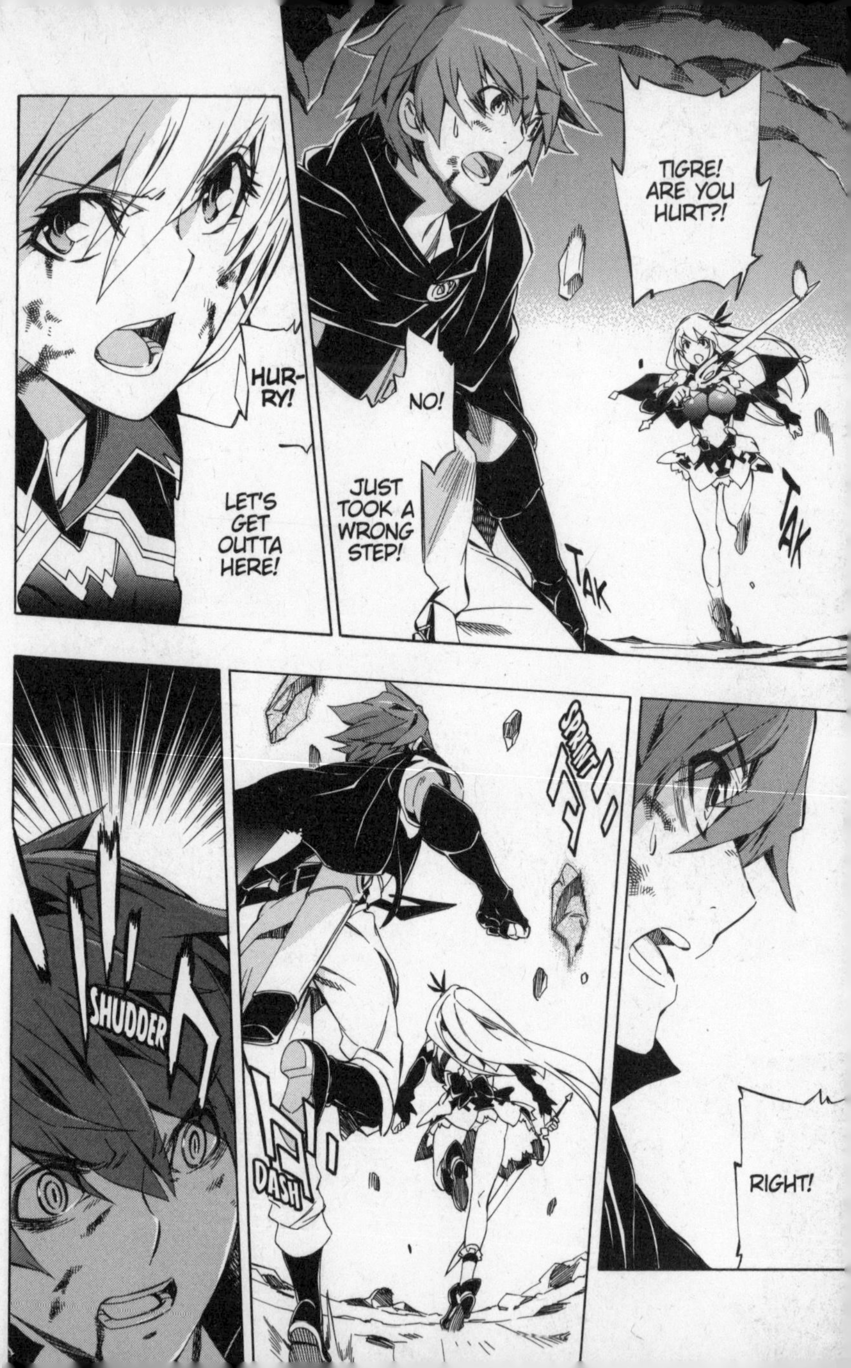
TIGRE! ARE YOU HURT?!
TAK
TAK
NO!
JUST TOOK A WRONG STEP!
HUR-RY!
LET'S GET OUTTA HERE!
RIGHT!
SPRINT
DASH
SHUDDER

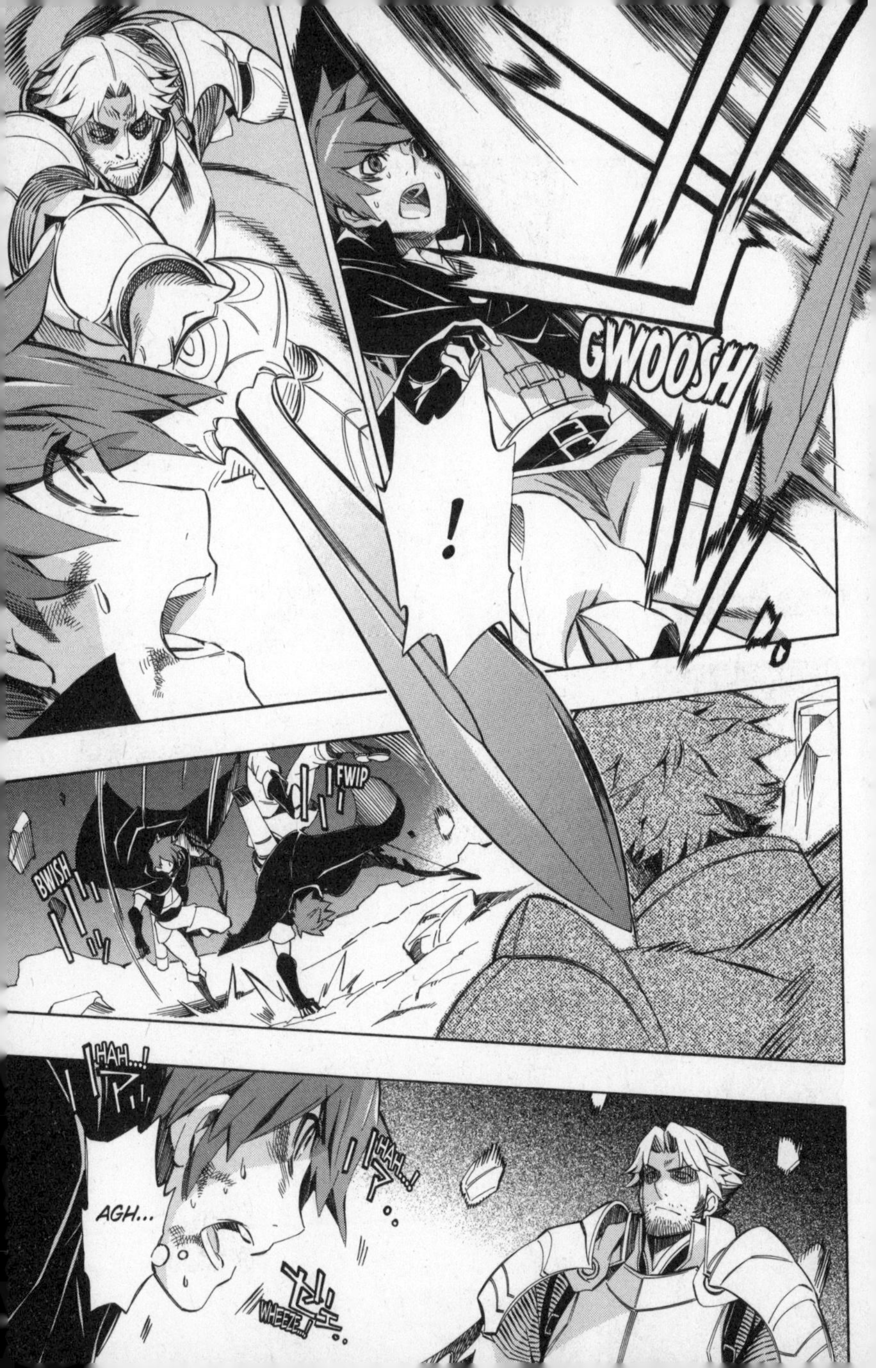
GWOOSH
!
FWIP
BWISH
HAH...!
HAH...!
AGH...
WHEEZE...!

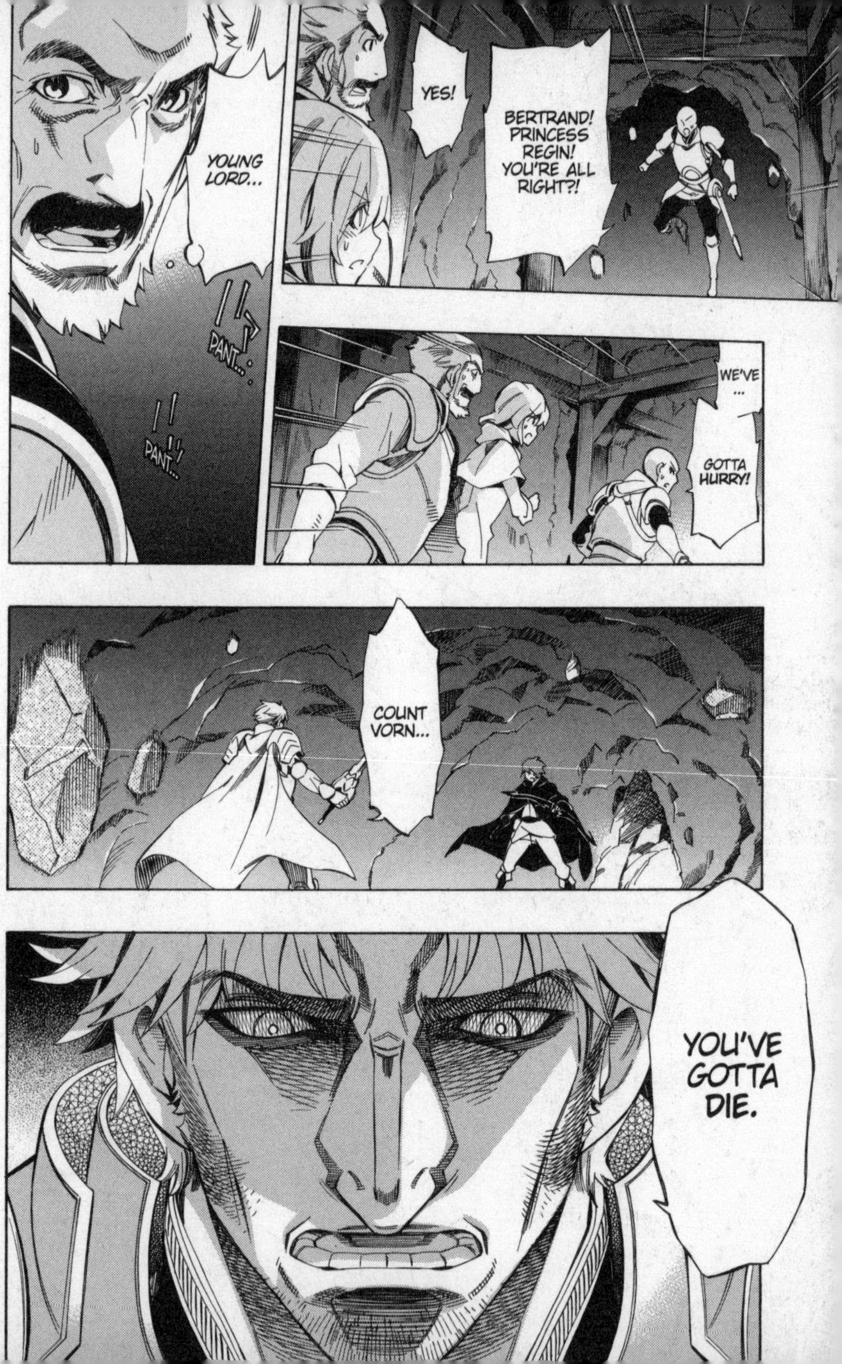
BERTRAND! PRINCESS REGIN! YOU'RE ALL RIGHT?!
YES!
WE'VE ...
GOTTA HURRY!
YOUNG LORD...
PANT...
PANT...
COUNT VORN...
YOU'VE GOTTA DIE.

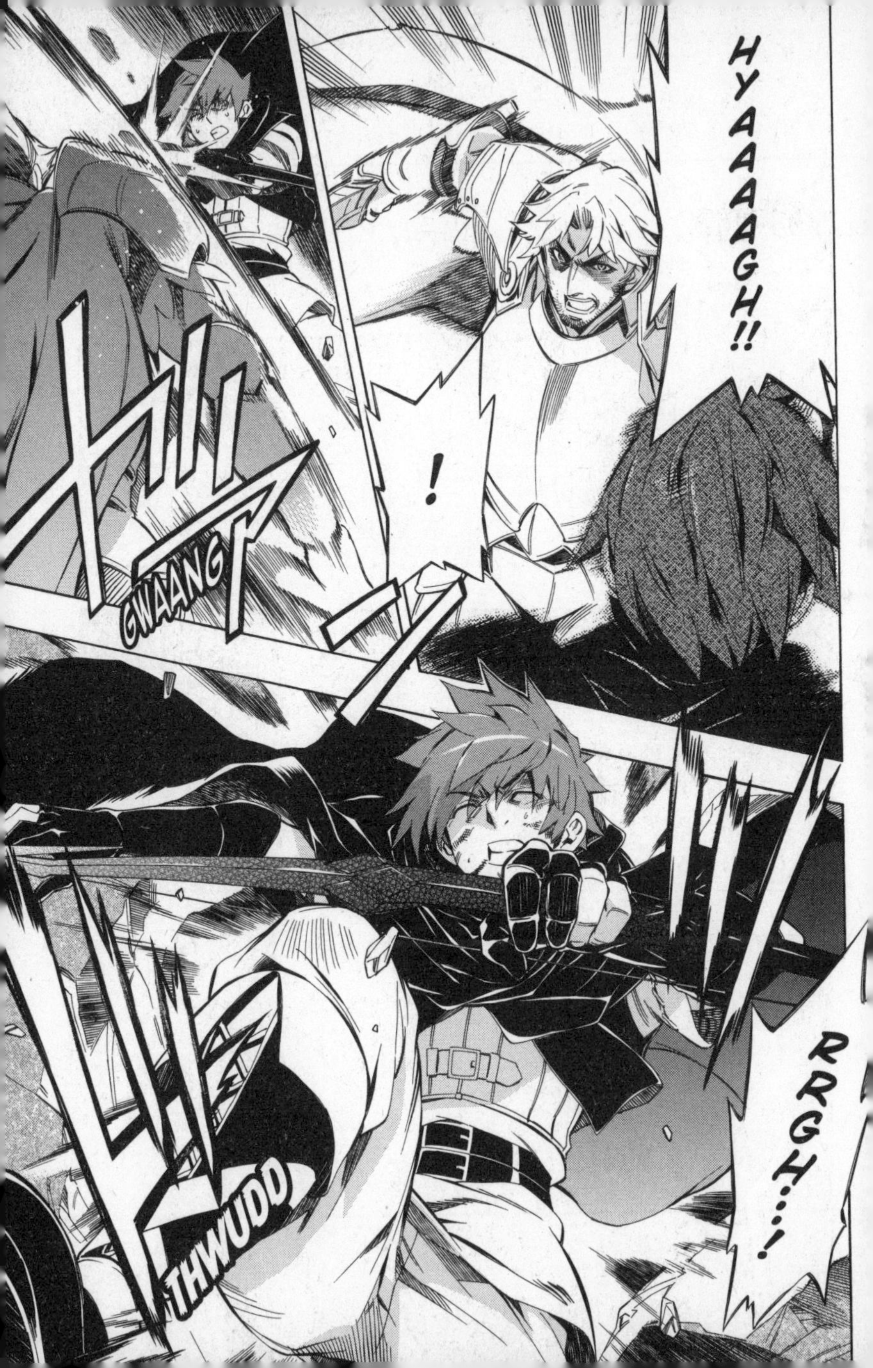
HYAAAAAGH!!
!
GWAANG
RRGH...!
THWUDD

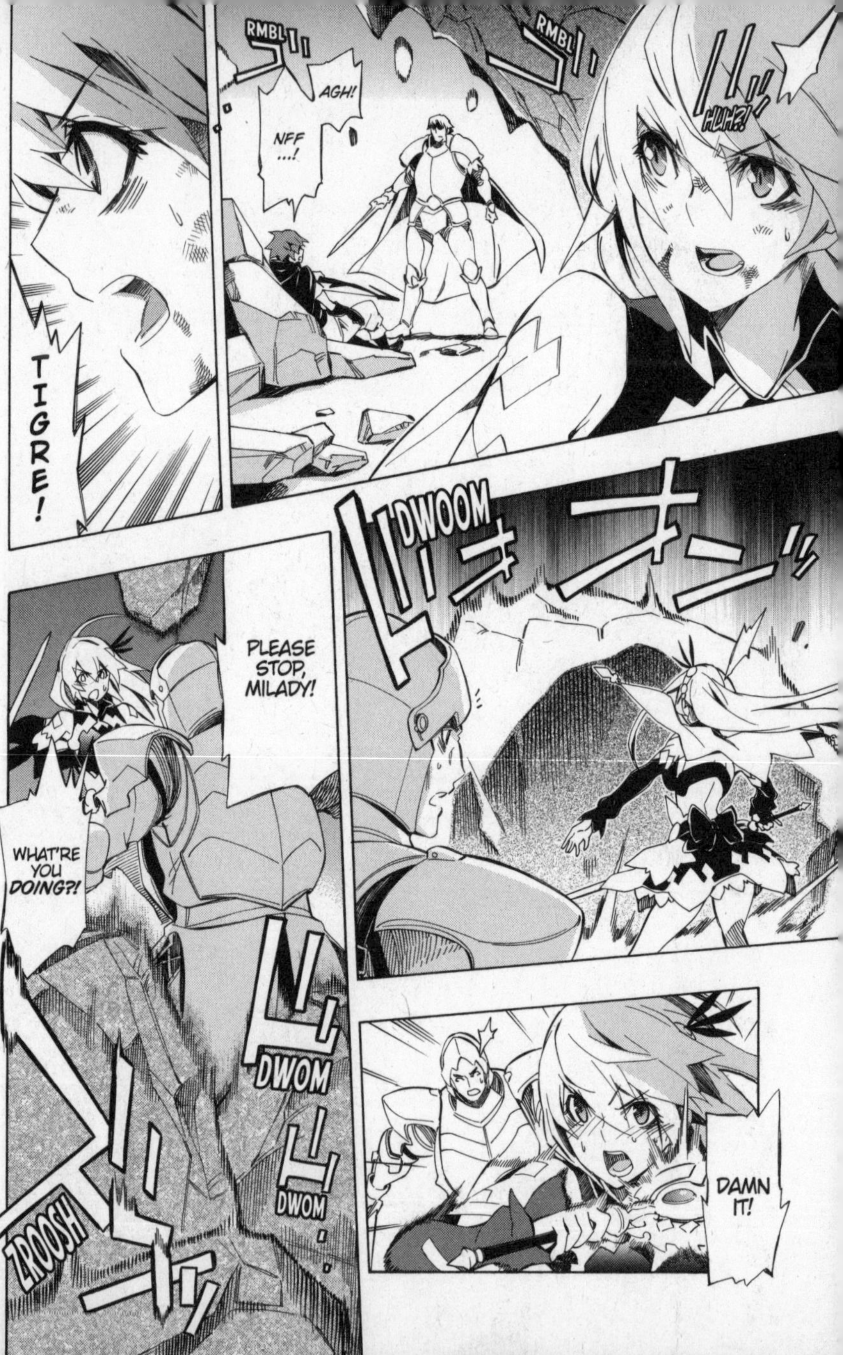
RMBL
HUH?!
RMBL
AGH!
NFF ...!
TIGRE!
DWOOM
DAMN IT!
PLEASE STOP, MILADY!
WHAT'RE YOU DOING?!
DWOM
DWOM
ZROOSH

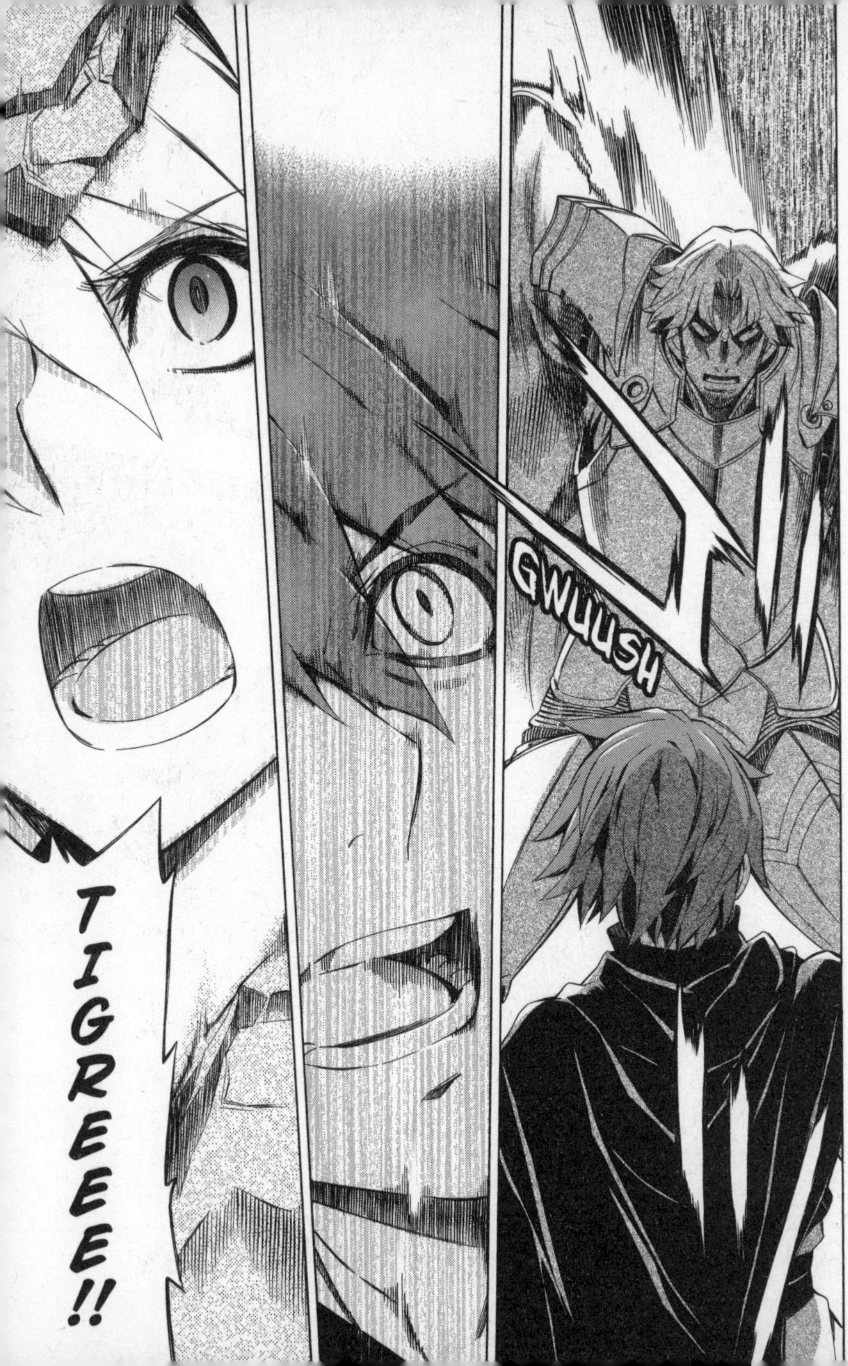
GWUUSH
TIGREEE!!

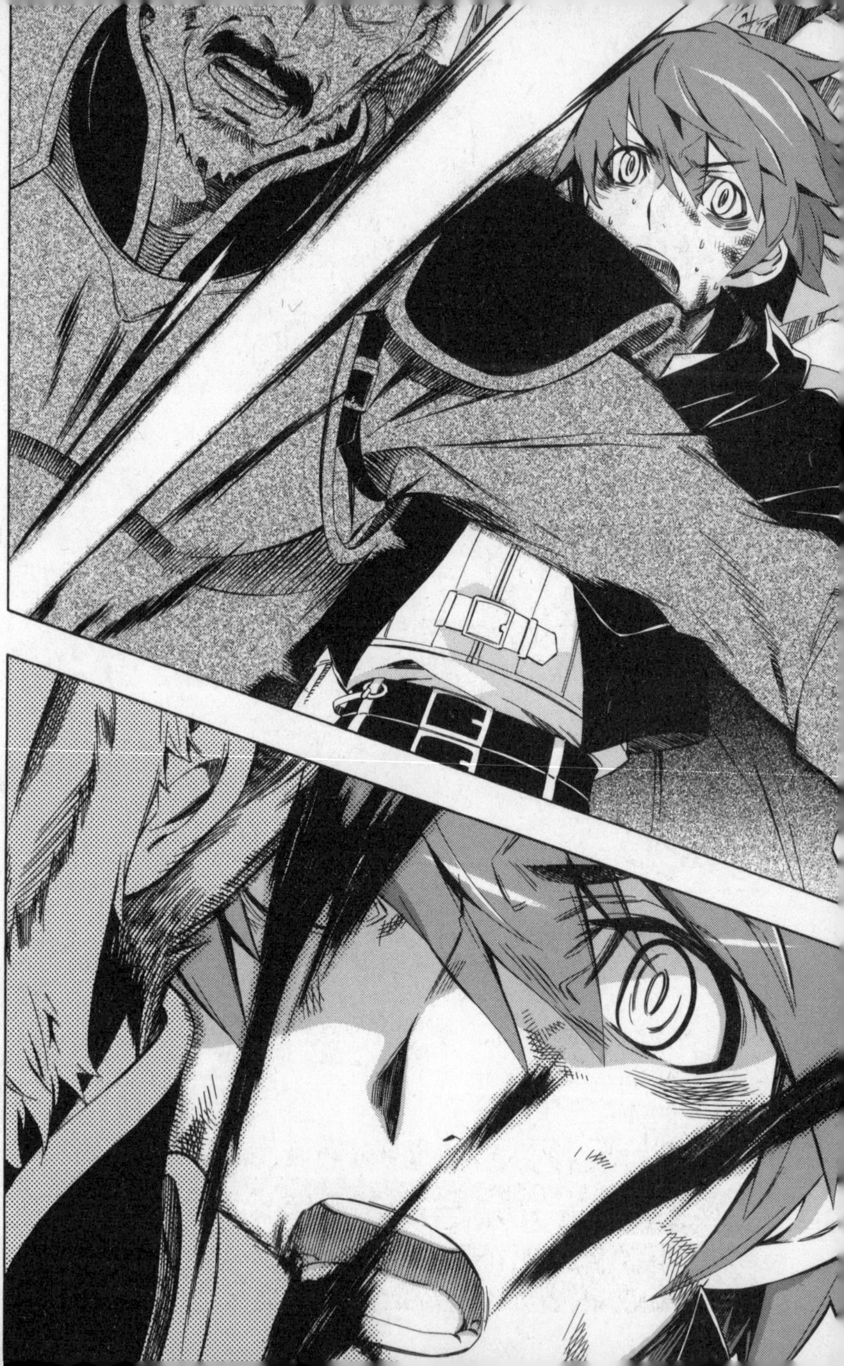

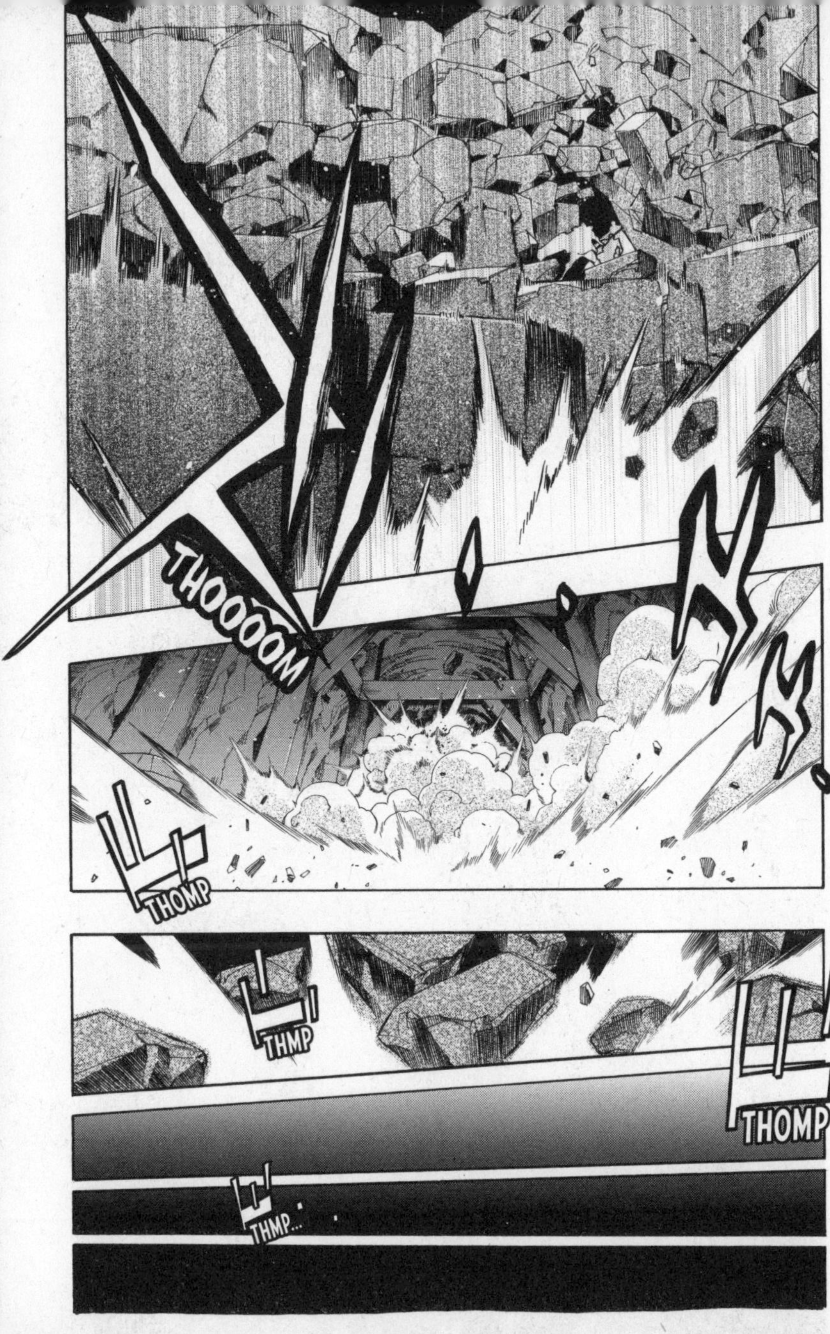
THOOOOM
THOMP
THMP
THOMP
THMP...

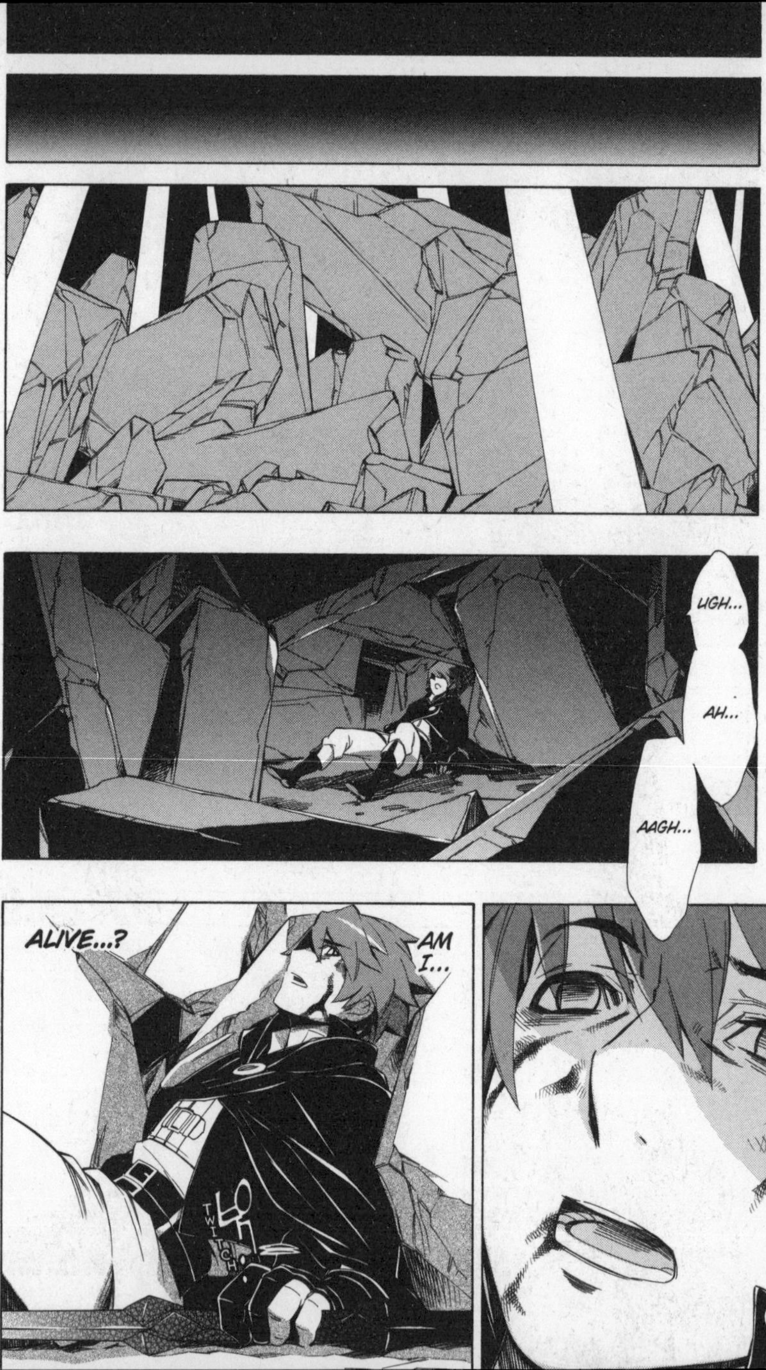
UGH...
AH...
AAGH...
AM I...
ALIVE...?
TWITCH

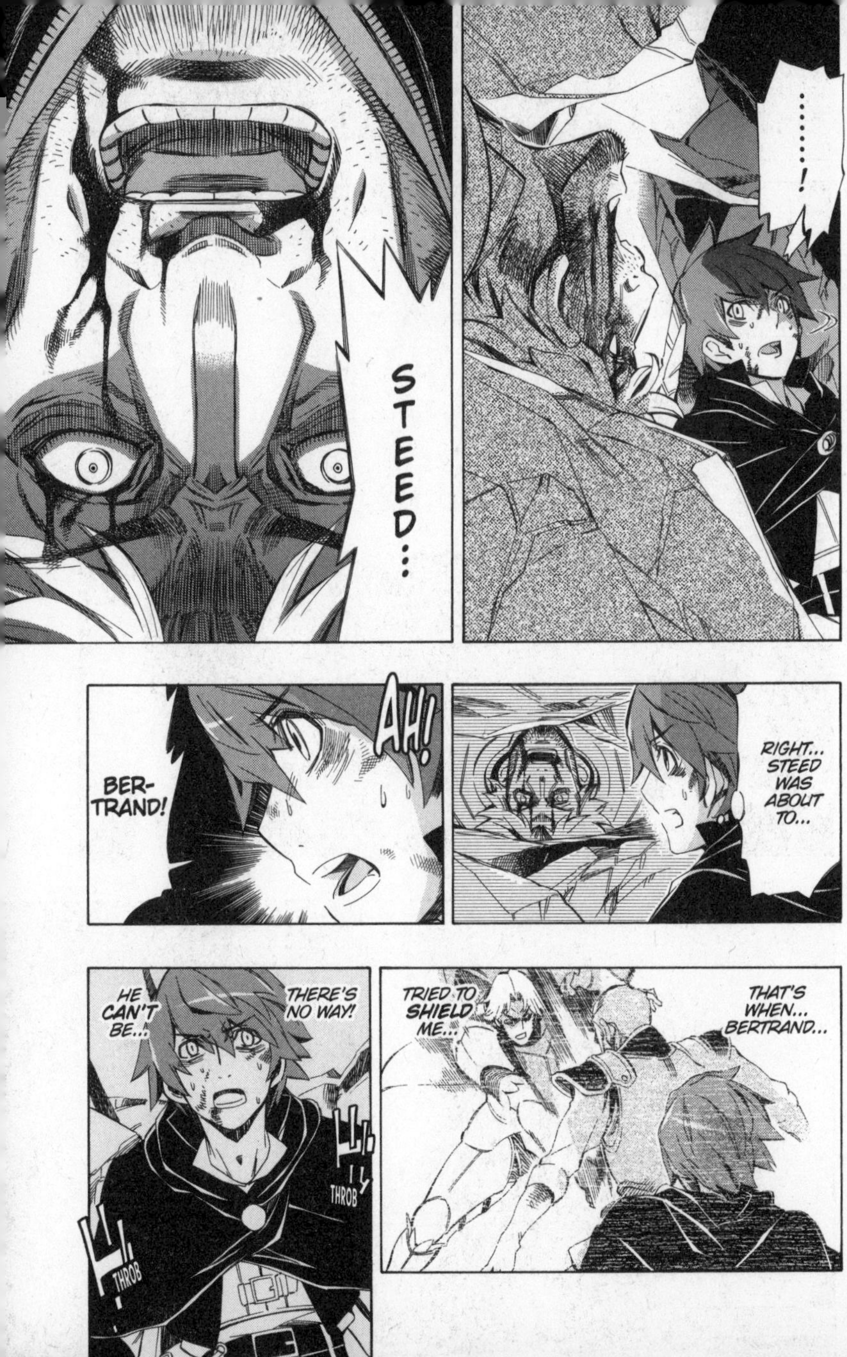
......!
STEED...
RIGHT... STEED WAS ABOUT TO...
AH!
BER-TRAND!
THAT'S WHEN... BERTRAND...
TRIED TO SHIELD ME...
THERE'S NO WAY!
HE CAN'T BE...
THROB
THROB

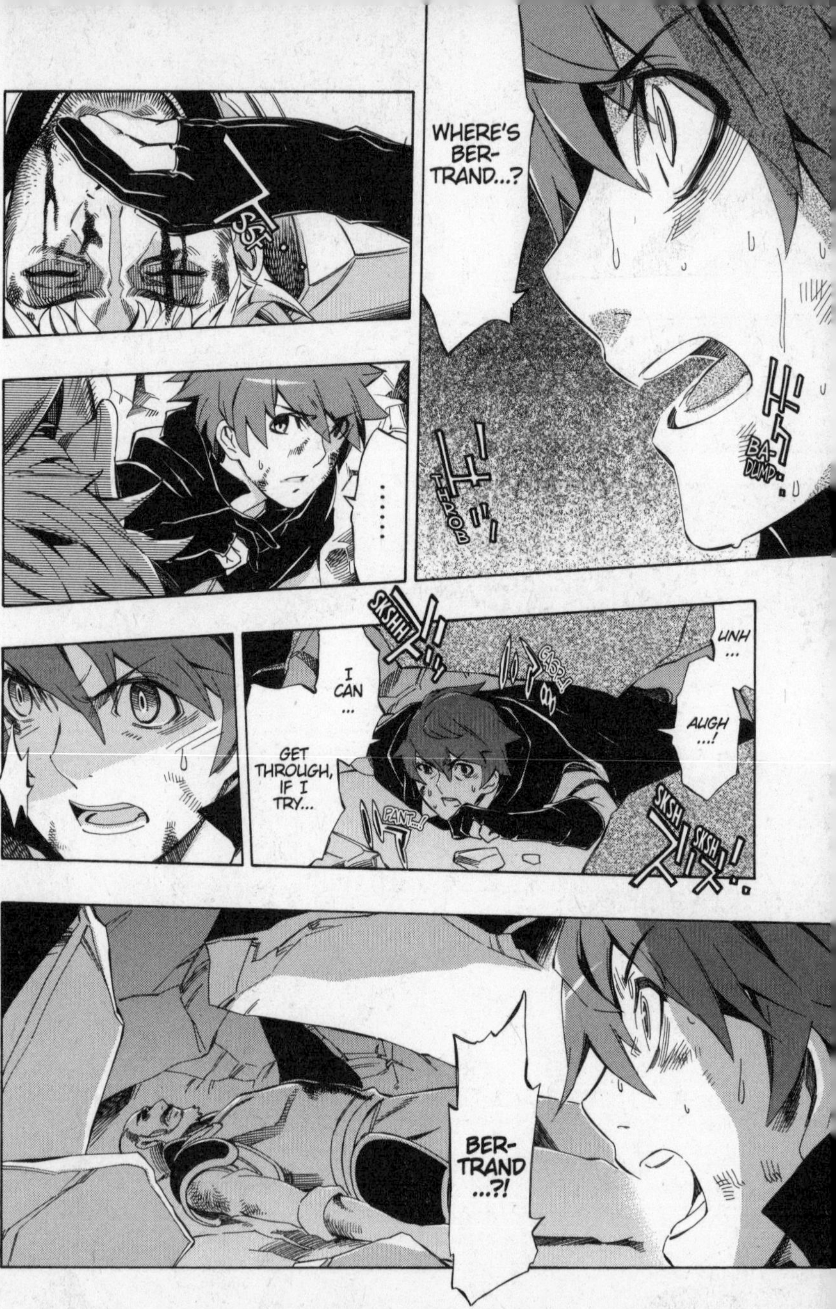
WHERE'S BER-TRAND...?
BA-DUMP!
THROB
SSF
......
UNH...
SKSHH
GASP!
I CAN...
AUGH...!
GET THROUGH, IF I TRY...
PANT...!
SKSH SKSH!
BER-TRAND...?!

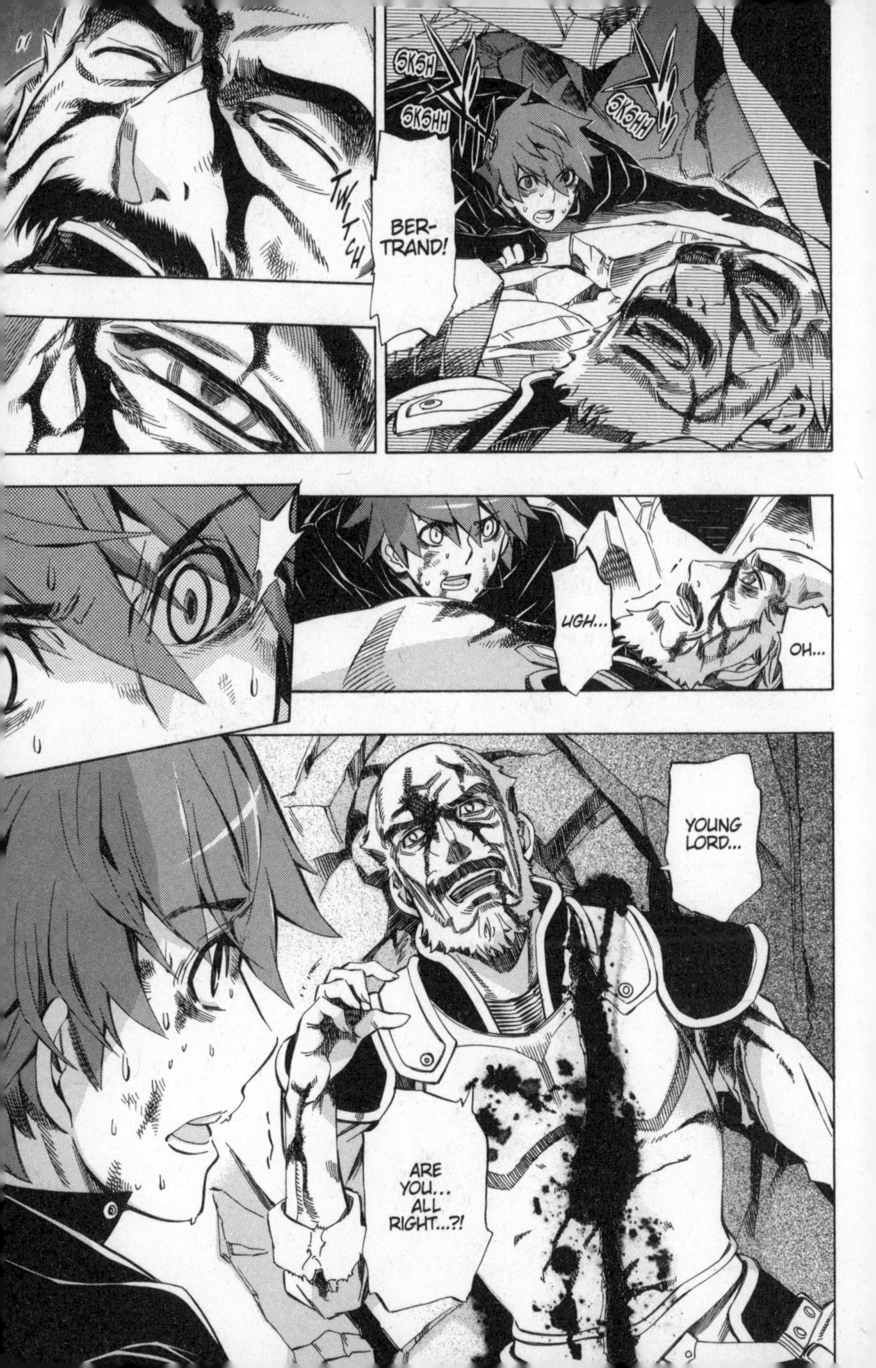
SKSHH
SKSH
SKSHH
BER-TRAND!
TWITCH
UGH...
OH...
YOUNG LORD...
ARE YOU... ALL RIGHT...?!

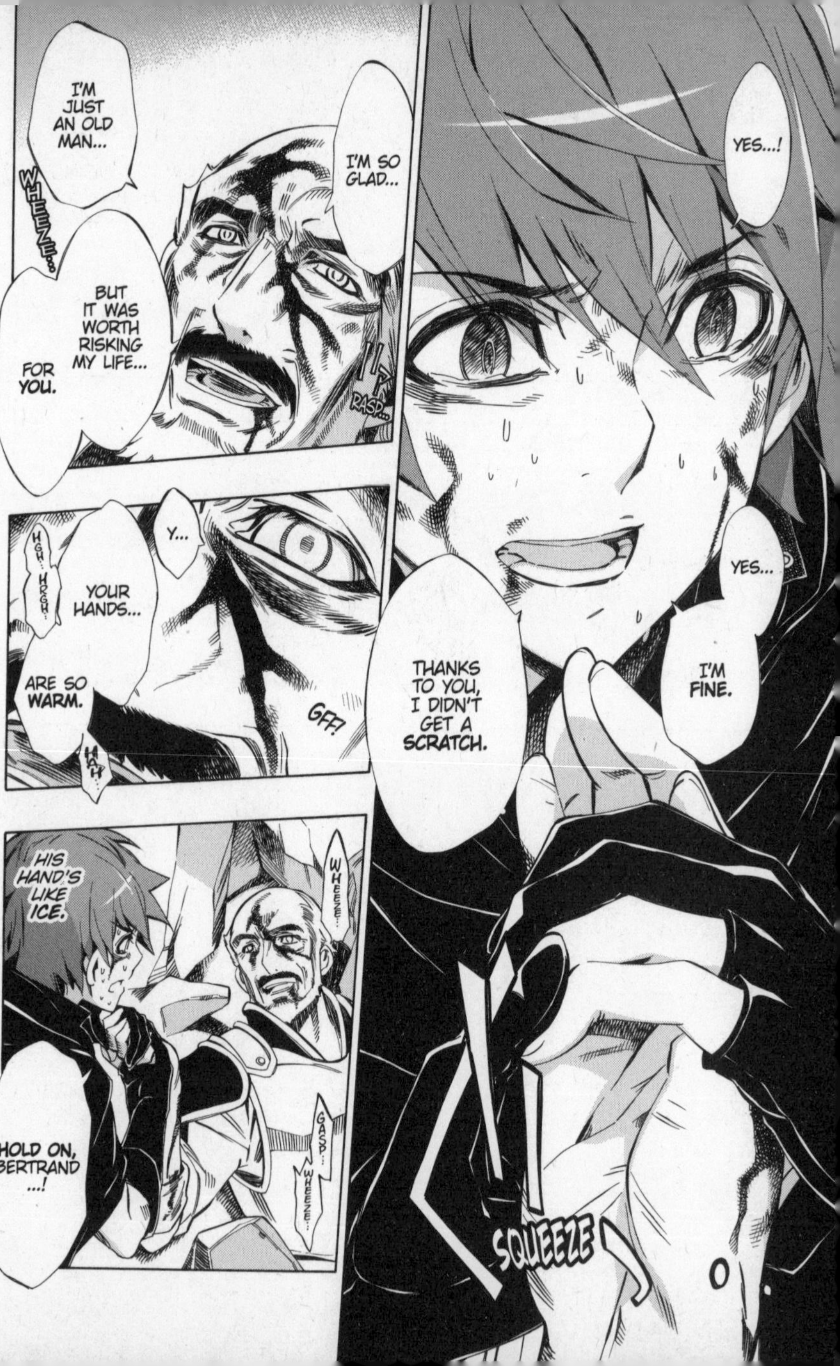
YES...!
YES...
I'M FINE.
THANKS TO YOU, I DIDN'T GET A SCRATCH.
SQUEEZE
I'M SO GLAD...
I'M JUST AN OLD MAN...
WHEEZE...
BUT IT WAS WORTH RISKING MY LIFE... FOR YOU.
RASP...
Y...
YOUR HANDS... ARE SO WARM.
HGH... HRGH...
GFF!
HAH...
WHEEZE...
HIS HAND'S LIKE ICE.
GASP... WHEEZE...
HOLD ON, BERTRAND ...!

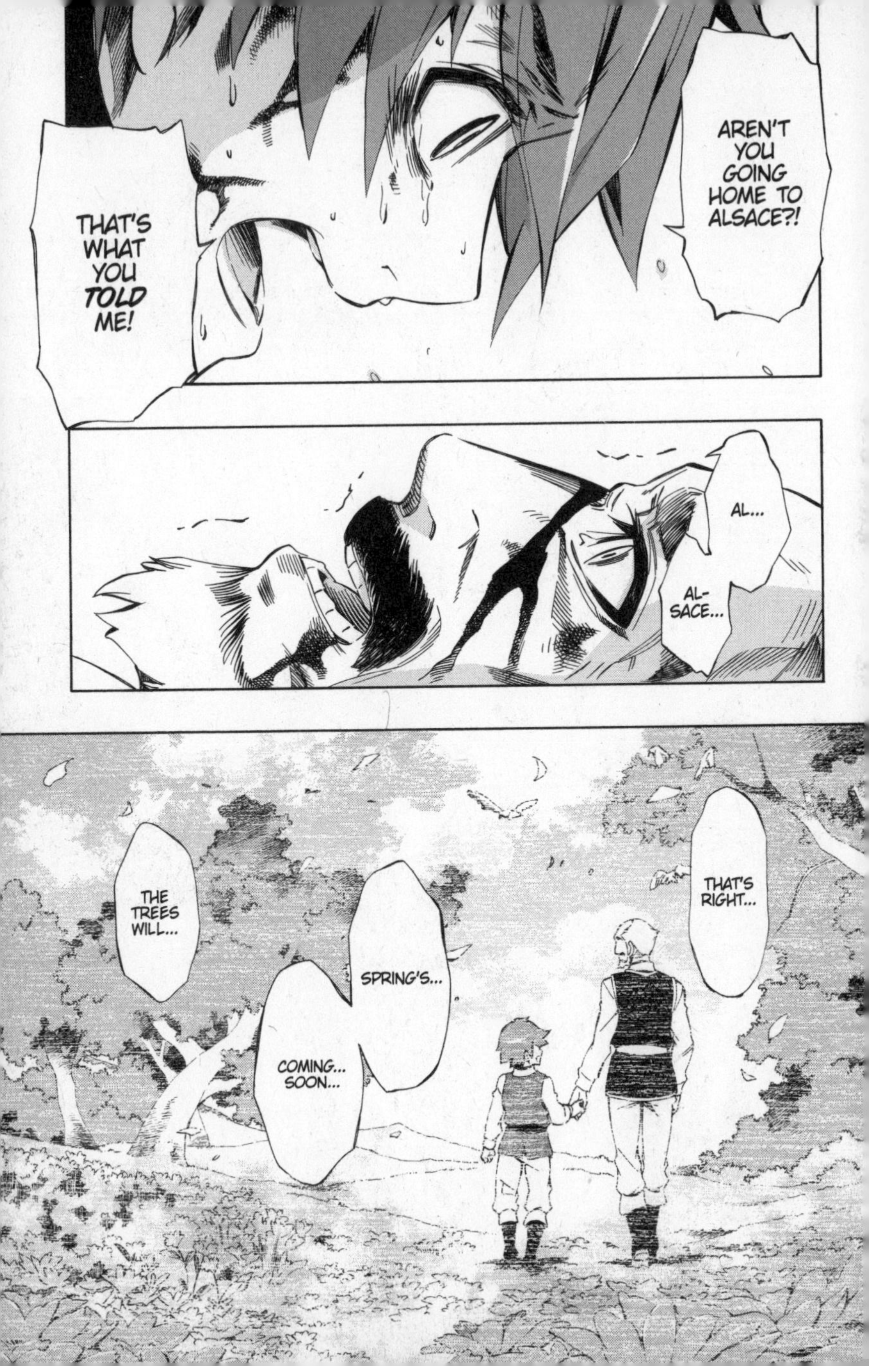
AREN'T YOU GOING HOME TO ALSACE?!
THAT'S WHAT YOU *TOLD* ME!
AL...
AL-SACE...
THAT'S RIGHT...
SPRING'S...
COMING... SOON...
THE TREES WILL...

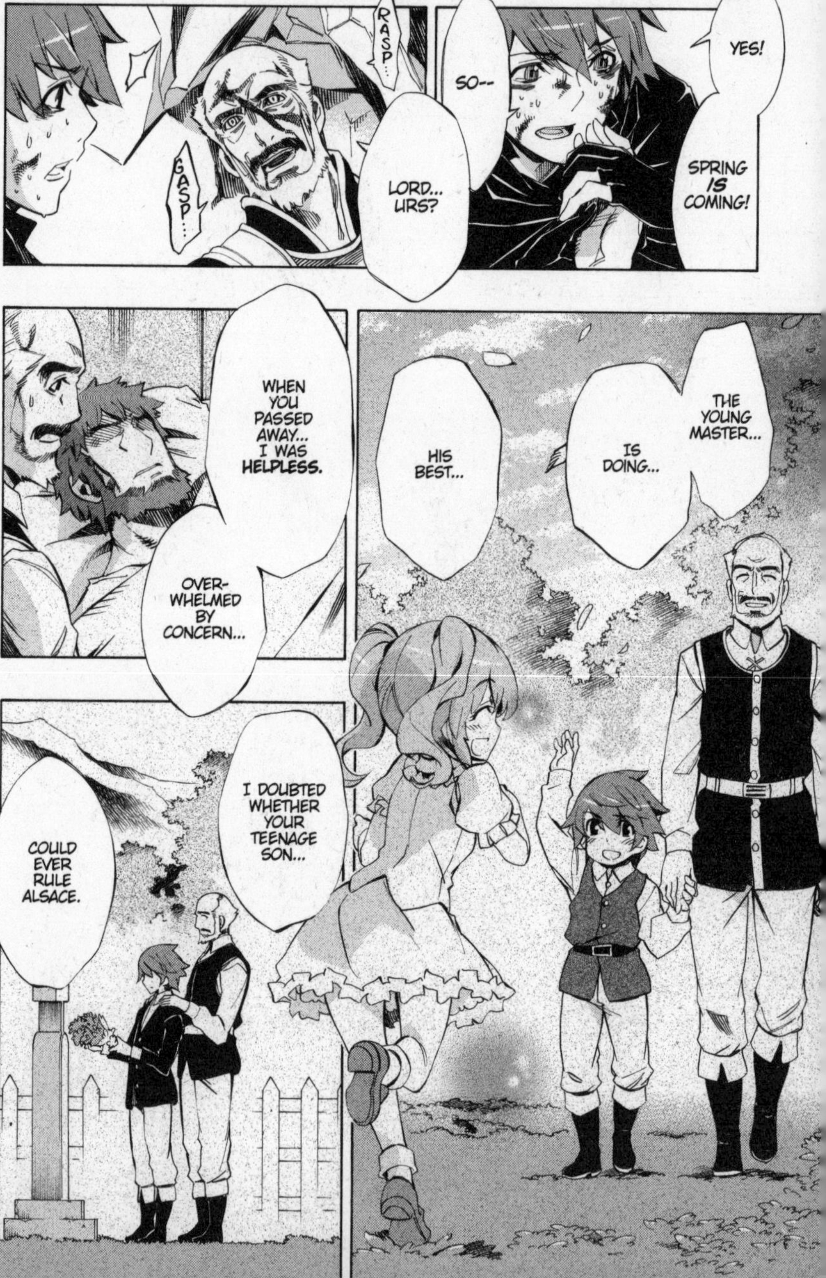
YES!
SPRING **IS** COMING!
SO--
RASP...
GASP...
LORD... URS?
THE YOUNG MASTER...
IS DOING...
HIS BEST...
WHEN YOU PASSED AWAY... I WAS **HELPLESS.**
OVER-WHELMED BY CONCERN...
I DOUBTED WHETHER YOUR TEENAGE SON...
COULD EVER RULE ALSACE.

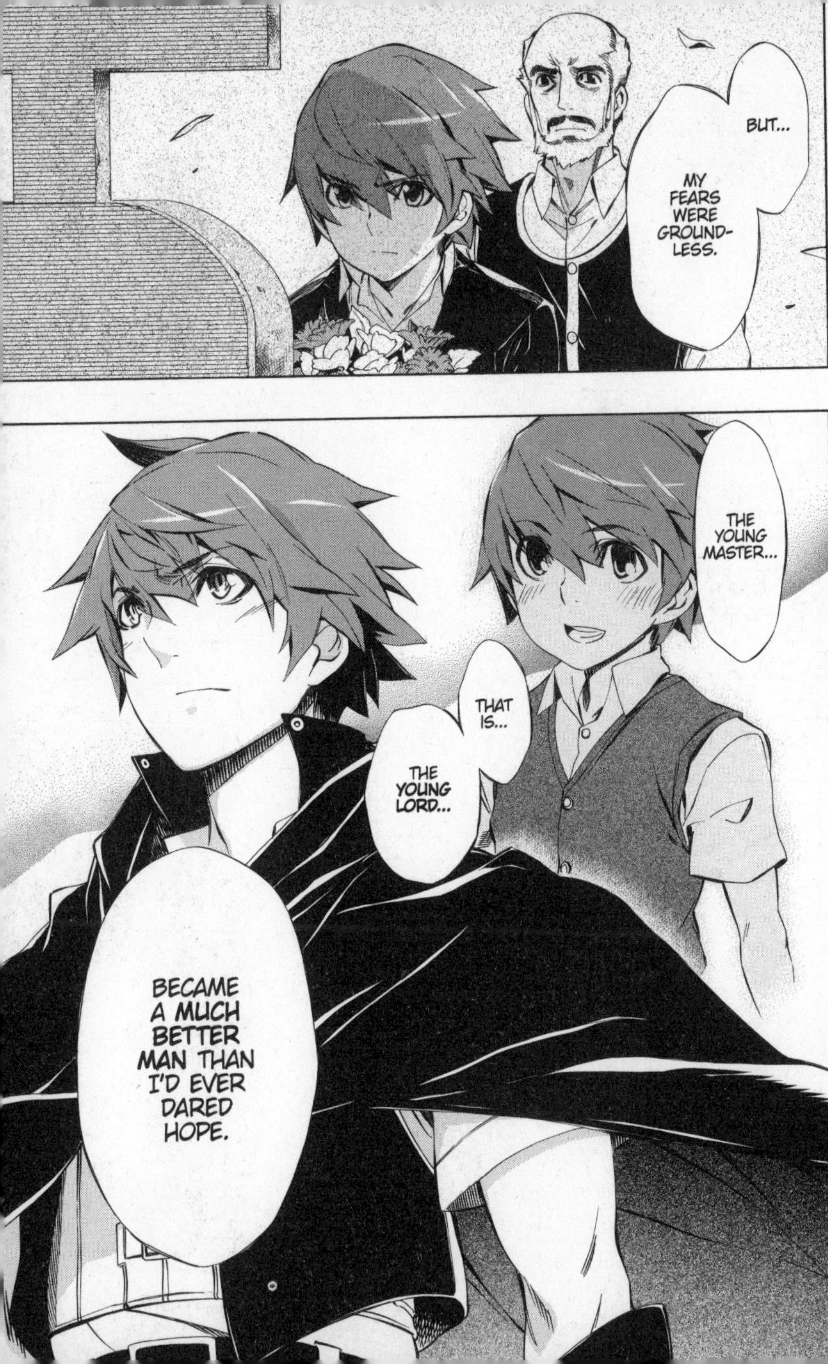
BUT...
MY FEARS WERE GROUNDLESS.
THE YOUNG MASTER...
THAT IS...
THE YOUNG LORD...
BECAME A MUCH BETTER MAN THAN I'D EVER DARED HOPE.

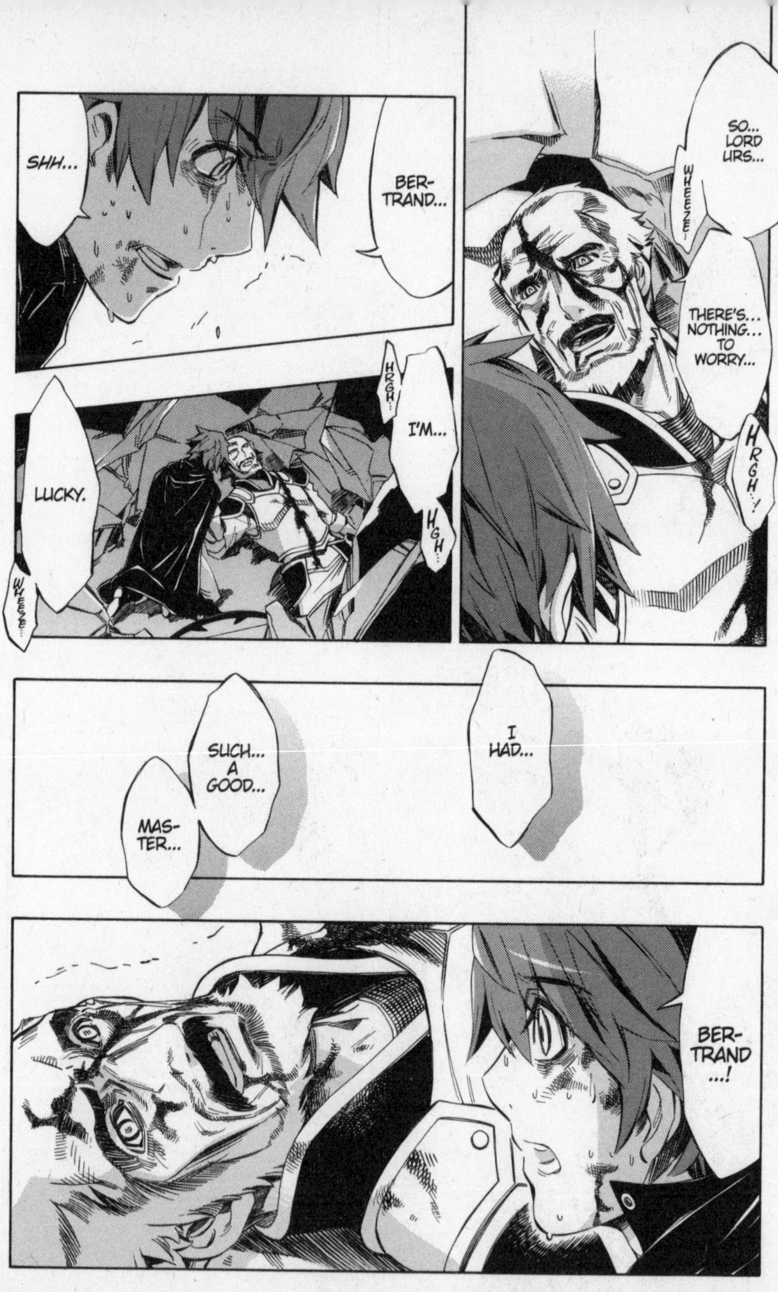
SO... LORD URS...
WHEEZE...
THERE'S... NOTHING... TO WORRY...
HRGH...!
BER-TRAND...
SHH...
HRGH...
I'M...
HGH...
LUCKY.
WHEEZE...
I HAD...
SUCH... A GOOD...
MAS-TER...
BER-TRAND...!

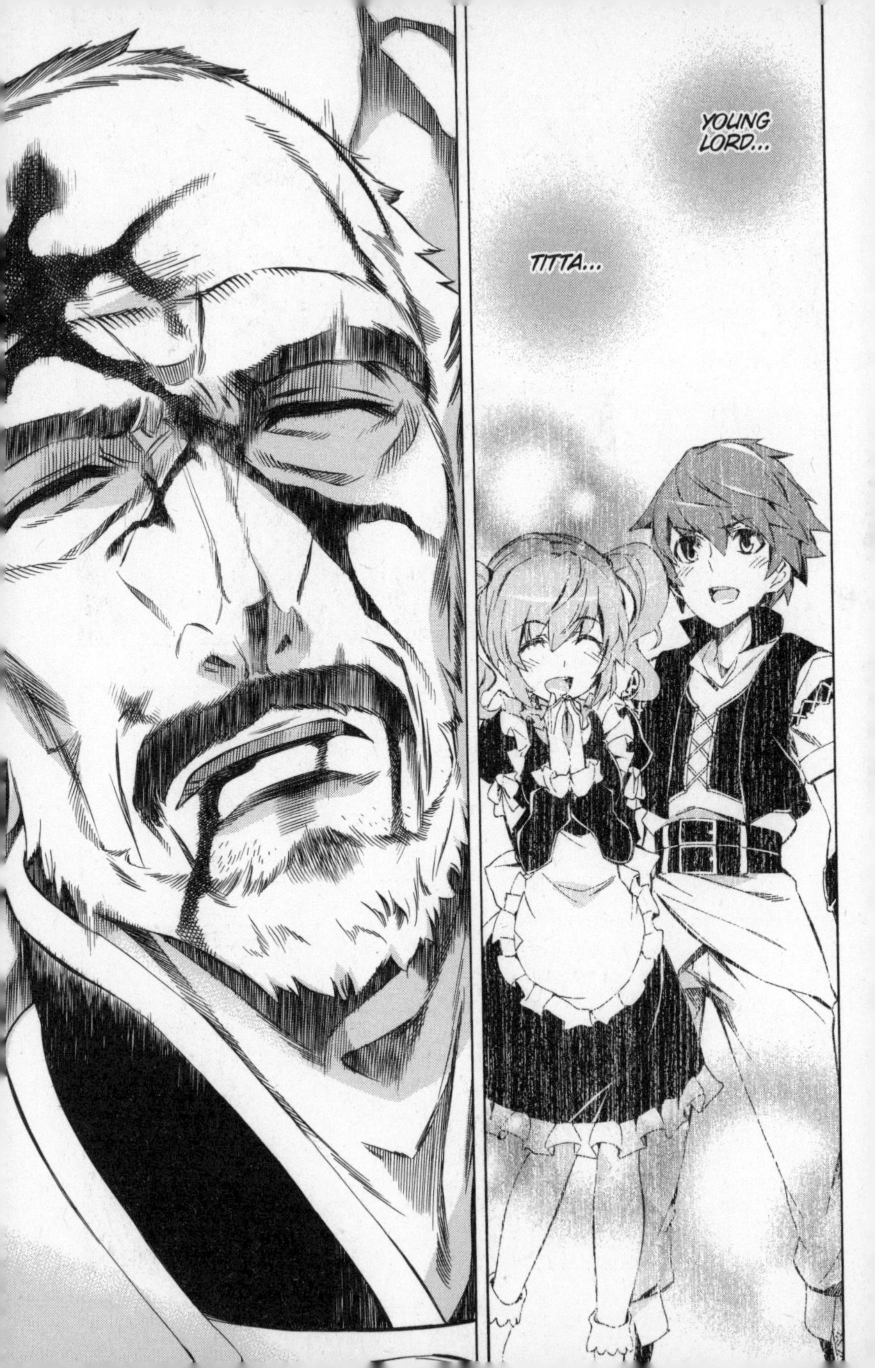
YOUNG LORD...
TITTA...

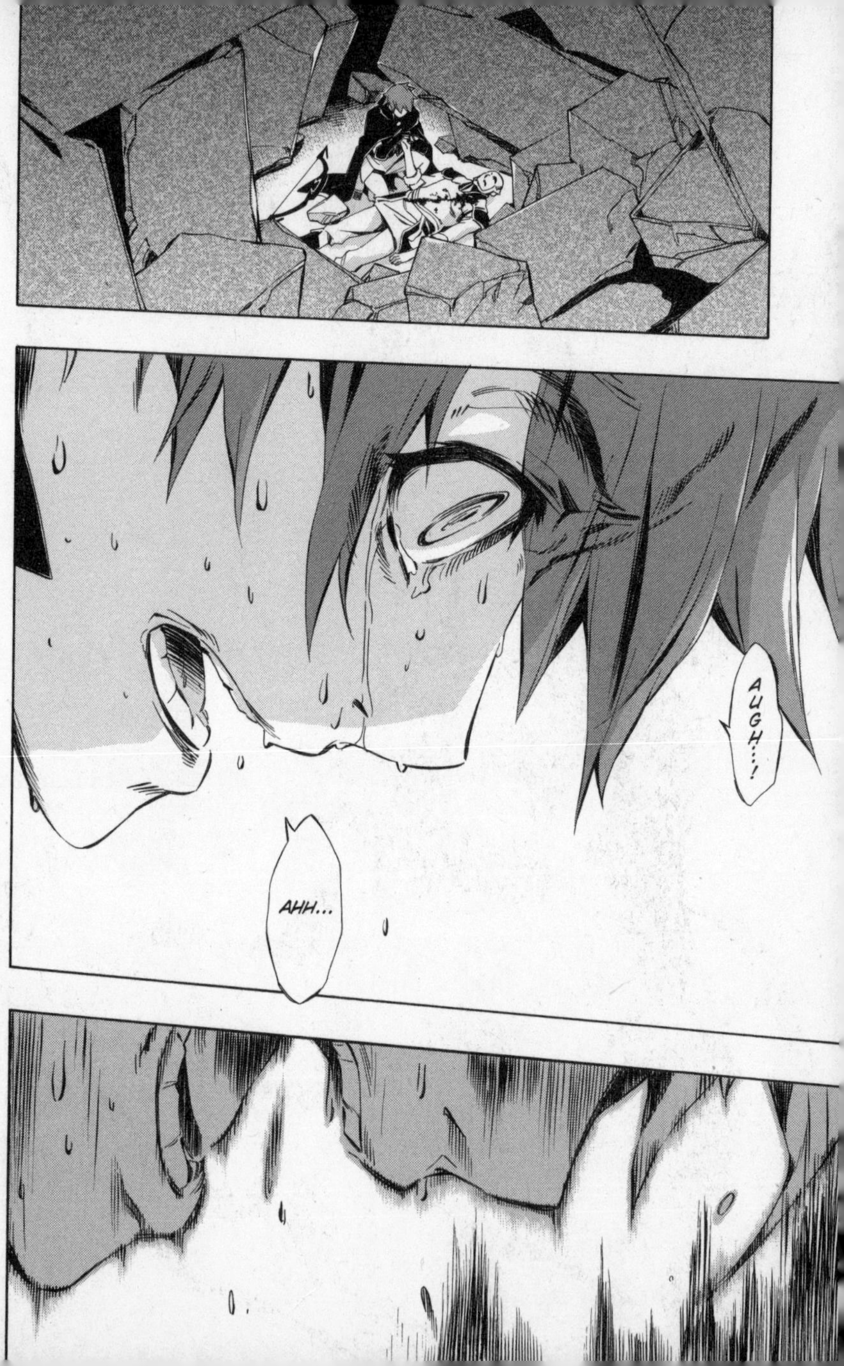
AUGH...!
AHH...

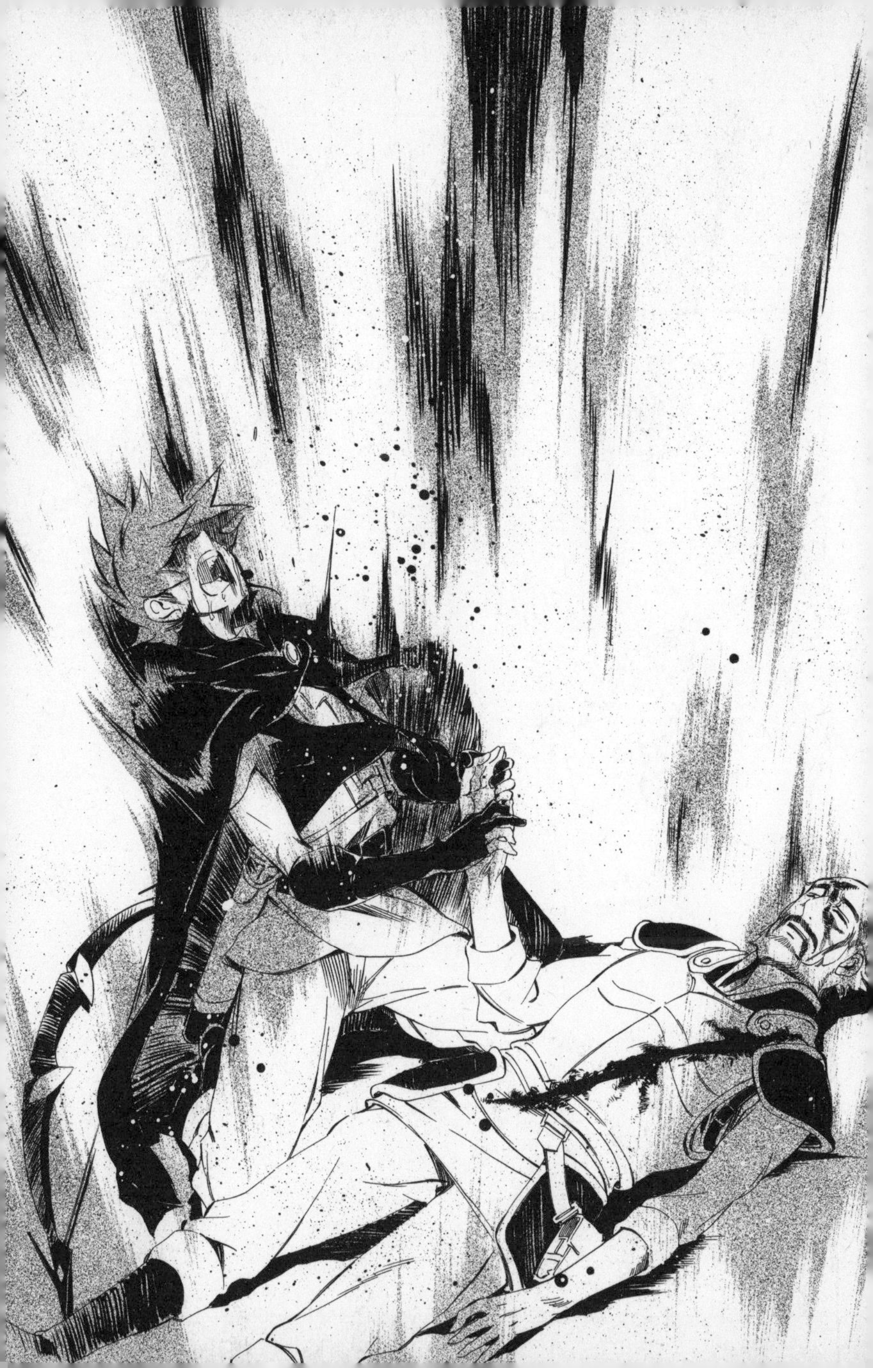

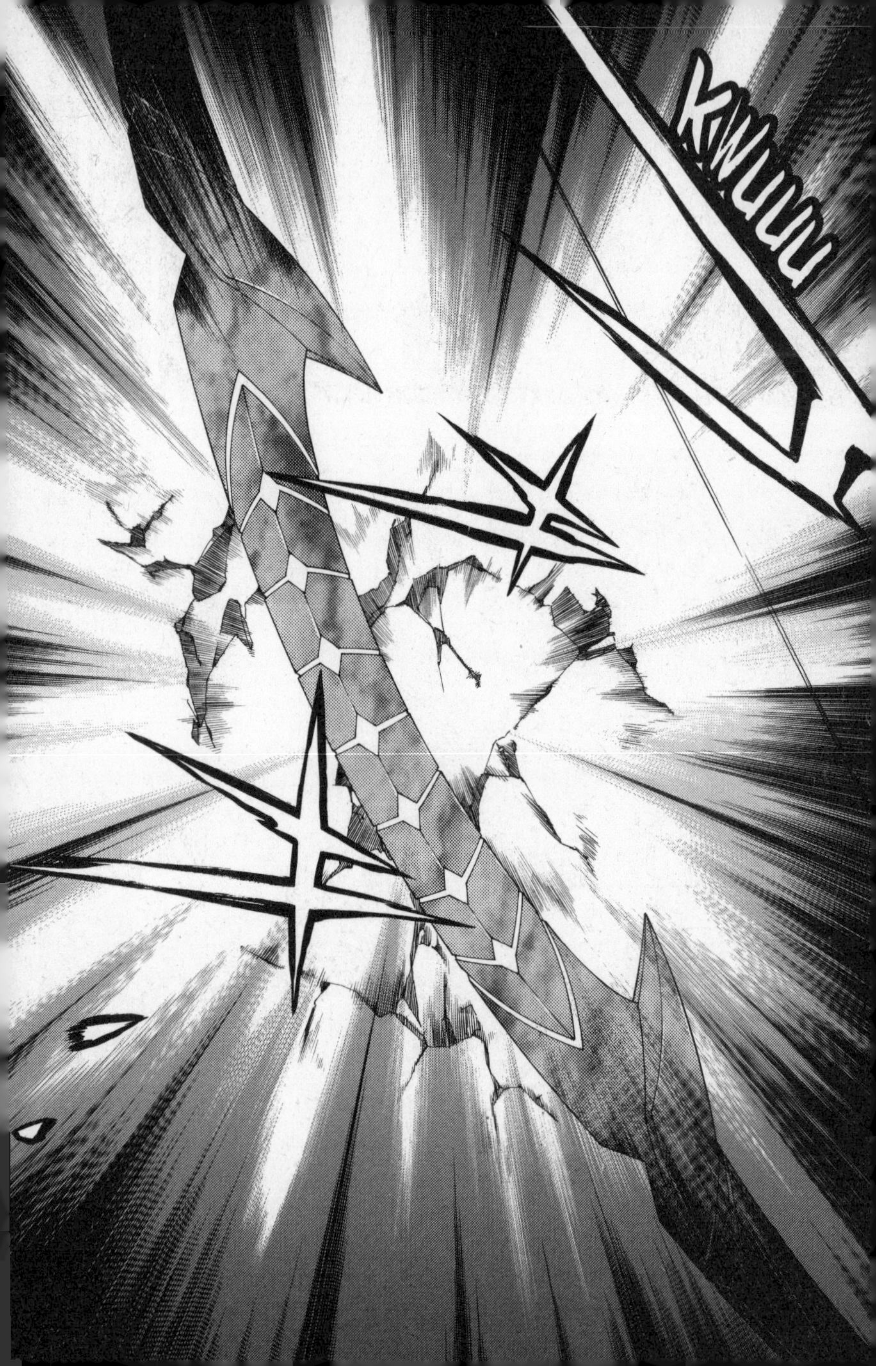
KWUUU

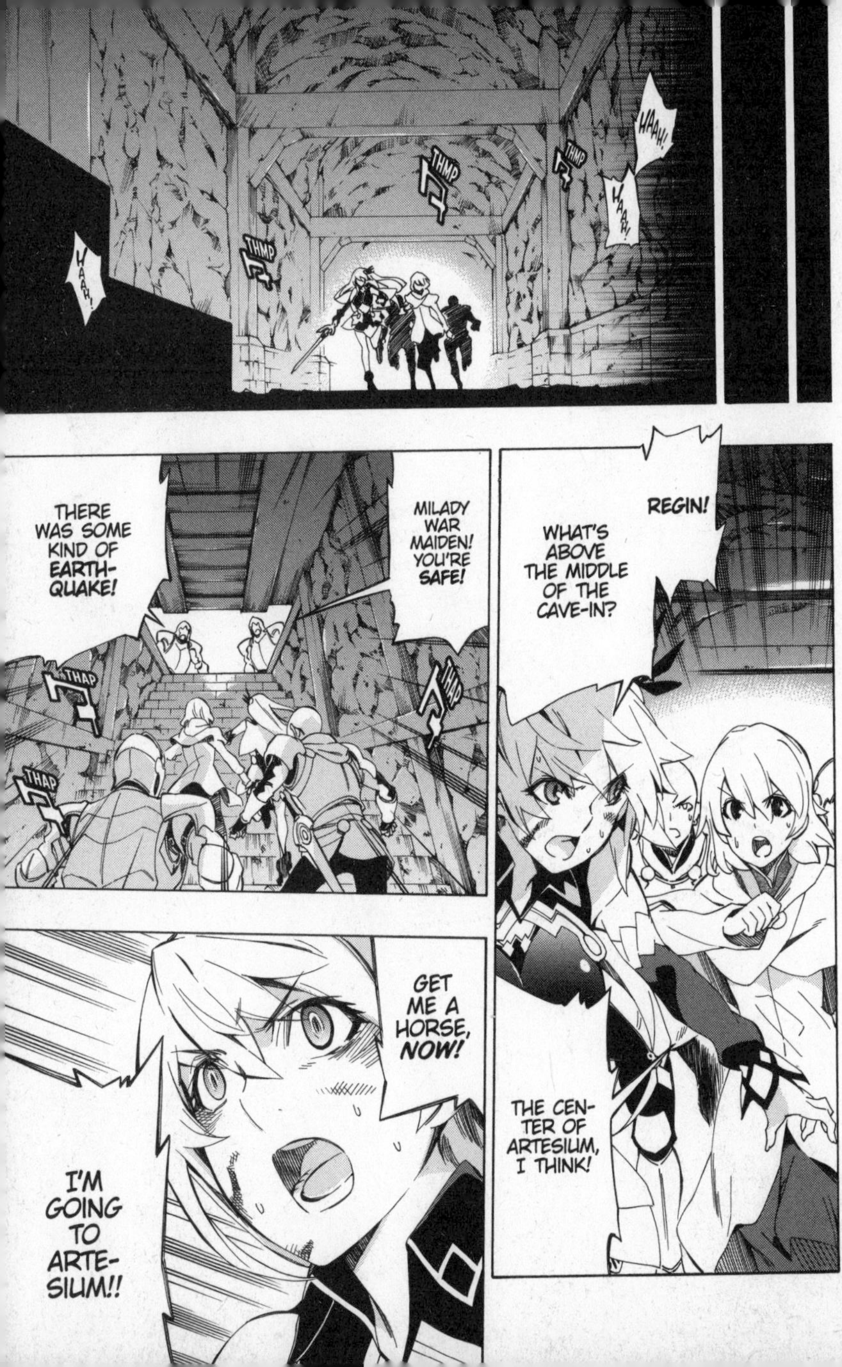
HAAAH!
HAAAH!
THMP
THMP
THMP
HAAAH!
REGIN!
WHAT'S ABOVE THE MIDDLE OF THE CAVE-IN?
THE CEN-TER OF ARTESIUM, I THINK!
MILADY WAR MAIDEN! YOU'RE SAFE!
THERE WAS SOME KIND OF EARTH-QUAKE!
THAP
THAP
THAP
GET ME A HORSE, NOW!
I'M GOING TO ARTE-SIUM!!

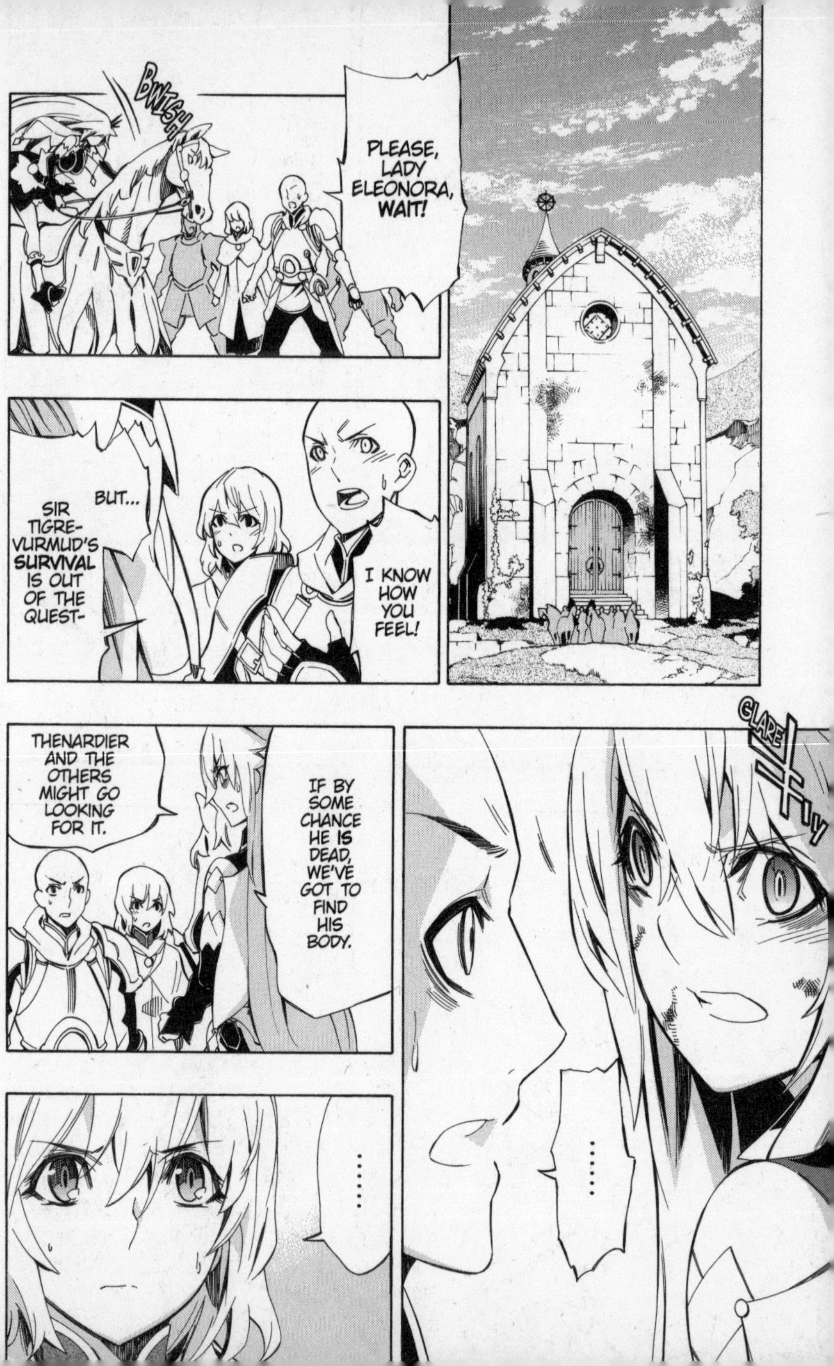
BWISH
PLEASE, LADY ELEONORA, WAIT!
I KNOW HOW YOU FEEL!
BUT...
SIR TIGRE-VURMUD'S SURVIVAL IS OUT OF THE QUEST-
GLARE
......
IF BY SOME CHANCE HE IS DEAD, WE'VE GOT TO FIND HIS BODY.
THENARDIER AND THE OTHERS MIGHT GO LOOKING FOR IT.
......

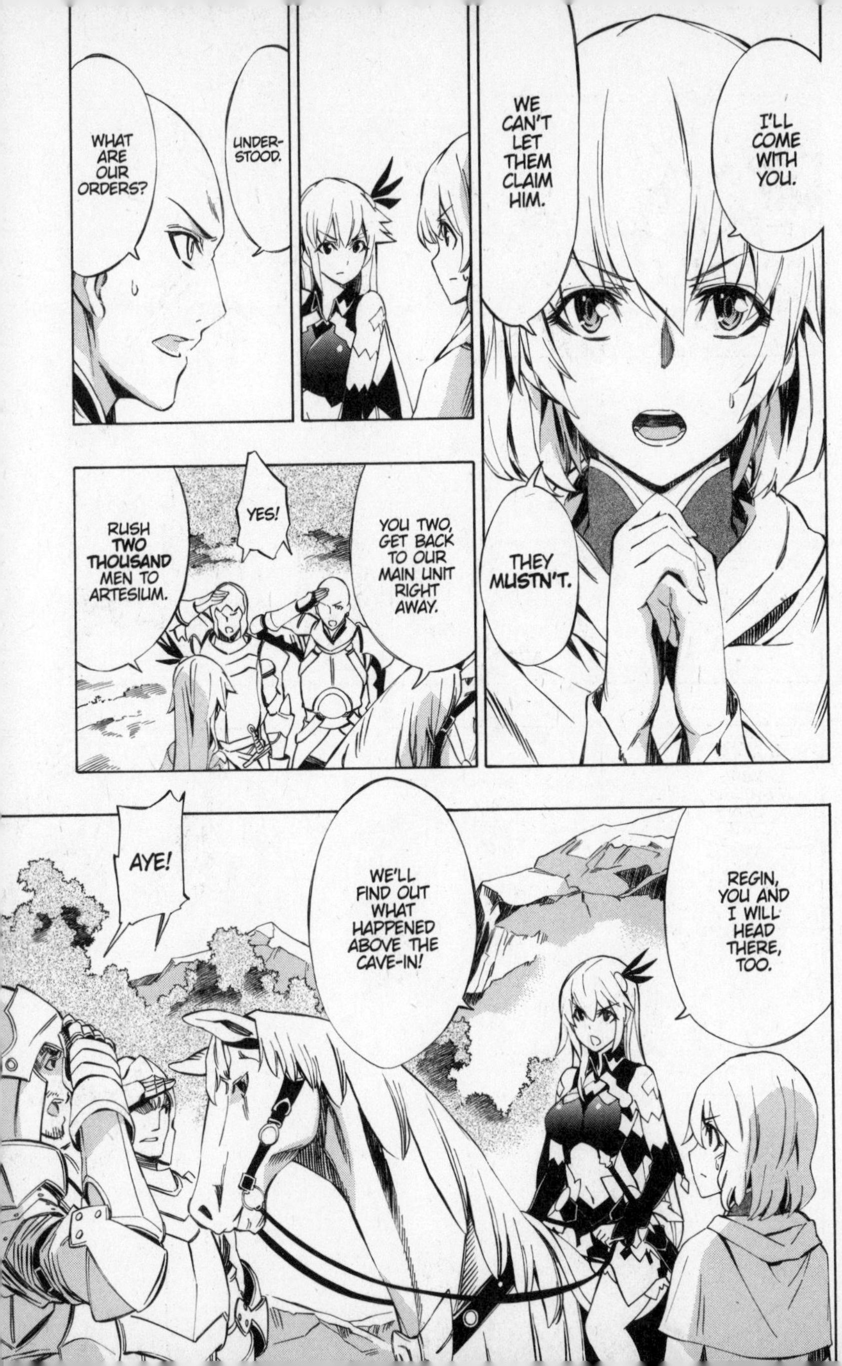
I'LL COME WITH YOU.
WE CAN'T LET THEM CLAIM HIM.
THEY MUSTN'T.
UNDER-STOOD.
WHAT ARE OUR ORDERS?
YOU TWO, GET BACK TO OUR MAIN UNIT RIGHT AWAY.
YES!
RUSH TWO THOUSAND MEN TO ARTESIUM.
REGIN, YOU AND I WILL HEAD THERE, TOO.
WE'LL FIND OUT WHAT HAPPENED ABOVE THE CAVE-IN!
AYE!

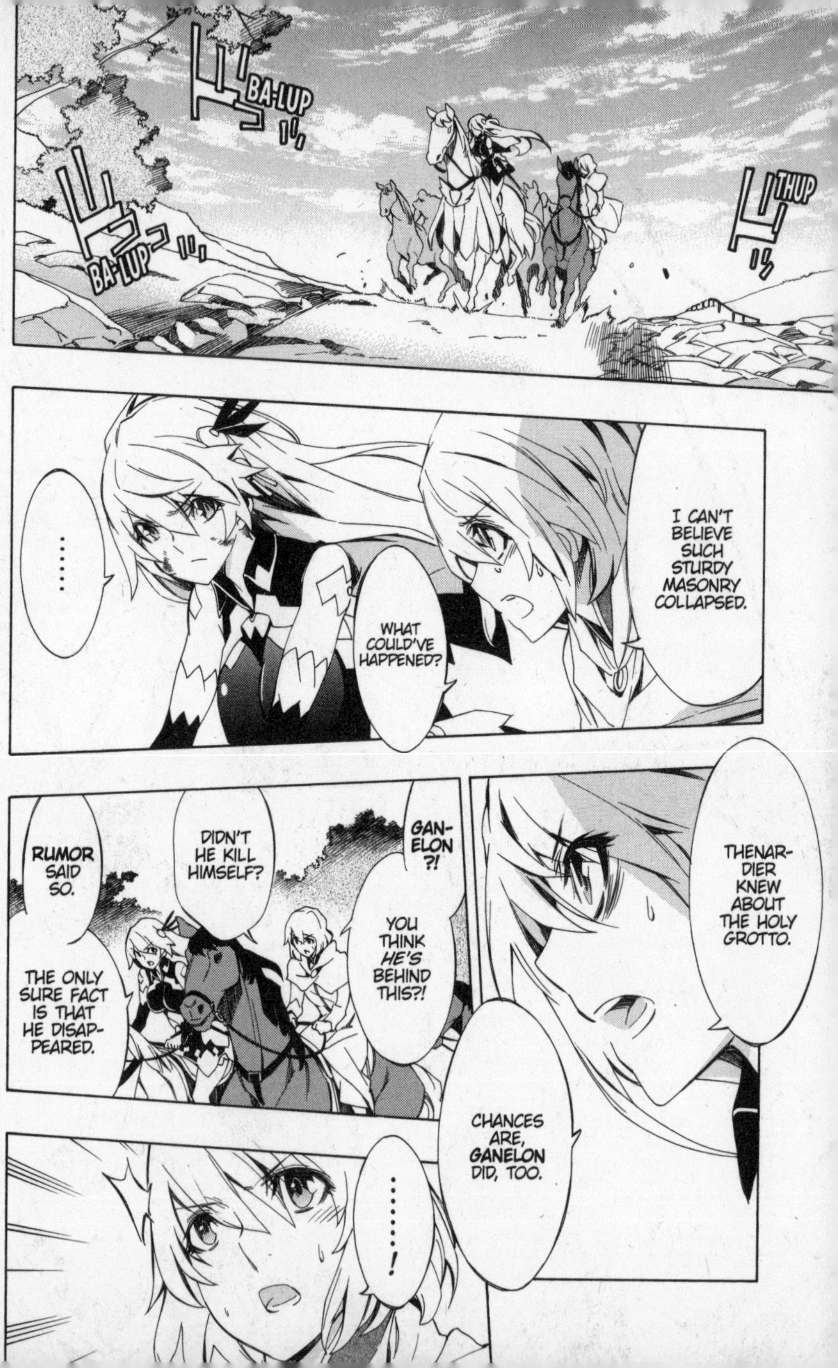
THUP
BA-LUP
BA-LUP
I CAN'T BELIEVE SUCH STURDY MASONRY COLLAPSED.
WHAT COULD'VE HAPPENED?
......
THENARDIER KNEW ABOUT THE HOLY GROTTO.
CHANCES ARE, GANELON DID, TOO.
GANELON?!
YOU THINK *HE'S* BEHIND THIS?!
DIDN'T HE KILL HIMSELF?
RUMOR SAID SO.
THE ONLY SURE FACT IS THAT HE DISAPPEARED.
......!

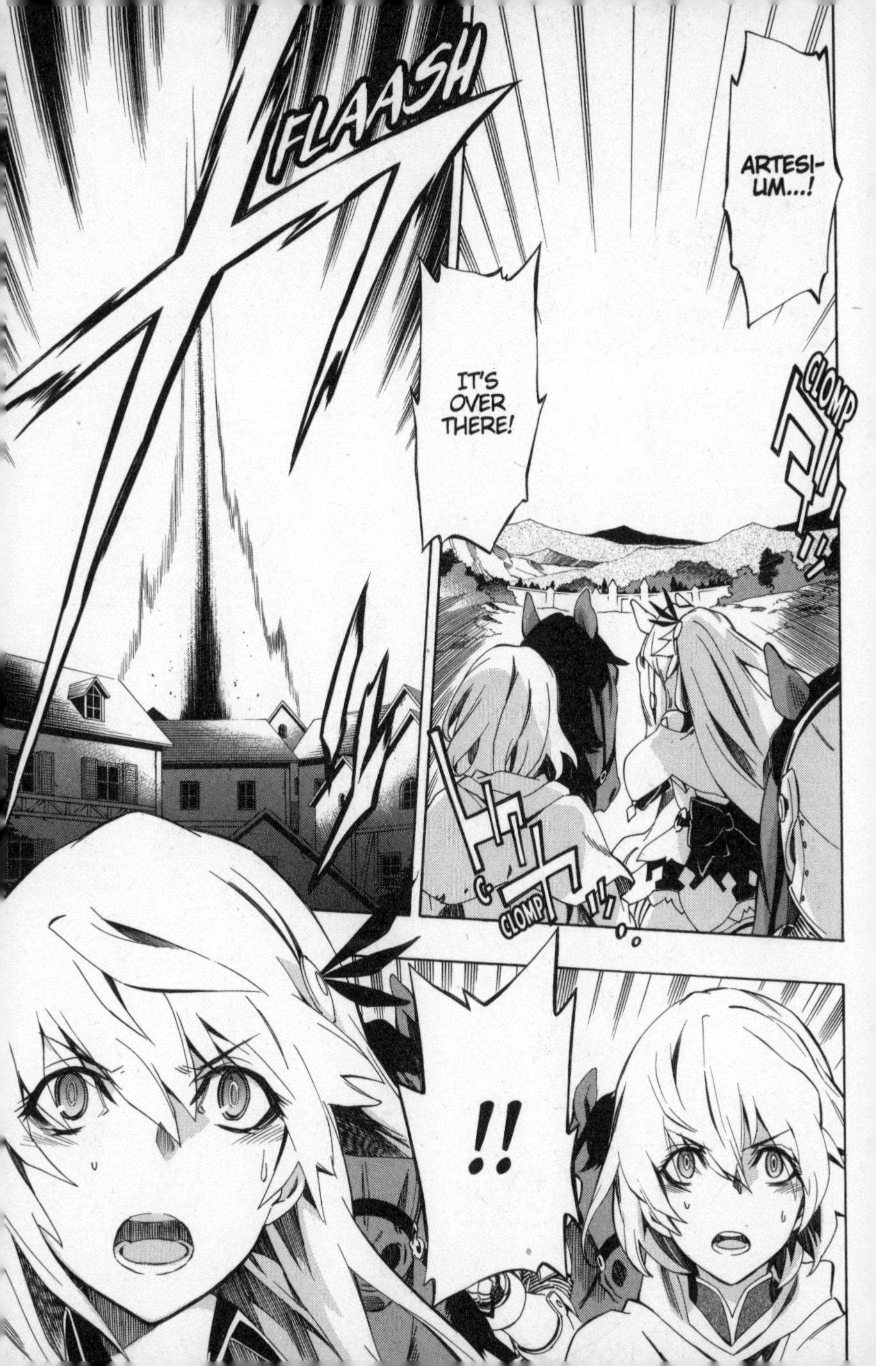
ARTESI-
UM...!
IT'S
OVER
THERE!
CLOMP
CLOMP
FLAASH
!!

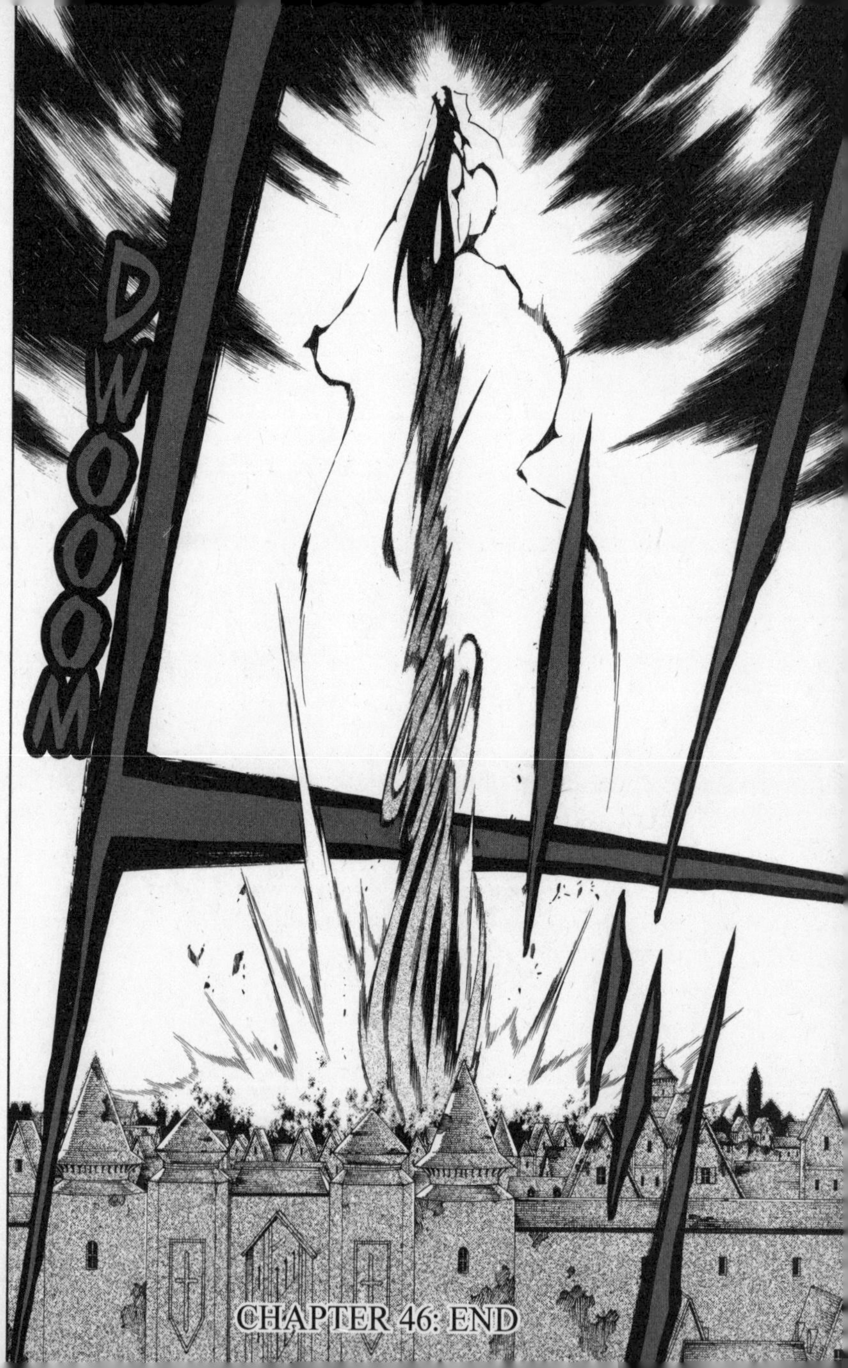
DWOOOOM
CHAPTER 46: END

Lord Marksman
and Vanadis

TO BE CONTINUED...

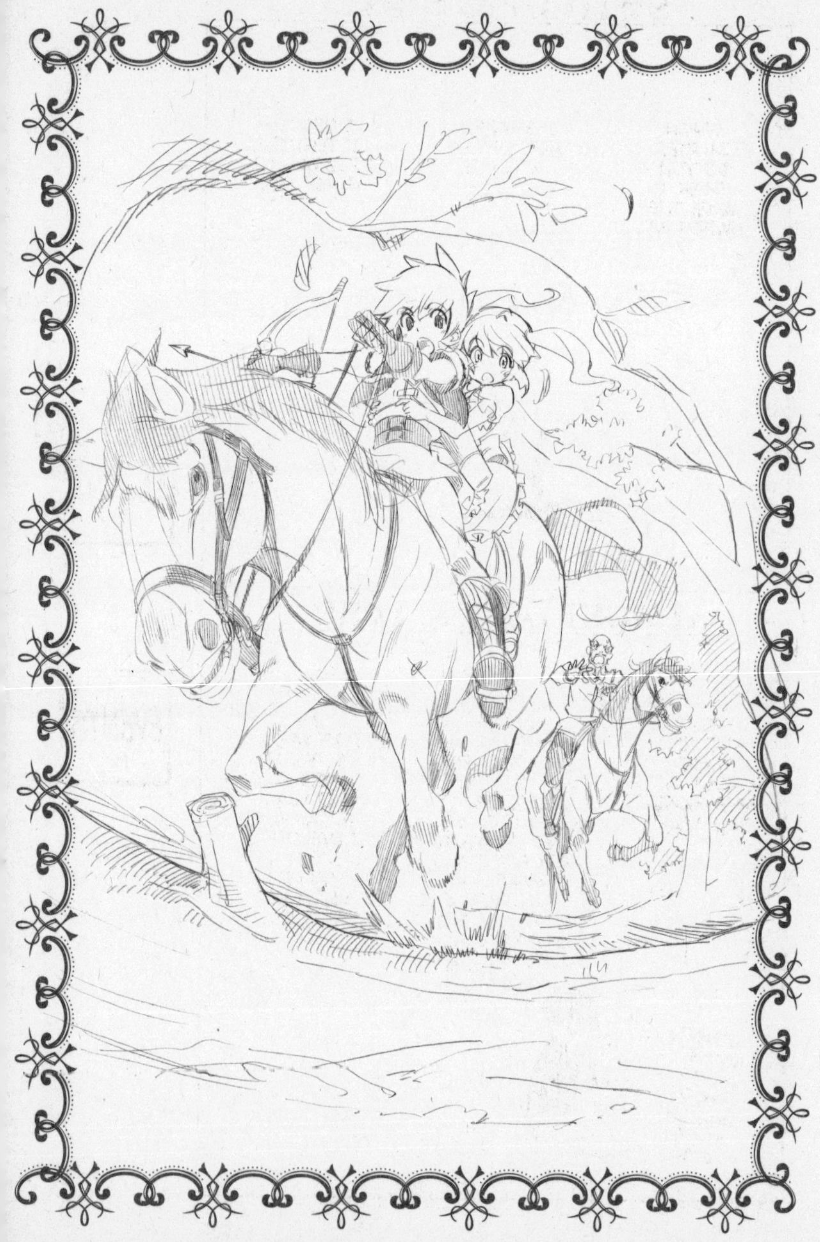

AFTERWORD: RECENT EVENTS

SWITCHING NIBS...

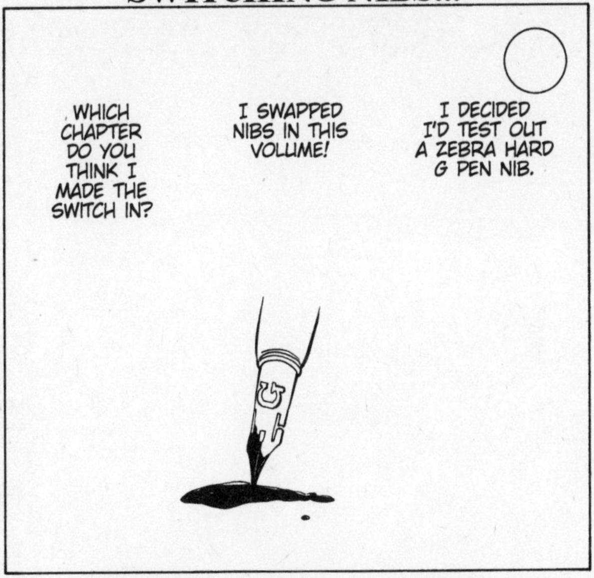
I DECIDED I'D TEST OUT A ZEBRA HARD G PEN NIB.
I SWAPPED NIBS IN THIS VOLUME!
WHICH CHAPTER DO YOU THINK I MADE THE SWITCH IN?

ALMOST LOSING PEKO...

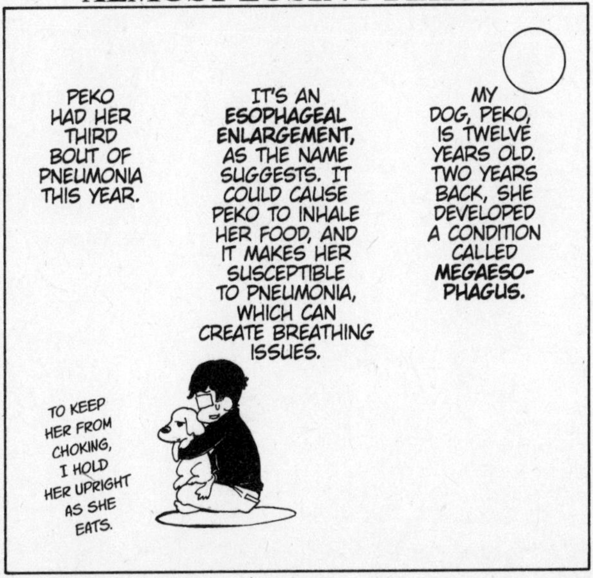
MY DOG, PEKO, IS TWELVE YEARS OLD. TWO YEARS BACK, SHE DEVELOPED A CONDITION CALLED MEGAESOPHAGUS.
IT'S AN ESOPHAGEAL ENLARGEMENT, AS THE NAME SUGGESTS. IT COULD CAUSE PEKO TO INHALE HER FOOD, AND IT MAKES HER SUSCEPTIBLE TO PNEUMONIA, WHICH CAN CREATE BREATHING ISSUES.
PEKO HAD HER THIRD BOUT OF PNEUMONIA THIS YEAR.
TO KEEP HER FROM CHOKING, I HOLD HER UPRIGHT AS SHE EATS.

ENJOYING DARK ROAST...

SINCE I STARTED GRINDING MY OWN COFFEE BEANS, I'VE BEEN SAMPLING LOTS OF VARIETIES.

I WAS NEVER A FAN OF ACIDIC FOODS...

SO I DISCOVERED THAT I PREFER **DARK ROAST** COFFEE.

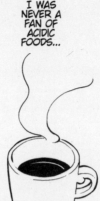

UNTIL I STARTED DRINKING BLACK COFFEE, I THOUGHT YOUNG PEOPLE WHO TOOK THEIR COFFEE BLACK WERE **SHOW-OFFS**. SORRY!

DRAWING BERTRAND WITH PASSION

BERTRAND'S DEATH SCENE STANDS OUT IN THIS VOLUME.

I WASN'T HAPPY WITH THE ORIGINAL ART FOR THE PART WHERE TIGRE SCREAMS, SO I REDREW IT RIGHT BEFORE THE DEADLINE.

[STAFF]
Aoki-san and Matsuo-kun

[SPECIAL THANKS]
Special Thanks To:
Koutarou Yamada-sensei,
Tsukasa Kawaguchi-sensei,
Hinata Katagiri-sensei,
Nishizawa-san, Rushi-kun,
Kajiyama-san, my editor,
I-buchi-san...
and my readers!

YOUNG LORD!
TITTA!

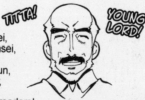

魔弾の王と戦姫（ヴァナディース）

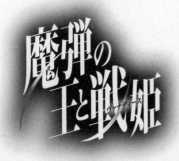

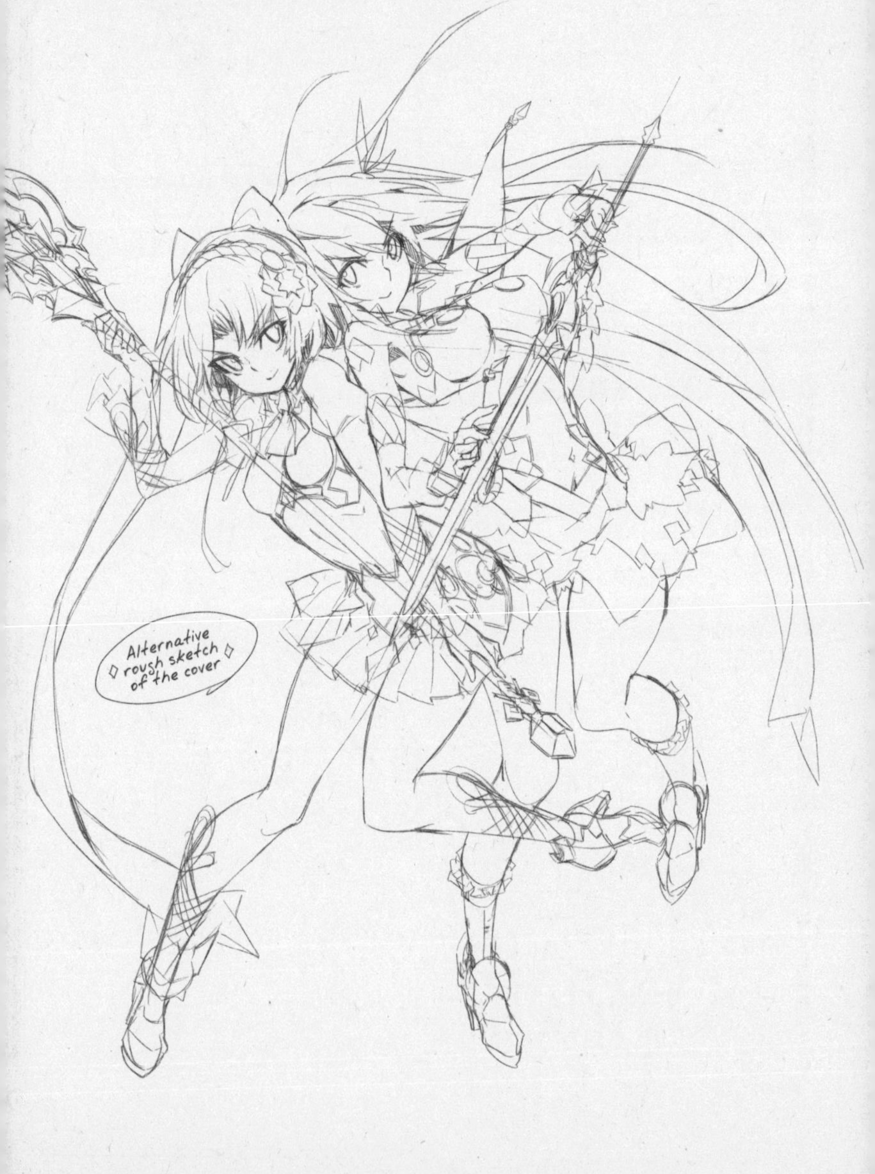
Alternative rough sketch of the cover

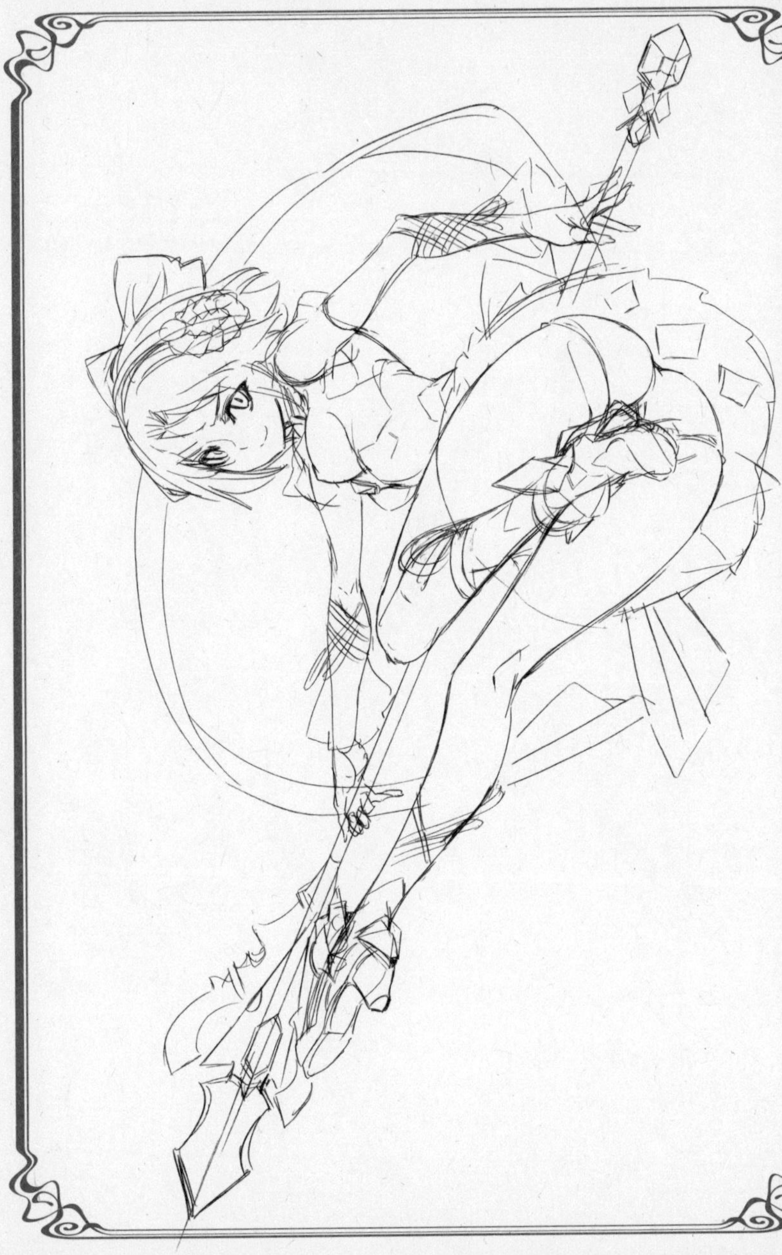

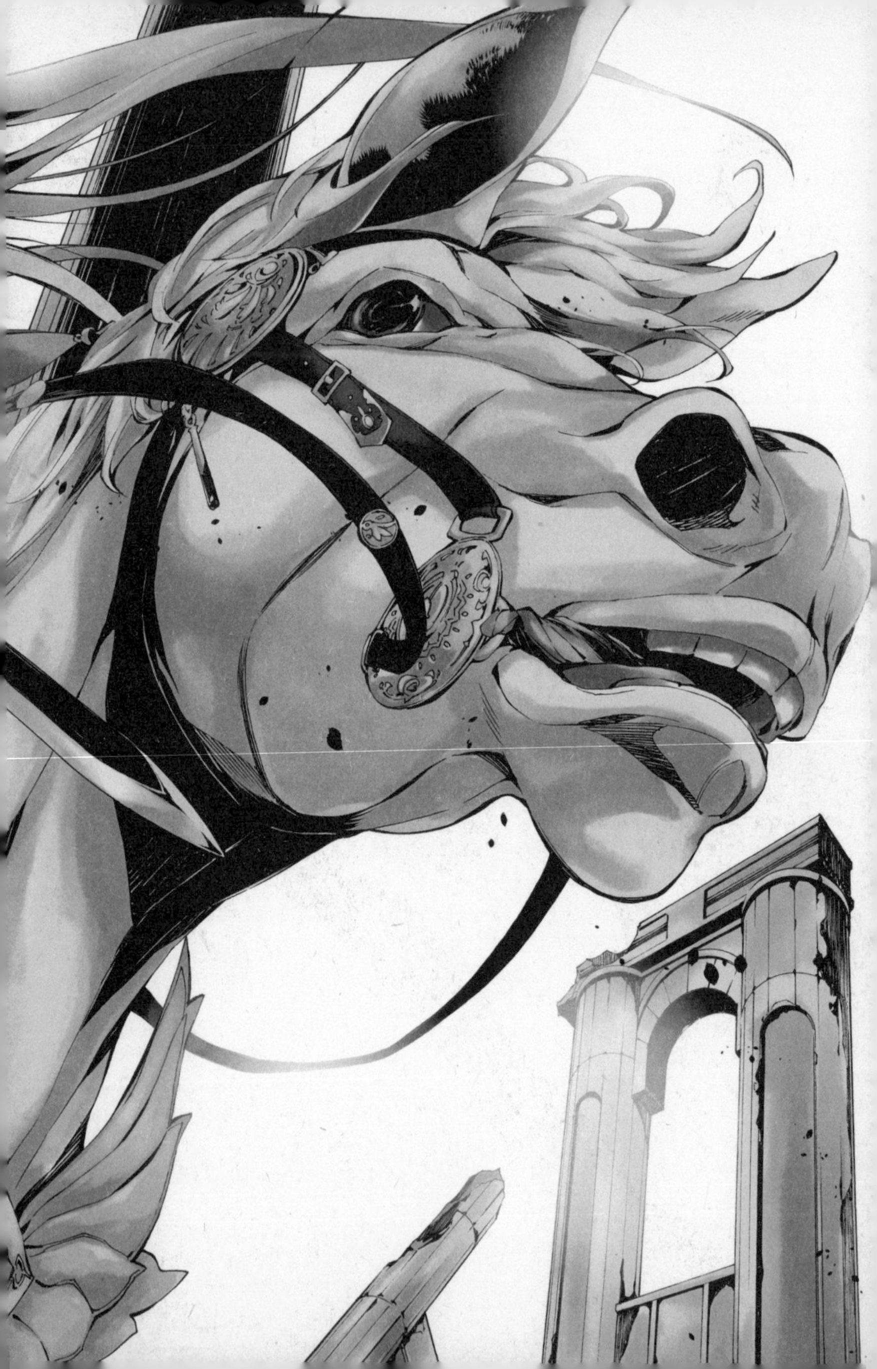

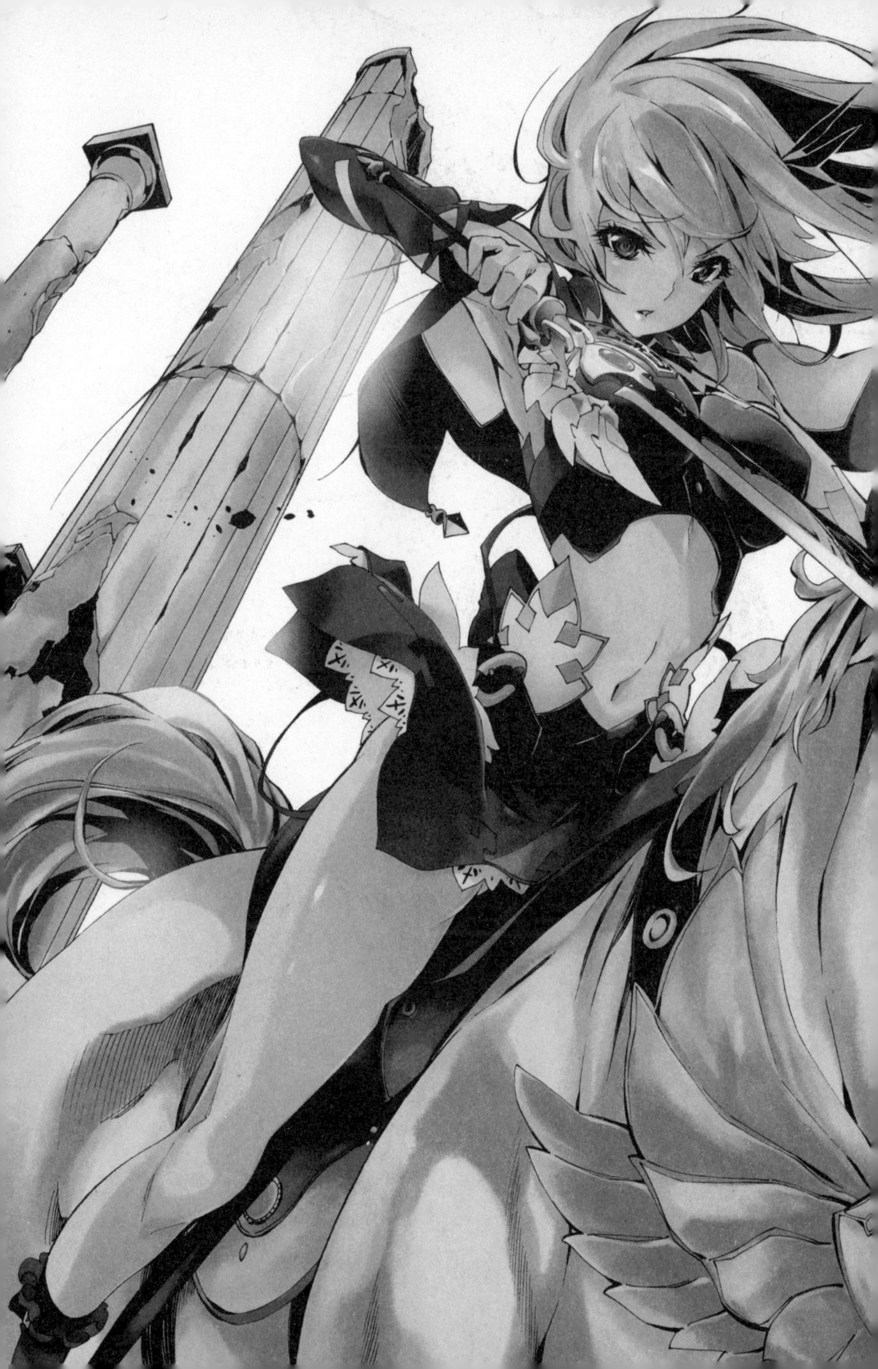

Lord Marksman and Vanadis

SEVEN SEAS ENTERTAINMENT PRESENTS

Lord Marksman and Vanadis VOL. 9

original story by TSUKASA KAWAGUCHI / art by NOBUHIKO YANAI
character design by YOSHI☆WO & HINATA KATAGIRI

TRANSLATION
Elina Ishikawa

ADAPTATION
Rebecca Spinner

LETTERING
James Gaubatz

COVER DESIGN
KC Fabellon

PROOFREADER
Danielle King
Tim Roddy

EDITOR
J.P. Sullivan

PRODUCTION ASSISTANT
CK Russell

PRODUCTION MANAGER
Lissa Pattillo

EDITOR-IN-CHIEF
Adam Arnold

PUBLISHER
Jason DeAngelis

LORD MARKSMAN AND VANADIS VOL. 9

ISBN: 978-1-626929-57-9

Printed in Canada

First Printing: January 2019

10 9 8 7 6 5 4 3 2 1

READING DIRECTIONS

This book reads from ***right to left***, Japanese style. If this is your first time reading manga, you start reading from the top right panel on each page and take it from there. If you get lost, just follow the numbered diagram here. It may seem backwards at first, but you'll get the hang of it! Have fun!!

1
2
3
4
5
6
7
8
9

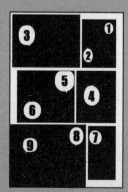

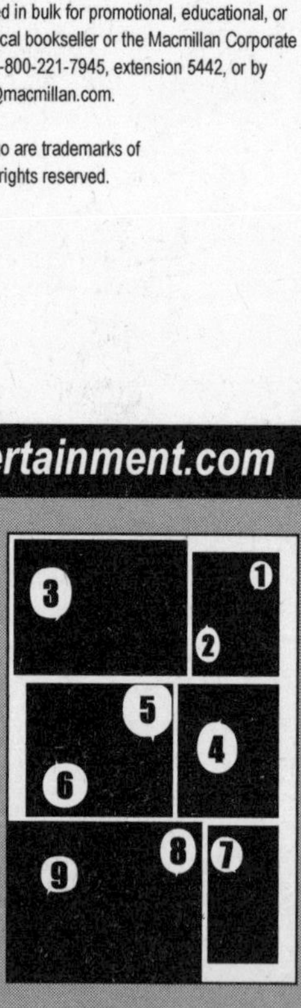